W9-CGO-770

THE
LEADERSHIP
CONTRACT

THE
LEADERSHIP
CONTRACT

THE FINE PRINT TO BECOMING
AN ACCOUNTABLE LEADER

THIRD EDITION

VINCE MOLINARO

WILEY

Cover Design: Wiley
Cover Images: Pen image: © Gunnar Pippel/Shutterstock
Paper image: © mirojurin/Shutterstock

Published by John Wiley & Sons, Inc., Hoboken, New Jersey
Published simultaneously in Canada

For general information about our other products and services, please contact our Customer Care
Department within the United States at (800) 762-2974, outside the United States at (317) 572-3993
or fax (317) 572-4002.

Wiley publishes in a variety of print and electronic formats and by print-on-demand. Some material
included with standard print versions of this book may not be included in e-books or in print-on-
demand. If this book refers to media such as a CD or DVD that is not included in the version you
purchased, you may download this material at http://booksupport.wiley.com. For more information
about Wiley products, visit www.wiley.com.

Library of Congress Cataloging-in-Publication Data:
Names: Molinaro, Vince, author.
Title: The leadership contract: the fine print to becoming an accountable
   leader / Vince Molinaro.
Description: Third edition. | Hoboken: Wiley, 2017. | Revised edition of the
   author's The leadership contract, [2016] | Includes index. |
Identifiers: LCCN 2017033423 (print) | LCCN 2017036344 (ebook) | ISBN
   9781119440611 (pdf) | ISBN 9781119440499 (epub) | ISBN 9781119440536
   (hardback)
Subjects: LCSH: Leadership. | Organizational change. | BISAC: BUSINESS &
   ECONOMICS/Leadership.
Classification: LCC HD57.7 (ebook) | LCC HD57.7 .M635 2017 (print) | DDC
   658.4/092–dc23
LC record available at https://lccn.loc.gov/2017033423

Printed in the United States of America

To my wife, Elizabeth—thank you for helping me be
a better person, husband, and father.

To my children, Mateo, Tomas, and Alessia—for
your daily inspiration and humor.

To my parents, Camillo and Maria—for always
supporting me as I pursued my dreams and goals.

CONTENTS

FOREWORD

As chief executive officer of The Adecco Group, the world's leading workforce solutions provider, I see the profound changes that are transforming business and the world of work around the world. Automation, robotics, and artificial intelligence are dramatically altering business models, and the rise of the so-called "gig" economy is transforming workforces and working relationships. There has never been a more important time to build a strong culture of leadership in organizations.

Yet, while the world and its foremost corporations are crying out for strong and clear leadership, there are worrying signs of turmoil in both business and politics. Despite significant investment in leadership development, many companies believe the majority of their leaders don't have the skills they need to take their company into the future.

That is why it gives me great pleasure to write this foreword to the third edition of Vince's bestselling book *The Leadership Contract*. Many have written about leadership, its importance, and its challenges, but few have done so as convincingly and authoritatively as Vince—a position now acknowledged by this expanded and updated version of his best-known work.

The solution, as Vince shows, is that we need leaders to be truly accountable. *The Leadership Contract* offers compelling and practical ideas for leaders to embrace and organizations to implement. Such proposals have been put into practice with great effect in companies around the world, including within The Adecco Group itself.

With more than 20 years advising companies and executives, Vince Molinaro has carved out a commanding position as a strategic thinker. As global managing director of the leadership transformation practice at Lee Hecht Harrison—the Adecco Group's specialist talent development and career transition subsidiary—Vince is uniquely positioned to comment on leadership and its pitfalls, thanks to his work with leaders of some the world's most forward-thinking companies.

Alain Dehaze
Chief Executive Officer, The Adecco Group

INTRODUCTION

What does it mean to be a leader? It's the question I believe every single one of us in a leadership role needs to answer.

Why? Because what it means to be a leader today is very different than it was a generation ago. You know this to be true. The world in which you lead is more dynamic and complex.

But there's more. Since releasing the first edition of this book in 2013, I have continued to see signs that leadership is still in trouble. Consider some of the following examples:

- A founder and chief executive officer (CEO) of a Silicon Valley company is publicly embarrassed when a video leaks of him berating and demeaning an employee in public. Many senior executives and employees leave based on the toxic corporate culture in the organization.
- Millions of people take to the streets to protest bribery and corruption among prominent CEOs and political leaders. It leads to the impeachment of the country's president.
- A former industry-leading innovator in the technology sector loses its market dominance in a matter of months and now struggles to survive.
- The CEO of a retailer is forced to resign after having an inappropriate relationship with a co-worker. The founder and chair of the board of that same company is pushed out after it's revealed that he knew about the relationship and did nothing to inform the board.
- No fewer than 18 executives connected with a major international organization are indicted for their participation in a culture of systematic, cynical, and constant corruption.

- A global study by a major research firm finds that 51 percent of leaders have essentially checked out, which means they show up every day, caring very little about their jobs, their people, and their company.
- Another research firm finds that close to two-thirds of the general population do not have confidence that current leaders can address their country's challenges. Furthermore the credibility of CEOs fell by 12 points in one year to only 37 percent.

What is going on?

Stories of ineffective leadership, corruption, and scandal are now so commonplace that we don't even react to them anymore. Our trust and confidence in senior leaders have been destroyed. Survey after survey finds employee engagement is chronically, cripplingly low. Managers say the new generation of workers is unmotivated and entitled, while many Millennials say they're simply not interested in rising through the ranks in the traditional way. They are looking for purpose, meaning, and inspiration. But they are not finding it. As Generation Z begins to enter the workplace, they will have even higher expectations of leaders. Meanwhile, you and your colleagues feel overworked and pulled in a dozen directions at once.

These aren't separate problems. I believe they're all part of one crisis, a crisis that companies worldwide are spending an estimated $65 billion trying to solve—and getting nowhere.

It's a crisis in leadership.

At a time when our world is more complicated than ever, is changing faster than ever, and is more radically transparent than ever, we desperately need our leaders to be stronger than ever. And they're not. They're failing us. They are unaccountable and untrustworthy. And we're becoming disillusioned.

In all the years I've been thinking and talking about leadership, I've come to realize that the desperate need for accountable leaders is the fundamental challenge organizations are facing today. It's at the heart of every other problem we face.

"Accountability is as important as the concept of leadership, and those who are granted power must be held accountable." This observation came from John W. Gardner—former Secretary of Health, Education, and Welfare under President Lyndon Johnson—in his book *On Leadership*, published by The Free Press in 1990. He clearly understood the connection between accountability and leadership almost thirty years ago. Yet it's clear as we see the crisis in leadership we face today, we must also realize that it's a crisis of accountability.

We have, quite simply, a significant *leadership accountability gap*, and it is a global problem in our society, in corporations, and in politics. Truly accountable leadership is the only way to build an organization that can not only survive in our increasingly complicated world, but also grow and thrive. And yet, based on my research, this is a challenge that few organizations are facing head-on.

I've been studying leadership for almost my entire career. As an employee, I've worked for some great leaders and some not-so-great ones. I know firsthand the effect leadership has on employee engagement and organizational performance. Through my academic studies and research, I have focused on learning what sets the few truly great leaders apart from the many mediocre ones. As a consultant, I've worked with hundreds of leaders and organizations worldwide. I've also held leadership roles myself—at the front-line, middle management, and C-suite level. I know at a personal level how challenging leadership can be if you want to do it well consistently. I also know how great it can be when you get it right.

Over the last few years, I've had the privilege to speak around the world to leaders like you. These conversations confirmed that leadership accountability is a critical business issue in almost all organizations.

A while back, I set up a Google Alert for the word *accountability*. It became immediately clear from the search results that the world is in dire need of real accountability. I read about cries for accountability in the banking sector, from a corporate governance perspective, in education, at all levels of government, in the military, in health care, in police forces, in the media—you get the picture. It doesn't matter what facet of our society you look at, real accountability is lacking. What is also clear is that there appears to be a lot of talk about the need for accountability but little action to make things better. I find the same dynamic inside organizations. Every CEO I work with wants to drive real accountability, but making it a reality is not easy.

I have also learned that we are paying a real price for bad leadership. I appeared on a radio talk show a while back. I was asked to share my thoughts about how and why so many people have lost trust and confidence in their leaders.

I was struck during the radio show to see just how deeply this problem affected everyday people. The host took calls from listeners, several of whom had very moving stories about how they had been personally let down by bad and ineffective leaders. Most were cynical and very disappointed with their experience of leadership.

One call came from a woman named Marian, who talked about how she had just quit her job to escape an awful leader. Her voice trembled as she described this painful decision. Her emotions were still raw. It was a courageous move—to leave her job—but in taking a stand, she demonstrated just how damaging poor leadership can be to an organization. Unfortunately, Marian felt she had no choice but to quit.

I believe that a generation ago a company could get by with bad leadership. Most workplaces were dominated by Baby Boomers, who were more likely to put up with bad and ineffective leaders. As difficult as it is to believe, tolerance for bad leadership was considered a badge of honor for them.

The business world is much different today. People expect more from leaders. They also demand much more accountability from them. The workforce is now also populated with a new generation of employees who, in general, won't put up with bad or mediocre leaders like the Boomers did. Like Marian, they'll just leave. The employees who choose to stay will simply become disengaged. Sure, they will show up at work, but they will do so with little real commitment.

I talk to leaders every day who recognize that the world has changed for them. Some feel they are not keeping up. Others believe there is something fundamentally wrong with how we have come to think about leadership. They know their organizations are struggling just to stay abreast of a changing world, and they know that in their desperation they're *settling*. When everything on your to-do list is urgent, things like inspiration and motivation seem like luxuries. You feel like the leadership parts of your role are just that: parts, something separate that you do from the corner of your desk.

But leadership is not a luxury. You can't settle or accept mediocrity in yourself or you risk becoming a lame leader. Your organization needs great leaders at all levels, now more than ever. You need to be the best leader you can possibly be.

The Pressures Leaders Face Today

The reason is clear—the world is more challenging and demanding. As a leader, you are now under more pressure than ever before. Let's look at a few of the big ones:

1. *The Pressure to Differentiate:* Whether it's a private-sector company or a public-sector organization, every enterprise is trying to differentiate itself. All organizations have competitors, whether for market share or government funding, and that competition is fierce. Whatever competitive advantage you thought you had seems to have a shorter and shorter shelf life as rivals copy it almost overnight. You face unrelenting pressure to innovate and look for ways to stand out from the crowd.
2. *The Pressure to Execute Strategy:* You face tremendous pressure to execute strategy. If you've been a leader for a while, you know how hard this can be. Success is hard to come by for many organizations. Research repeatedly shows that only 10 to 30 percent of organizations ever succeed at executing their strategy. I believe the reason is that many organizations don't fully appreciate the deep connection between strategy and leadership. It's leaders who create the strategy, and they need to work together to align the organization. Leaders need to ensure that everyone from the front line to the senior team understands the plan. If leaders fail to live up to this responsibility, there will be gaps in strategy execution.
3. *The Pressure to Lead Transformational Change:* A recent report by the Boston Consulting Group called "A Leader's Guide to "Always-On" Transformation,"[1] states that leaders today often feel like they are running on a steep treadmill with the speed and incline set on their maximum levels. This idea of "always-on" transformation really captures what I hear from leaders I work with. They are working through some kind of complex transformation. Then something else comes along that now requires them to drive even more change. As one leader explained to me, "We aren't just leading one large transformation project; it feels like we are doing ten all at once."
4. *The Pressure to Create Enduring Value:* You are also under continuous pressure to deal with ever-increasing expectations from customers, boards, and shareholders. The scrutiny you are under is intense.

Customers want value and will go wherever they must to get it. Their loyalty is fleeting. Boards and shareholders want a short-term increase in share price *and* long-term enterprise value—not an easy tension to manage for senior leaders.

5. *The Pressure to Build Future Talent:* You also cannot focus solely on the present. You are being called upon to build the next generation of leaders. The challenge you face is that after years of shedding costs and people, organizations are now realizing there are significant gaps in their leadership pipelines and succession plans. It seems like everyone finally understands that leadership does matter. The problem is that we have a new generation of employees who aren't necessarily that keen on taking leadership roles. We have demographic trends working against us. Many of these younger employees want to work with leaders they admire and who create meaningful work opportunities.

If you are like the leaders I work with every day, you personally feel the impact of all these pressures. You feel the increased ambiguity of your business environment. You can feel the scrutiny you are under. You understand the high level of accountability you have for the success of your organization. You are keenly aware of the impact you need to have on customers, employees, and other stakeholders.

Take a moment and reflect on these five pressures. How are they affecting you in your leadership role?

Redefining How You Lead to Meet Ever-Increasing Expectations

Taking all of these pressures together, it's obvious that old models of leadership just won't cut it anymore. It's time to redefine leadership for the new world we're living in. What worked in the past isn't going to work in the future. All of us need to start demanding more from ourselves as leaders. What has become clear through all my client work is that expectations for all leaders are increasing—more is expected of each of us in leadership roles.

For example, since launching the first edition of this book back in 2013, my team and I have been running one-day Leadership Contract learning programs with thousands of leaders around the world.

We begin a session with a simple exercise—participants must answer the following question: What does it really mean to be a leader today? Now here's the catch. They must answer the question using only one word.

Here are the most common words that are shared: leaders today must be inspirational, trustworthy, courageous, agile, humble, transparent, decisive, collaborative, resilient, risk-takers, strategic, visionary, possess integrity, proactive, team players, confident, and accountable.

As these words are shared, the facilitator captures them on a flip chart. The participants are then encouraged to add to the list throughout the day as new ideas emerge. By the end of the day, the list that started with fifteen or twenty words expands to fifty, sixty, and at times even seventy words or more. This long list of words answers the question: What does it means to be a leader today?

When I have looked at those lists, I'm always surprised by a few trends. First, it's remarkable how consistent the words are globally. It doesn't seem to matter where in the world the program is delivered; we have a common way of thinking about what it means to be a leader today. Second, by the sheer volume of words generated, it's clear that we have very high expectations of leaders. Being a leader isn't easy. It is an extremely challenging role. The expectations are very high. Third, these expectations are for all leaders, regardless of their level in an organization. They aren't just for CEOs or executives. In fact, we recently surveyed hiring managers from around the world to quantify and rank their expectations across 21 different competencies for three levels of management: front-line, mid-management, and senior executives. The results showed that while senior leaders still carry the greatest expectations of all, leaders at other levels of an organization's hierarchy are not absolved of the responsibility of being good at their jobs—sometimes they are expected to be just as good as the most senior executives. We asked the question: "How important is each of these core leadership competencies when assessing managers?" Remarkably, the survey results showed that expectations around leadership competencies were incredibly consistent from the front line to the senior levels of an organization.

Now when I look at those lists and reflect on those great expectations, I often wonder: Can any one person be and do all those things consistently well, every day of the week, while they are leading?

At the end of the day, this is what you have to understand when you are in a leadership role, or want to move into one: The expectations are extremely high and you must commit to living up to them as a leader.

Based on my research over the years with organizations, I've seen this expanding set of expectations. We need our leaders to do more. To be more. As a leader, you will need to take accountability to:

- *Align and engage.* You need to understand your company's strategy and your role in executing it. You must then align and engage employees so they can effectively deploy the strategy in a way that ultimately delivers value to customers, shareholders, and society.
- *Take an enterprise-wide perspective.* You must define success at the company level. This means you will need to collaborate across silos and do what's right for customers and the entire organization. All leaders in your organization need to share this *one-company* mindset.
- *Build relationships.* In our interconnected and interdependent world, relationships matter more than ever. You have to invest time in getting to know internal and external stakeholders. You must also build relationships with a foundation of trust and transparency.
- *Master uncertainty.* Today's increasingly complicated business environment creates a lot of challenging situations and risk. Many companies are attempting to transform. Your role as a leader is to create focus and help employees deal with ambiguity and the stress it brings, especially in a time of disruption.
- *Develop other leaders.* You must leave a legacy of strong leadership within your organization that goes beyond yourself. It's about making your leaders stronger so that they can make your organization stronger.
- *Model the values.* You cannot be focused exclusively on your own personal agenda or team goals. The organization's vision, values, and goals trump ego and self-interest. This means balancing strong self-confidence with humility. You need to set the bar high for yourself as a leader because mediocrity in leadership isn't acceptable anymore. It never was.

All leaders today are being called upon to redefine how they lead. This process starts with you, and it starts now. Are you ready?

The Leadership Contract

Let's begin with an analogy. You know that experience you have when you're online planning to buy a product or a service? At some point in the transaction, an online contract appears. To complete the purchase, you have to click that Agree button. Almost everything you do online today requires you to click an Agree button, and when you do, you also know you are agreeing to pages of tiny single-spaced text outlining a set of complicated terms and conditions. You go ahead and click Agree. But do you actually read those terms and conditions? If you are like most people, you don't. You simply click away without really thinking about it.

Studies show that only 7 percent of people ever read those terms and conditions of online contracts.[2] Yet with that simple click, you are agreeing to quite a lot. You have some sense that you have just agreed to a contract, but you don't know what it entails. You don't understand the fine print.

I believe something similar is happening in leadership today. A lot of leaders have clicked Agree to take on a leadership role without thinking through the terms that come with what I call the *leadership contract*.

You may have clicked Agree for a valid reason—to get the promotion, the higher salary, the perks, the power, or the opportunity to have a real impact—but if you don't fully appreciate what you have signed up for, you won't be effective in leading through the pressures of today's business environment.

Redefining leadership for the future begins with recognizing that there is in fact a leadership contract. It's not a legal or formal contract that you sign. It's a personal one. It represents the commitment you must personally make to be an accountable leader. It's a deep commitment to redefine how you lead and become the leader for the future. And when you sign the leadership contract, you are agreeing to a set of terms that you must live up to.

Here they are. Here's the fine print to becoming a truly accountable leader.

1. Leadership Is a Decision

Every leader's story begins with a decision. I have heard lots of people describe a moment in their career when they made the conscious decision to be a leader, whether it was their first promotion or the day they stepped into the executive suite. These moments demand that we reflect on why we want to lead, whether we are ready for a new role, and how committed we are to becoming great leaders. This term of the leadership contract demands that you make the personal commitment to be the best leader you can be.

2. Leadership Is an Obligation

Once you decide to lead, you quickly learn you are going to be held to a higher standard of behavior. You also realize that you have obligations that go beyond yourself. It's not just about what is best for your career anymore. You are obligated to your customers and employees, your organization, and the communities in which you do business. This term of the leadership contract demands that you step up to your accountabilities and live up to your obligations as a leader.

3. Leadership Is Hard Work

Leadership is hard, and it's getting harder. We have to stop pretending that it is easy or that some quick-fix idea is going to make things better. You need to develop the resilience and determination to tackle the hard work of leadership. You need personal resolve and tenacity to rise above the daily pressures and lead your organization into the future. This term of the leadership contract demands that you get tough and do the hard work that you must do as a leader.

4. Leadership Is a Community

In our complex world, no one leader will have all the answers. The idea of the lone hero who can save us all was yesterday's model of leadership. Today, we need to build a strong community of leaders. Imagine if you and your colleagues were all fully committed to being great leaders and focused on supporting one another to be better—this would set your organization apart. This term of the leadership contract demands that you connect with others to create a strong community of leaders in your organization—a community where there is deep trust and support, where you know everyone has your back, and where all leaders share the collective aspiration to be truly accountable leaders.

Why I Wrote the Third Edition of This Book

In January of 1990, I left a stable and secure job with a public-sector organization to start my own consulting business. I was young and naïve, but full of optimism and enthusiasm.

Most of my initial work came from individuals who wanted career advice. They were trying to navigate their lives in turbulent times. The economy was struggling. Uncertainty was high.

What I quickly found was that many of my individual clients brought me into their organizations. They wanted me to help their employees deal with change. I then found much of that work focused on helping leaders develop the skills they needed to lead change at a personal, team, and organizational level.

As I reflect back on that period of time, it is fascinating how much the word "change" was part of the lexicon of companies and individuals. And yet, I can tell you that change was nothing compared to what companies are facing today.

There is something more fundamental going on in our economies and our workplaces. Whether it's fueled by all things digital, fundamental shifts in how we will work, or new competitors who are turning industries upside down, I can tell you that today's change isn't like what we saw in the 1990s. It's something more profound. Disruption is everywhere.

And how are companies responding?

Well, the ones who are quick and agile have already positioned themselves for success. Take the example of Cisco. In a recent interview conducted for McKinsey Insights, John Chambers, the chairman of the company, eloquently described what companies are facing today, but also talked about how Cisco has responded. He described the world in which leaders lead today as one of "brutal disruption," where many companies will not even exist in ten to fifteen years.

He also argued in the interview that most companies will need to reinvent themselves. They will need to be fully digital in five years. And here's the real point—he believes most will fail.

Why? Because leading today is very different than leading was yesterday. Leaders need new skills that allow them to work more horizontally, across functions and departments. Cisco began its transformation by focusing on leaders with those crucial skills. What has been the impact of those organizational changes? In the McKinsey interview, Chambers shared that they changed 40 percent of their top leaders over the last couple of years. As he reflected on this, he said, "This isn't something I'm proud of, but it's something we had to do so we could disrupt, rather than be disrupted."

I've seen more and more companies pursuing radical change like this, just since publishing the second edition of this book. Many of my clients now need my company's help and the expertise of my colleagues to successful transform their organizations. Like Cisco, these organizations understand that successfully transforming your company starts by transforming your leaders.

This is why I was driven to write the third edition of *The Leadership Contract*. Leaders and organizations around the world have found the ideas in this book extremely relevant and important as they begin to transform themselves.

And this is where things get personal for each one of us in a leadership role. Chances are, your organization is going through a transformation. Are you going to help lead that transformation, or will you be a casualty of it?

The ideas in this book will help you understand how to step up and be truly accountable to help your organization thrive in a time of change and disruption.

A Word of Warning

I believe leading an organization is one of the greatest honors and challenges that any individual can assume. But it's not a job for everyone. And there is only one way to ensure that you have what it takes to be a truly accountable leader—you have to make a conscious decision to lead, with full awareness of what that means.

So this book is going to ask a lot of you. It has to because leadership matters more than ever. Your organization needs you to be the best leader you can be, especially if your organization is transforming itself.

There may be times when you feel overwhelmed by the ideas in this book. You may feel they are completely unrealistic. But you'll also realize something else—these ideas are ones you've already thought about. Deep down, you know that we all must redefine how we are leading today. We all have to. It's not just you. We all need to be more accountable as leaders.

You will also have to think hard about whether you are ready to commit to accepting the four terms of the leadership contract and becoming a great leader, the kind of leader your company needs you to be. You can't be a good or average leader any longer. You can't make leadership just a part of your job, something you focus on only when you have a few minutes of spare time. You must make leadership your whole job. It's time to aspire to more. It's time for you to be a great leader. But this is going to take some serious work on your part.

To help you through this, you will find a section at the end of each chapter called "The Gut Check for Leaders." Inspired by my weekly "Leadership Gut Check" blogs, I'll ask you a series of reflective questions based on the ideas in each chapter. They will be tough questions that I believe all of us in leadership roles need to think about. I believe it is critical to reflect on what it means to be a leader today and how you can transform yourself to be a truly accountable one. I encourage you to pause when you get to this section and think about your answers to the gut check questions.

If you want to take your leadership even further, then consider getting *The Leadership Contract Field Guide* (Wiley, 2018). It is full of practical activities to help you apply the leadership contract at a personal and organizational level.

Now if you're *not* ready to challenge yourself and hold yourself to account, you might want to put this book back on the shelf for a while. But if you believe, as I do, that we desperately need great and accountable leadership in the world today, then read on. If the ideas in this book speak to you, I hope you'll join others who share your passion at www.theleadershipcontract.com.

CHAPTER 1

My Personal Leadership Story

Great leaders aren't born; they are made—made and shaped by their experiences. Gandhi's mother was very religious and influenced by Jainism, a religion founded on the idea of nonviolence toward all creatures. A village schoolteacher refused to teach a young Susan B. Anthony long division because she was a girl. Margaret Thatcher gained experience weathering criticism when, as education minister in the early 1970s, budget cuts earned her the nickname "milk snatcher." When Richard Branson was about seven years old, his mother, Eve, left him three miles away from his home on the way back from school so he would be forced to figure out how to get home on his own. She did it to help him overcome his crippling shyness. It took him ten hours, but he did it; and it helped him become the person and the leader he is today.

Like Gandhi, Anthony, Thatcher, and Branson, every leader has a story. But most leaders aren't fully aware of how their experiences have shaped them to be the leaders they are now. I believe it's crucial for leaders to take time to think about their history and their own personal leadership stories.

Take a moment to think of the key experiences that have shaped you as a leader. I hope some stories are already coming to mind for you. Some will be stories of peak experiences when you had a significant impact—when you were at your best. Others will be more negative—moments when you struggled and your personal resolve was tested. Reflecting on all of these moments of leadership will give you a clearer vision of who you are as a leader and why you lead the way you do.

I have seen it hundreds of times in my work. In leadership development programs, my team and I take people through an exercise that helps them build a Personal Leadership Timeline: a list of the key experiences, both positive and negative, they believe have shaped them as leaders. These stories can come from childhood, school, work, or life in a community. This kind of personal reflection is easier for some people than for others, but everyone I have worked with has come away from this exercise with a renewed sense of enthusiasm and commitment for his or her leadership role.

My own leadership story is based on several key experiences. I'm going to share my story with you because it's important for you to understand where the ideas in this book come from and because I hope it will help you reflect on your own personal leadership story.

Is Leadership Worth Dying For?

Most leaders don't ever have to ask themselves this question. I did very early in my career, soon after I started my first full-time job.

Do you remember how you felt when you first started your working life? If you were like me, you wanted to change the world, to really show the value you could bring to an organization. I got a job as a caseworker with a large public-sector organization that helped some of the neediest people in society, providing financial support and services to help people get back to school or find a job.

Most of my colleagues were nice people. They were very dedicated to their clients. But they weren't that dedicated to the organization. Most showed up at 8:30 AM and left at 4:30 PM sharp every single day. Maybe they had been turned off by the bland working environment. Everything in the office was beige—the walls, the floors, even the desks and chairs. Even the people seemed beige—or at least bland.

The supervisors and managers were decent individuals, too, but they weren't very inspiring. They did what they were told. They respected the hierarchy and their place in it. Senior management seemed distant. Few employees had direct access to them, and as far as I could tell, they didn't have much impact on the organization.

A month after I started, I was already wondering whether this was really the place for me.

I had done what I was supposed to do. I went to college, got good grades, and landed a solid full-time job. All I had to do now was be loyal, and the organization would take care of me until I retired. This was the old-fashioned concept known as job security. But I was soon realizing it wasn't enough to build a career on. I wanted not just to have an impact on my clients' lives but also to make a difference to the organization as a whole. This was the moment I learned how much the culture of an organization can undermine an employee's sense of engagement.

Things improved a little when I started a new role working as a career counselor. This role was better aligned with my own interests, not just in giving a handout as a caseworker but also in giving a hand up. I actually started to feel like I was running a new start-up within a large organization. I soon learned I had a strong entrepreneurial side. I was a builder—not a maintainer.

My work captured the attention of a senior manager named Zinta. She was a quiet and reserved person whom I had only known from a distance. She started coming by my office to talk about my work and the new programs I was building. In those discussions, I told her some of my ideas for improving our work environment. One day, she said, "We need someone like you in management. You're a big-picture thinker. You have a strategic mind and you know how to get things done. This would really help our management team."

Nobody had ever said anything like that to me before. That conversation made me think about myself differently. I began reading books on management. I wanted to learn more about what Zinta saw in me.

A few weeks later, Zinta dropped by my office again. This time she shared an idea she had. She suspected that I wanted to have a greater impact on the organization, and I agreed. She then told me she was setting up a committee to find ways to make our work environment more positive. She asked whether I would be interested in helping her out, and I jumped at the opportunity.

Much to my surprise, as the work of our committee began to take effect, things actually started to improve. Employees became more enthusiastic. The organization was starting to feel more positive. Everyone was more engaged. You could feel the changes starting to happen in that place. While the walls, floors, and desks were still all beige, the workplace had more life and vitality. This was the moment I learned that the culture of an organization could be changed for the better, and that one person could make a difference.

Things were going pretty well for me. My job was fulfilling. The work environment was more positive and energizing. I was feeling like I was having a real impact. Then disaster struck. Zinta was diagnosed with lung cancer, and she had to leave immediately to start treatment.

She was gone for several months. As soon as she left, the changes we worked so hard to create began to slip away. Upper management disbanded the committee Zinta had started. They told those of us on Zinta's committee to focus on doing our own jobs and leave the organizational stuff to them. Those of us who worked with Zinta started to be passed up for promotions. I was told I didn't have what it took to be a manager. My engagement eroded even further. I was frustrated, but even more than that, I was confused. I couldn't understand why upper management wouldn't want us to create a better work environment. Plus, I was getting some seriously mixed messages about my future with the organization.

As the weeks continued to pass, I heard that things weren't looking good for Zinta, so I decided to visit her at home. As I approached her porch, I could see her waiting for me behind the screen door. I immediately saw that the disease was getting the best of her. My heart sank.

I had brought her a fruit basket and she thanked me. She offered me some tea. We sat down and started talking about her treatments. She seemed confident in her ability to fight her disease, but she quickly changed the subject. She wanted to know how I was doing. At first, I kept things superficial; after all, I was there to talk about her. But she kept pressing, so I opened up and shared my experiences, my frustration, and my confusion with my role.

Then she started talking. She told story after story of her experiences as a manager. She described at length the petty office politics, the discouraging atmosphere, and the lack of genuine trust among her fellow managers. She described her regular battles with upper management who resisted her every effort to make the organization better. I could feel her anguish. Then she said something that took me by surprise. She said, "You know, Vince, I've always taken care of my health. I've never smoked a cigarette in my life, and I have no history of lung cancer in my family. I believe the disease I'm fighting today is a direct result of all the stress I have experienced being a manager in this organization."

I was stunned. As I left Zinta's house, I grieved for her. I felt angry about why she had to endure what she did. As the days passed, I couldn't get Zinta's words out of my mind. I started to wonder what they meant to me and whether I would ever be prepared to pay the price she had paid.

Two weeks after my visit, I received an envelope in the mail from Zinta. When I opened it, I found a card thanking me for the visit and the fruit basket. There was also a letter folded inside, and here's what it said:

> *Vince,*
>
> *I understand you may have received a mixed message recently regarding your objectives. Success is a funny thing. Like physics, every action has a positive and negative reaction. On one hand, success has the effect of giving one a sense of achievement, pride in the accomplishment, affirmation of skills, and promotes a desire to expand to the next horizon.*
>
> *The other side is the reaction from others. Some will rejoice in your achievements. Others, perhaps because of their own insecurities, will feel threatened. These people will inadvertently or purposefully make moves to discourage you, undercut the significance of your success, or redirect you to paths that are less threatening to them. Some people are jealous of others' success. (Why does he get all the "breaks"?) Little do they realize that opportunities exist for everyone.*
>
> *The choice remains yours. Which of the above will influence you? I encourage you to always be the best you can be and take advantage of opportunities as you find them. You have everything to gain.*
> *Hope this helps,*
> *Zinta*

When I think about what it means to be a leader, I think about Zinta and her letter. In the midst of her struggle to survive, she took the time to reach out to a young colleague who needed some encouragement.

Zinta died two weeks after I received this letter, and the organization died along with her. That was the moment I learned that although one leader can make a difference, one leader can't sustain culture change on his or her own. Weeks and months after, I reflected on Zinta and her experience. I had many questions. Was her cancer really a result of the stress she endured in that organization? I don't know for sure. But she believed it was, so strongly that the stress must have had some negative effect on her health.

I often asked myself, "If things were so bad for her, why didn't she just leave the organization?" Over the years, I've been surprised to find how many leaders have lived in working environments almost as bad as the one Zinta put up with. I also discovered the one common factor—they were all Baby Boomers. This generation grew up expecting to persevere and put up with whatever they had to. If you worked for a jerk, you put up with it. If you worked in a dreadful work environment, as Zinta did, you just put up with it. In a weird way, putting up with all the bullshit was like a badge of honor for many Boomers.

I knew I was wired differently from Zinta. That letter forced me to reflect very early on in my career on two important questions: What is leadership? Is it worth dying for?

I learned from Zinta's example that I wasn't prepared to sacrifice the way she had, not for an organization that didn't deserve it—not for an organization that didn't aspire to greatness. An organization like that doesn't deserve the commitment and energy of its employees. That was as clear to me early in my career as it is today.

Zinta's experience also taught me that there isn't an artificial division between our work lives and our personal lives. We each have one life, and there's no reason to spend it in a dreadful organization led by uninspiring managers and leaders. Moreover, work is a big part of our lives. We spend a lot of time at work, and for most of us it's the main way we contribute to society. So I believe it's critical that we make it the best experience we can. And if we do, we all win—employees, customers, shareholders, our families, and our communities. Organizations make our world work. We need them to be strong and vibrant, not uninspiring and soul-destroying. I have come to learn that it all begins with accountable leadership.

At the time I worked with Zinta, people didn't really talk about leadership. It was all about management, and being a good manager was about doing what you were told and ruffling as few feathers as possible. Respect the hierarchy. Do as you are told. Twenty-five years after Zinta died, I decided to start sharing her story because I believe we need to do a lot better when it comes to leadership.

Zinta's letter changed the way I thought about my life's work. It also changed my life in a more practical sense: It inspired me to start my own consulting business. I didn't realize it then, but Zinta challenged me to make a critical decision—a leadership decision.

What I also didn't realize at the time was that the moment I made that decision, I began a quest—to learn how we can create compelling organizations with leaders who truly inspire others to succeed. I wanted to find and work with like-minded individuals who aspired to create something special in the organizations they led. Unfortunately, finding those people would not be easy.

When I started my consulting business, I focused first on providing private career counseling services to professionals. My work with these clients was gratifying. They began to invite me into their organizations to deliver workshops for their employees. I quickly found I enjoyed that work even more. I also learned that although career counseling let me have an impact at an individual level, leading seminars gave me the opportunity to have an organizational impact. This really appealed to me. Over time, I began to shift my business, relying less on individual career counseling and more on work inside organizations.

All the projects I worked on had one thing in common: change. I continually worked with organizations, individual leaders, teams, and business units that were at an inflection point. They needed to change to survive but didn't know how. That's when I learned that even people and groups who want and need to change tend to resist it.

As my work grew more complex and strategic in nature, I decided I needed to learn more about organization development, leadership, and change. This is when I began to pursue my graduate degrees. I continued to run my business while I was in graduate school, and I found being part of these two worlds at the same time fascinating. I would read about leadership theories and then test them out with my clients. I learned which ideas really were valuable and which were theoretically interesting but not connected to the real world. This was the moment I learned to always favor practical, actionable ideas.

My graduate courses made me think about my client work differently. I started to see organizations in a more systemic way. The more I learned, the more I could see what got in the way of success. I started to focus on what has become the central theme of my career: holistic ways of thinking about business and leadership. I was kind of a misfit in my graduate courses. I was self-employed, working with private-sector organizations while my fellow students worked in education, health care, or the public sector. This was the moment I learned that exposure to ideas from other fields can be immensely valuable. Being a misfit is perfectly fine; in fact, it may help you in ways you don't even appreciate at first. I eventually did my doctoral research on what I termed "holistic leadership." I found leaders who shared a common way of thinking about leadership and building compelling organizations. They became my research participants and my teachers. They became my beacon for hope. Little did I realize then how much I would end up relying on that hope to deal with the challenges I would face in my consulting work.

Why Are Some Leaders Such Jerks?

I worked with one company led by a CEO whom many employees described to me as the "classic asshole." Larry was a savvy business leader, but he was also arrogant and pompous. To make matters worse, he used fear and intimidation as his primary approach to leadership. People said that every time they interacted with Larry, they left feeling demeaned and deflated.

Human resources (HR) brought me in to run a leadership development program for mid-level and senior leaders. Larry was in one of my initial interviews, and within five minutes he set an adversarial tone. He went on a rant trashing HR and made it clear he was just putting up with this program. He didn't believe they needed it. When I asked him to describe his approach to leadership, he said, "It's easy. Fear. Your people have to fear you if you're going to be effective."

Once I started running the program, a lot of people wanted to talk about Larry. His senior leaders struggled with his style, but he was the boss. I told them that they had a responsibility to give Larry honest feedback. It would help him become a better leader. But nobody wanted to speak up—they just put up with him, and Larry continued to be, as many referred to him, "the classic asshole."

I ended up working with this organization through one of the biggest crises it had ever faced. Employees from a major supplier went through a nine-month strike, crippling my client. However, the leaders really stepped up and kept the organization going. They were struggling. They didn't achieve their financial goals—a failure they weren't used to.

But they managed to keep the company profitable, which was an amazing accomplishment in light of the crisis.

The leaders I worked with felt pretty good about themselves after the crisis was over. The company got positive media attention for the way it managed the situation. And the leaders came to trust one another more and work together better. Adversity can tear you apart or make you stronger; in this case, it made the leaders stronger.

About a week after the crisis was over, the senior leadership had a meeting with Larry. They were all expecting him to congratulate them for managing so well. But he didn't. Instead, he told them they were lucky to pull through, and he proceeded to point out all the times they had failed during the strike. When I talked to the leaders about this meeting, some of them had tears well up in their eyes as they retold this story. I heard them out and then asked, "Why didn't any of you stand up to Larry?" Complete silence filled the room.

I told them that leaders need to have the courage to call out bad behavior, no matter where it comes from. It's about speaking truth to power. It's not easy, but it is necessary at times. They told me that no one stood up because they were afraid—afraid of what Larry could do, afraid that they would lose their jobs. I felt for them. It was difficult to watch grown men and women talk about being belittled like that. Little did I know then that this theme of courage would become so prominent in my work with leaders.

I felt obligated to talk to Larry. I knew firsthand the negative impact that his behavior was having, and he needed to know. Someone had to have the courage to talk to him. I also knew he would not react well. He would probably retaliate by ending my contract. But that didn't bother me. I was more concerned that he would make things worse for his leaders once he found out what I had learned. Things were already bad enough for them. My contact in HR told me not to bother. He said the leaders would have to come to terms with Larry in their own ways. And over the next few months, they did—a few of them resigned, but most just put their heads down and kept putting up with it. No one had the courage to talk to Larry directly.

This experience weighed on me for quite a while. I kept asking myself what I could have done differently. But in the end, the real questions were: Why do organizations put up with leaders like Larry? Why are there so many people like him out there? What do they hope to achieve? Clearly, that company was very successful; it is possible to drive success through fear and intimidation, but that strategy can only get you so far. Leaders like Larry get the worst of their people. They waste the human potential of their teams. So much potential is left unrealized. So much potential is destroyed.

This is the moment I learned that, to change organizations, you need a little bit of naïve optimism. You have to believe in the potential of leaders and employees and what they can do to create great organizations. Unfortunately, great leaders and great organizations are the exception. The real work is in helping all those other leaders and organizations to be better. My personal resolve grew stronger. I became even more committed to my quest.

Why Are Many Leaders So Lame?

A little later in my career, I worked with a technology company whose founder and CEO, Jim, was a brilliant guy. He designed software for the financial services industry, and he was very successful. Customers came knocking on his door. His company grew quickly. But as a leader, he was a little rough around the edges. He could be hard on his people. But everyone knew his intentions were good, so it didn't bother them that much.

By the time I was brought in to build a leadership program, the company was struggling. New competitors had entered the market, and the company's software was starting to look dated. Talking to employees in the company, I learned that product development staff never communicated to those in marketing, and marketing staff never talked to those in sales. Success had made them lazy and complacent. Sales leaders were in the field promising release dates for new versions of the software, creating customer demand for a product that nobody was actually building. It was an absolute mess. How had these leaders let it get this bad?

The leadership forums I designed and ran were difficult meetings. The leaders only wanted to sit around and blame one another for the company's problems. They were too focused on their own small silos— they weren't operating as one company.

When the business had been doing well, the dysfunction didn't seem to matter—everything was easy. Cash kept streaming into the company.

This success had given the company a false sense of security and a false sense of how good it really was. That's when I learned that the numbers don't always tell the whole story.

Now that sales were lagging, everyone had noticed the cultural and organizational problems, but nobody knew what to do about them. Jim was at a loss, and the other leaders were stressed out, realizing that they were the ones who were going to have to figure out how to save the company. They were all under great pressure to turn things around. But they weren't responding. They were inept. They were helpless.

One day after another tough meeting with this group, I went to the parking lot and put my laptop bag and materials in my car. As I went to close my trunk, I looked up at the client's office building. I saw the floors where my client had offices. I pictured all those leaders who spent all their time fighting with one another, and then I pictured all the other floors with other companies in that office building, each one playing out its own self-created drama. It was only from outside the building that you could see how small those fights were, how much they distracted everyone, and how much they got in the way of success. This is when I began to understand that to create a strong organizational culture, you need to begin with a strong leadership culture.

In my experience as a consultant, I find many organizations have weak leadership cultures. Some are dreadful and others are completely dysfunctional. What's important to understand is that they are made that way, often by default, because few leaders pay attention to this thing called leadership culture.

However, I do find that there are a few truly exceptional leaders who have figured it out. They deliberately build strong leadership cultures in their organizations. I am fortunate to work with a few of those leaders. They show me that leadership culture can be a powerful and positive force in organizations. But it is also fragile. And the moment you stop paying attention to it, it begins to erode.

In the end, I have also learned that we all have a choice. We don't have to put up with uninspiring or toxic leadership cultures. We can create great ones. But it takes concerted effort to build and sustain them over the long term. It means you have to be relentlessly focused on keeping the cultures strong. It all begins with an aspiration for great leadership.

At that point in my journey, I also thought a lot about the quest I was on. I realized that as a consultant, I would always be on the sidelines, helping my clients but not really creating cultures myself. I enjoyed consulting, but I wanted to help build a business, too. I didn't just want to be a leadership expert—I wanted to be a leader. So I decided that I needed to go back into an organization, to take everything I learned from 10 years of consulting work, my graduate programs, and my research, and see whether I could actually make a strong leadership culture happen within a company.

Has Anyone Noticed That We've Stopped Talking about Our Values?

I never would have expected that my next opportunity would emerge so quickly. I was approached by a search firm to consider a role with a new start-up pharmaceutical company. The CEO, John, was an industry veteran. He had left a senior marketing job with a top-tier pharmaceutical company to start this new venture. He had a vision for creating a different kind of pharmaceutical company.

John had a great vision for the culture he wanted to create. The culture attracted me to the company. I decided to make the leap and became responsible for leading the learning and leadership function. It was a great experience with a great group of people. I had the opportunity that I was looking for: to go into a company and put my ideas into action. The good news was that John wasn't looking for the same old ways of working.

As a new company, we were pushing ourselves to think and act differently in all areas of our business. One of the things John taught me was a very subtle and important insight about leadership. John always believed that many leaders never really understand how a company actually makes money. He thought that was the cornerstone of all leadership, because once you understand that basic fundamental, it then drives all your behavior as a leader. That's when I began to learn about the deep connection between strategy and leadership.

Over the three years I was there, a subtle change took place in the conversations we had about our company. In the early days, we spent a lot of time talking about our values and the kind of culture we wanted to create. We were very successful at doing that. But then we stopped having those discussions.

Once in an all-staff meeting I shared my personal observation, "Has anyone noticed that we've stopped talking about our values?" It was a question that resonated with many. What I would learn later when I was back in consulting was that organizations do this all the time. Values and culture are closely connected to each other. Companies sometimes treat them as a project, something to be checked off the list. I would see this faulty thinking over and over again. Culture building isn't a one-time project or a simple to-do item; it's never-ending. You have to constantly work on it. If you don't, it will begin to erode.

Although my experience at this company was great and my team and I accomplished some good things, as the leader of a support function, I still felt one step removed from the core of the business. In just three years, I had already started to move into maintenance mode, and I knew that wasn't where I excelled. It was time to move on.

All along, the spirit of Zinta was still present as my inspiration. Then the chance I was really looking for finally arrived. I joined another consulting firm that was soon acquired by a new company called Knightsbridge Human Capital Solutions.

How Do You Create a Vibrant Culture?

David was the founder and CEO of Knightsbridge—a seasoned business leader who had a strong track record as a corporate CEO. David had an idea: He wanted to give organizations a more integrated way to address their human capital needs at every stage—from recruitment, selection, and talent attraction to employee and leadership development.

In addition, David stressed the importance of not only building a great professional services firm but also becoming a great operating company. This dual part of our vision created a healthy tension in our organization. David and the rest of the Knightsbridge employees were committed to making this goal a reality.

David also talked about building a vibrant company culture. He knew that would be critical to our success. And I knew that my vision of an integrated leadership practice would help play a role in making his overall vision a reality. I had found my opportunity to be the leader and put all my ideas about leadership and culture in place both within my business and externally with our clients.

In every organization, culture is both what binds you together and what propels you forward—but only if you get it right. If you don't, your culture becomes your fatal flaw. For a professional services business like Knightsbridge, culture has a real impact on the customer's experience. We defined our cultural uniqueness as our "K-Factor." It described our culture and the kind of employees who succeeded in our organization. It's what galvanized us. It's what made the organization special.

I held several roles of increasing responsibility in the early years. Then in July 2008, I was given the opportunity I was looking for: I was asked to lead a new Leadership Practice. My job was to integrate three separate businesses and redefine how we went to market. It was a great opportunity, and I immediately noticed something in me begin to change. As an executive, I now felt a greater sense of responsibility and accountability— more than at any other time in my career. I felt a direct obligation to our shareholders and board. I felt an even greater sense of accountability to our customers and employees. I was thrilled to have such an exciting opportunity to take on. I also knew it would take hard work to succeed.

But something happened in July of that year that would truly test my leadership—the financial crisis of 2007–2008.

As you might imagine, this was a very stressful time for all leaders in our client organizations. Knightsbridge fared well because our business model was tested and it was strong. Having a holistic business model with a collection of practice areas that can survive changes in economic cycles was a significant benefit for us. It was part of David's vision for the company and it worked.

It was also a big personal test for me. I learned that as a leader, you personally need resilience and resolve in difficult times. Not only do you need to manage your own reactions in those situations, but you also need to manage those of your team. And in our case, we also needed to be there for our clients in their time of need.

It was our collective obligation.

We stood by those who were struggling to deal with the fallout of the financial crisis. Many of our clients lost their jobs. Our career transition and outplacement services helped these clients in their time of need.

Others who managed to keep their jobs were working hard to make sure their companies remained intact during the crisis.

We also learned that many of our clients, particularly those who were new executives, had led only in good economic times. For them, this was their first experience leading through what would be one of the toughest economic periods in history. Our services became invaluable as we supported our clients through the crisis. I was proud of my colleagues and the impact they had on our clients during this difficult period.

Finally, what was fundamentally important to us was an idea I always believed in strongly: We couldn't just preach this leadership stuff; we needed to live it ourselves. We needed to work both to become great leaders and to model great leadership when working with our clients. If we did, they would notice and feel the difference. I believe we achieved this goal because we were able to build a strong leadership culture within my team. The other lesson is that building a strong leadership culture isn't just a destination you arrive at. You must remain committed in your efforts to sustain it.

How Do You Lead through Ambiguity?

Early in 2015, a new chapter in my personal leadership story began to unfold. Knightsbridge was acquired by The Adecco Group and Lee Hecht Harrison (LHH), global leaders in talent acquisition, development, and career transition.

This is the second time that I have worked for a company that was acquired. I have also been the acquirer and know at a personal level the impact these kinds of events have on employees and leaders.

Consolidation, mergers, and acquisitions have become commonplace in many industries. We've worked with many clients in these situations, and I find the first leadership challenge is to deal with all the ambiguity and uncertainty that arises. Leaders need to be exceptional at it, and if they aren't, then things break down quickly.

Now I found myself in the same situation as so many of my clients. In our case, the acquisition was a positive event. But even in our situation, there was ambiguity and a sense of disruption for employees and customers.

Customers want to be reassured that their world won't change. As a leader, you must communicate frequently to your customers and maintain high levels of service.

Employees always have varied reactions. Some will be upbeat and positive. Others will be concerned about their jobs and careers. All these reactions are legitimate and need to be addressed head-on by leaders.

The important thing to remember is that in all this ambiguity and change, you have an obligation to lead. During periods of uncertainty, everyone instinctively looks to the leaders for cues. The tone you set can either help or hinder how everyone else reacts. If you're running around fretting, it's quite likely your employees will do the same. On the other hand, if you project confidence and reassurance, this will be contagious as well.

But there's more. We evolved from being part of a privately held company to being part of a publicly held Fortune Global 500 firm. The Adecco Group is headquartered in Zurich, Switzerland, and has more than 33,000 full-time employees in sixty countries. The company is the world's leading provider of workforce solutions, transforming the world of work through talent and technology.

Through its global brands Adecco, Modis, Badenoch & Clark, Spring Professional, Lee Hecht Harrison, and Pontoon, The Adecco Group offers total workforce solutions including temporary staffing, permanent placement, career transition, leadership and talent development, and outsourcing.

Six months after the acquisition took place, I was asked to take on a global role to help drive compelling thought leadership in the market. I also established a leadership transformation team to help organizations build the accountable leadership they need to succeed in a world of change, disruption, and ambiguity. This role represented another unique challenge in my own unfolding leadership story.

How Do You Transform Your Leaders?

In my new role, I was given a tremendous opportunity to share the ideas in this book with leaders around the world. I spoke at close to one hundred events with customers, at conferences, and in small dinners with senior human resource executives and C-suite leaders. As I traveled in North America, South America, Europe, and Asia, I found myself running up against significant leadership stories that were unfolding in every part of the world. These events pointed to the significant leadership challenges faced by many companies and countries.

I spent a lot of time in the United States, as Donald Trump was being elected president after a campaign in which both he and Democratic nominee Hillary Clinton achieved infamy for being among the least popular politicians ever to vie for the White House. I traveled to thirty U.S. cities, and during the election, everyone I talked to asked "How did we get here?" After the election, many I spoke to asked "What are we going to do now?" I could sense the anguish and uncertainty in their voices. Others saw it as an opportunity for change.

Then I had an extraordinary and unexpected experience on another business trip. I arrived one Sunday morning in March, in São Paolo, Brazil, South America's largest country. Soon after my flight landed, I came to learn that millions of Brazilians were in the streets protesting and showing their disgust for government corruption. President Dilma Rousseff was eventually impeached amidst corruption allegations. Her successor, Michel Temer, was in the job less than six months before he too was drawn into a corruption scandal involving illegal payments from engineering companies looking for government work. In my discussions with Brazilian business leaders, I could tell they were deeply uncertain about the future of their country.

I also spent a week in Colombia, just weeks after Colombians voted to reject a peace deal between the government and former rebel group Fuerzas Armadas Revolucionarias de Colombia (Farc). The deal took over four years to negotiate and would have ended five decades of war. The country was shocked at the failure of the deal, and people were left surprised and uncertain about how to move forward.

I traveled through the United Kingdom soon after the shocking decision to leave the European Union. The "Brexit" vote not only rocked international markets, but it also led to a rash of political leaders' resignations—many of the anti-EU leaders and British Prime Minister David Cameron. Many Brits were stunned and are still feeling their way through the transition.

I was also in Italy, launching the Italian translation of my book, just before Italian Prime Minister Matteo Renzi resigned after his citizens rejected a series of constitutional reforms in a referendum. The resignation has set off a political crisis in Italy, with no clear choice among other party leaders to form a government.

All these events provided me with a fascinating series of real-world lessons that helped me better understand how leaders around the world were making sense of what it truly means to be a leader.

I also learned that my research around leadership accountability, and the ideas in this book, were connecting with leaders in a profound way.

When I first set off for all my travels, I really didn't know what to expect. However, I was surprised and humbled to meet many great people who were fully committed to being truly accountable leaders. It was an honor to share my ideas, and I'm grateful they were so meaningful to so many. As an author and leadership adviser, that's the kind of impact you hope your ideas will have.

Still, I asked myself: Why were the ideas of the leadership contract resonating so much? As I traveled, I learned that many companies find themselves at critical inflection points. Fundamental changes in technology, markets, and demographics are forcing companies to transform themselves. And that kind of transformation must start with leaders.

Leadership and workforce transformation, then, is the work that companies must excel at if they hope to survive in the future. Interestingly, when I think about the best work that my teams and I have done in the past with our clients, it's always been with an organization looking to transform itself. We have rarely done what I call steady-state leadership development. Instead, we have always helped companies build truly accountable leaders during times of significant change and transformation.

Leading during transformation is not an easy task. I believe it represents the greatest leadership challenge that one can face. I believe more and more organizations in the future will need leaders who are agile and responsive—leaders who can quickly evolve and transform themselves so they can set the tone for the rest of the employees in their companies.

Reflecting on My Leadership Story

In fact, as I now reflect on my personal leadership story, I feel that I have been fortunate to have carried out Zinta's vision from all those years ago. I didn't realize it at the time, but Zinta was trying to start a transformation. She enlisted my help and we began to have some impact. But she ran out of time. She wasn't able to see the transformation she started to the end.

To make matters worse, she was trying to change an organization that didn't want to change. She worked in a toxic leadership culture.

I know I've been lucky to be part of organizations where growth and change were the expectation, and where we shared a collective aspiration to build a truly great organization. I never take this for granted, because I have learned over the years how rare this can be.

And that's the final lesson of my leadership story: Don't waste your time in an organization that doesn't deserve your investment. Remember Zinta. You aren't just investing your time or your career—you're investing your life.

As a leader, you need to determine whether your organization is worthy of that investment. If it is, then roll up your sleeves and get busy making it the best organization it can be. Your organization desperately needs you and your personal leadership. It needs you to make the leadership decision to become a truly accountable leader. It needs you to step up to your obligations as a leader. It needs you to tackle the hard work that you must do as a leader. It needs you to build a strong community of leaders so you can collectively transform it. Are you ready?

The Gut Check for Leaders—Your Personal Leadership Story

As you think about the ideas in this chapter, reflect on your answers to the following gut check questions:

1. What is your personal leadership story?
2. What critical leadership experiences have shaped you as a leader?
3. With whom can you share your personal leadership story?
4. How might you help a fellow leader better understand his or her own personal leadership story?

CHAPTER 2

What's Wrong with Leadership Today?

During the 2012 U.S. presidential race, the Republican Party attempted to paint a picture of Barack Obama as an ineffective leader who let down the American people. It did this in part by using the metaphor of an empty chair leader. Then *The New Yorker* picked up on the metaphor and ran a cover showing Republican candidate Mitt Romney at a presidential debate standing next to an empty chair. The cover struck a nerve with readers. E-mails flowed in. Some readers were outraged, believing the image to be disrespectful to the office of the president. Others were strongly supportive, believing it was time to call out poor leadership.

What was particularly telling about this cover was the strong reaction that readers of *The New Yorker* had to the metaphor of empty chair leadership. In fact, I believe it is a common human response. We all react viscerally when our leaders don't perform the way they should—when they don't fill their chairs effectively—and hold a title but don't really lead. We are filled with a sense of disappointment and even despair. In the worst cases, we become disillusioned.

We all hope to be great leaders, to be led by great leaders, and to be part of the great organizations that we collectively build. But too often, our leaders let us down. Many fail to live up to the obligations of the role. If we are honest with ourselves, we all know that stories of great leaders leading great companies act as beacons of hope, but these stories are the minority. More common are stories of empty chair leaders—those who are inept or motivated solely by personal ambition. These leaders fail to live up to their leadership accountability.

We as leaders can't ignore what is happening. Since publishing the first edition of this book, things seem to have only grown worse.

We need to work together to bring back a sense of hope about leadership. But before we can do that, we need to really understand where we are failing. We need to face the harsh reality that leadership today is still disappointing, disconnected, and disgraceful.

Leadership Is Disappointing

What made the people of Spain take to the streets in 2013 to protest their royal family? After all, the country's unemployment rate was hovering just below 30 percent at the time. The unemployment rate among young people was a whopping 57 percent. Surely Spaniards had more important things to worry about.

Actually, that economic trouble was part of the reason people were so fed up with the royal family. They appeared woefully out of touch with the realities of Spaniards' lives. In a country experiencing a prolonged depression, with a lost generation of youth, to flaunt one's riches is in bad taste. The same is true within organizations. When senior leaders appear completely out of touch with the realities of their employees, disgust sets in. The fact that the king's son-in-law apparently embezzled millions of dollars from charities that he ran only served to further fuel the fire.

You don't have to look very far to see examples of leaders who disappoint us. It could be that sense of disappointment when we read of corporate leaders who have behaved badly or bilked their companies and shareholders out of millions. It could also be that moment when you are in the voting booth during an election, looking at the slate of candidates, and asking yourself: Is this the best we can do? Sometimes it feels like we are disappointed even before we elect our politicians—even before they take office and really begin to disappoint us.

For the vast majority of us, disappointing leadership also happens in more personal ways. This has become apparent to me over and over again in my work with leaders.

A couple of years ago, in a leadership development program I was leading, a participant named Nate was struggling. He was resisting everything and didn't want to be there. Then something changed in him when he completed the Personal Leadership Timeline activity.

As participants were busy working away, I noticed that Nate was just sitting there. I assumed he was still resisting and choosing not to participate. When I approached him, however, I realized he was deep in thought. He shared with me that one of the patterns he had observed over his personal leadership timeline was that every negative experience in his career came about when he worked for a boss who was a jerk. One such boss in particular was very difficult and would routinely yell, scream, and belittle employees. Nate said he remembered how it eroded his personal sense of engagement as an employee.

Then he asked himself the question that really made him think hard about his own approach to leadership. It was his own leadership gut check question. He said, "If my team was completing this activity, where would I show up as their leader? Would they see me as a leader creating a positive experience or a demoralizing one?"

I could see now why Nate was so deep in thought. He'd just realized, for the first time, that he was probably the jerk on his employees' personal leadership timelines, and he didn't like that reality at all. At that moment, something changed in Nate. He became completely engaged in the program. He stopped resisting because he realized he didn't want to be the leader who demoralized his team and colleagues. He no longer wanted to be the leader he had become.

This is an important insight for leaders like Nate to gain, because emerging research suggests there is a price to pay if you are a jerk and a disappointing leader. An infographic in *Inc.* magazine recently focused on "The Real Productivity-Killer: Jerks."[1] It synthesized the findings of several studies on the real costs of lame leadership and bad bosses. For example:

- Seventy-five percent of employees report that their boss is the worst and most stressful part of their job.
- Sixty-five percent of employees would take a new boss over a pay raise.
- Fifty percent of employees who don't feel valued by their boss plan to look for another job.
- Thirty-three percent of employees with bad bosses confess to not putting in full effort.
- Twenty-nine percent took sick days when they were not ill.

Even worse, bad leaders are bad for your health. Employees who have poor relationships with their bosses are 30 percent more likely to suffer from coronary heart disease. Maybe my colleague Zinta was right after all. Her disease may well have been a function of being in that dreadful organization led by lame and bad bosses.

As leaders, we never want to hear that we are disappointing our employees. It's certainly not something I want to hear. But it's important for us to be honest with ourselves so we can stop letting everyone down.

If you learned that 38 percent of your employees were chronically poor performers, you'd be moving fast to fix the problem. Yet, a recent report released by the Institute for Policy Studies documents that 38 percent of CEOs studied (of 500) perform poorly—and little is being said or done about the problem. To be sure, some of those underperforming CEOs end up getting fired, but all too often, their companies pay massive fines or costs—or need to be bailed out. Or they simply go under.

Many of the poor performers represent some of the highest-paid CEOs in the world. And many walk away with huge severance packages after they were bailed out, booted, or busted.

Personally, I don't have an issue with CEO compensation when the individual is a strong and consistently high performer. I've worked with many of these CEOs, and I know the tremendous value they create in terms of strengthening the economy, creating jobs for thousands, and providing valuable products and services. They are not the problem. The problem lies with the CEOs who are chronicly poor performers. They tarnish the great work of the hardworking and high-performing ones.

Ultimately, it doesn't matter whether you're the CEO or a front-line manager. When you are a disappointment as a leader, you erode the engagement of your followers. They won't go the extra mile for you or your organization. They will never give you their full discretionary effort. Think of your own personal experience when you have worked with a disappointing leader. There's a good chance that you never gave that leader your best. In fact, there's a good chance you purposely withheld your most creative ideas, your passion, and your full discretionary effort.

As I've shared this idea with other leaders, it seems I've somehow uncovered a secret that we are all carrying: We all consciously withhold a part of ourselves when we're stuck with a boss who disappoints us. It's not how we want to behave, but it's how we are forced to behave in the face of disappointing leadership.

I believe this is the price that organizations pay when they have empty chair or mediocre leaders. Your employees come to work each day thinking: *How much effort do I really want to put in today? Is my boss worth my full engagement?*

This is why organizations have a chronic problem with employee engagement. Only one in five employees is ever fully engaged. Although we know that working for an admired leader is the number one nonmonetary motivator of employees, we don't seem to appreciate the impact bad leadership has on engagement. Empty chair leaders create unmotivated employees. The employee experience is a function of the quality of the leadership experience. As a leader, you need to understand the price your organization pays for having disappointing leadership.

Leadership Is Disconnected

I talk to many leaders in my work, and many tell me they feel like they are working in isolation. As leaders, they feel disconnected from employees, peers, and colleagues. They are trying to do their best, but they don't feel supported and don't have a real sense of community with their fellow leaders. A survey of 83 CEOs at public and private companies found that half reported feeling a sense of isolation that could hinder their ability to carry out their jobs effectively.[2] The survey also found that first-time CEOs were particularly vulnerable: 70 percent of them reported feeling lonely in their roles.

Although this research focused on CEOs, I believe this experience is more widespread. It's not just lonely at the top. It's lonely throughout all leadership ranks.

We should acknowledge that leadership roles by their nature do impose a sense of separation. Leaders need to do difficult things at times. They need to hold poor performers accountable, make decisions to close down companies, and fire people. Even when these actions are necessary, they serve to distance leaders and cut them off from others. That's a reality. We should also acknowledge that in large organizations, leaders often don't know one another. They're so busy that they rarely have time to connect and build relationships.

But I believe that our leadership experience doesn't have to be so isolating. We certainly don't obtain the best from our leaders this way.

Consider the story of Simon, a young product manager who worked in a pharmaceutical company. Simon was smart, well liked, and very good at his job. As soon as the senior leaders noticed him, they promoted him. Suddenly, Simon was responsible for the company's most successful and profitable product.

For a while, things went really well. Simon excelled in his new role. For about a year and a half, sales and market share were strong. Simon became *the golden boy*. He was held up as a model of what other employees should aspire to become. Other product managers were measured against him. He received a lot of positive attention and adulation.

Then the trouble started. A competitor launched a new product at a dramatically discounted price. It surprised everyone; the market in that therapeutic area had changed overnight. Simon was now under a lot of pressure to come up with a response. No matter what he tried, nothing seemed to help. He started to feel isolated and unsupported. He was no longer the golden boy. He quickly realized he wasn't being invited to the same meetings any longer. He was purposely being cut off. He knew it, and so did everyone else.

Unfortunately, Simon wasn't able to come up with a solution that worked. Market share took a significant hit; six months later, Simon was fired. The company believed that Simon had failed it. And to some extent, it was right: He did fail to meet that unexpected challenge.

Simon also failed because he began to believe all the hype that was being generated about him. He quickly went from hero to zero. But I also believe that the company failed Simon. Management was mesmerized by its new star, but it failed to support him when he needed it the most. Maybe it promoted him too quickly. Maybe it focused too much on the short-term results he was getting and didn't bother to show him how to translate his initial success into a sustainable long-term plan. Simon failed because he was isolated and unsupported.

Leadership Is Disgraceful

The International Federation of Football Association (or FIFA as its commonly referred to) is the world's governing body of soccer (or football, depending on where you are in the world). In 2015, the organization experienced a scandal. Many executive members and senior officials of the organization began to fall, like soccer players faking injuries on the field, as they faced multiple arrests and criminal charges for corruption. Sepp Blatter, the beleaguered president, had no place to hide and finally had to resign his post.

By the time he resigned, Interpol had already issued warrants for multiple FIFA officials on corruption, racketeering, and conspiracy charges. The Federal Bureau of Investigation (FBI) was also formally investigating Blatter.

It was clear that FIFA, as an organization, was rotten to the core.

From a leadership perspective, Blatter's long and checkered 17-year history with FIFA makes for an interesting study in ego, uncontrolled power, and greed. As does his initial refusal to step down as president when senior members of his team were being arrested. Even when he finally decided to quit, Blatter maintained he was stepping down only because the football community had lost faith in him, not because he was involved in the corruption.

"FIFA needs profound restructuring," Blatter said in his speech. "I decided to stand again to be elected because I was convinced it was the best option for football. Although the members of FIFA gave me a new mandate, this mandate does not seem to be supported by everyone in the world."

Only on his way out did he claim to have recognized the organization that he led needed restructuring. Could he really have been leading an organization that was rotten to the core and not have noticed?

And what if he had? Even then, his story is still one of failed leadership. How could a leader not know about the money, influence peddling, and rampant greed at the root of FIFA's extensive corruption?

It's not just FIFA. Leadership today has become disgraceful. You don't have to look very far to see that many leaders have lost their way. It's all over the front page: Enron, Lehman Brothers, the global financial crisis, and the Libor scandal. Corruption is everywhere. And many of the leaders at the center of these stories often seem to walk away free and clear—with big severance packages. How is this possible?

Our leaders have let us down. Employee trust and confidence in senior leadership, organizations, and boards of directors have been in a steady decline. The most pessimistic survey results show that only 7 percent of employees have confidence that the senior leaders in their organizations are looking out for their best interests.[3]

In fact, every time I start working with a new client, I ask to see the most recent employee engagement survey. I then find the one question that asks about employee trust and confidence in senior leadership. I know that if the percentage is low, I immediately have a sense of the state of that organization. Low trust in senior leadership has a price.

Scandals can weaken the entire leadership culture of a company. We recently launched a large leadership development initiative with an organization. Weeks before the pilot program began, the company came under fire for a financial scandal.

When we were kicking off the pilot session, the corporate scandal quickly became the elephant in the room topic. It wasn't long before we realized we had to discuss it with those leaders. They needed the forum to express their personal views on those events. What we found was that the leaders felt a deep-seated anger over the events.

Many of the participants admitted they were embarrassed to work for the company now. Others were devastated because they were once so proud to be part of that company and now felt empty inside. Another group of leaders felt a real sense of resentment because they feared that the scandal negatively tainted the reputation of all the company's leaders. They were already seeing a change in relationships with customers and vendors. Trust was eroded.

When stories of corporate scandal break out in the media, the attention is often on the bad leaders involved or the damaged reputation of the company. Few stories dig deeper to understand the impact on other leaders and employees. What I learned from this organization is that a scandal can rock the culture of an organization to its core. It affects all employees in significant ways. In fact, there is new research to suggest that the impact is far more significant than previously thought.

In a paper published in the journal *Social Psychological and Personality Science*, researchers Takuya Sawaoka and Benoît Monin of Stanford University report that the personal reputations of good and ethical leaders are in fact damaged in companies embroiled in corruption or a scandal. The researchers call this the "moral spillover" effect.

What it means is that if you happen to find yourself in a company experiencing a major scandal, there is a high probability that your own personal reputation will be marred, even if you had nothing to do with the wrongdoing. The researchers go on to say that not only are personal reputations damaged, but careers also can be derailed completely. It seems the negativity of being associated with a corrupt organization can linger for a long time and diminish one's chances of being hired by another firm.

I doubt that leaders engaging in bad or unethical behavior really care about the collateral damage from their actions. They certainly don't care about the personal reputations of their fellow employees. But the fact remains that when these scandals happen, all of us as leaders are tarnished. I know firsthand that the majority of CEOs with whom I have had the privilege of working take their roles seriously and lead ethically, with integrity and humility. These are the CEOs I admire. They are not the problem. But the few who act in a disgraceful manner erode the trust we need in our leaders. The public just doesn't trust its leaders anymore, and we have to do something about it. We need to collectively find our way back and restore the trust and confidence that people have in us. We have to stop making leadership a disgrace.

How Did We Get Here?

Leadership has become lame in many organizations. Many of the mid-level leaders I work with say they feel complacent in their roles because they aren't inspired by the leaders above them. Employees will say that most leaders they have worked with are average at best. And we as leaders know that being an average leader isn't good enough in today's world.

So how did we get here? There are four primary reasons for today's crisis in leadership accountability, which I will review below.

We Have Relied on the Heroic Model of Leadership

The story of Simon shared earlier in this chapter has been repeated countless times in countless organizations. At the core is a belief in the heroic model of leadership. It's a model we all know too well—the idea that one leader, usually at the top of the organization, has all the answers and can single-handedly lead the way.

This model may have occasionally worked in the past if the person was truly extraordinary, but it certainly won't work in today's complex and uncertain world. The old heroic model of leadership just isn't sustainable anymore. No one leader could possibly have all the answers—and yet we're constantly watching our leaders today, waiting for them to slip up, waiting for them to demonstrate that they, in fact, don't know everything.

Take Claudio Ranieri, the former manager of the Leicester City football (soccer) club in England. He was the darling of the football world when he led his underdog team to win the championship in 2016 for the first time ever in the team's 132-year history. Ranieri was praised as an inspirational leader. Some people started calling him "King Claudio."

Then his second season with the club began. The team lost six of their first twelve games. In those first twelve games, they only managed to secure one point while on the road. Obviously, that's a disappointing comedown after an improbable and exhilarating victory—but is it proof that the system that worked one season doesn't work anymore?

Leicester City seemed to think so. They fired Ranieri midway through his second season despite a brilliant first year, when he couldn't repeat his miraculous performance in his second year. He was out and went from hero to zero.

If you are a senior leader, your every move, your every decision, and your every action are open to commentary, debate, and criticism. We have created a world in which you are either a hero or a zero.

However, it is important to realize that it actually is risky to put all your faith in just one individual. And this kind of constant scrutiny focused on only one leader at the top actually takes attention away from other leaders in an organization. Emerging leaders, mid-level leaders, and executives all contribute to the success of an organization, but if we focus on only the few at the top, we fail to support and grow the leaders we need for the future.

We Have Glorified Charismatic Leaders

Unfortunately, the problem is amplified because we don't just focus on a few heroes at the top; we then turn them into celebrities. Think of all those charismatic celebrity CEOs out there. We adore them. Jim Collins warned against the dangers of charismatic CEOs in his book *Good to Great*. Yet here we are today, still adoring them. In the process, we give them too much money and power. I'm not saying that charisma is bad, not at all. All leaders need a certain amount of it, but charisma can have a dark side too.

Author Geoffrey Nunberg, in his book *Ascent of the A-Word*, dubs this the "age of assholism," because some of the world's nastiest leaders have become the most successful.[4] He cites Steve Jobs as one of the most famous examples. Walter Isaacson, author of the bestselling biography *Steve Jobs*, describes him as a person who succeeded despite being a "colossal asshole."

Uber Technologies CEO Travis Kalanick sought forgiveness and redemption after an online video of him arguing and berating a driver was leaked on social media. He apologized for his actions, saying he was seeking coaching to learn how to be a better leader. This was admirable for him to do. But it soon became clear that his style of leadership had permeated the culture. More fallout ensued with the resignations of key executives, as well as charges of harassment. Eventually, Kalanick had to step down. At first, many cited that Uber often hired "brilliant jerks" known to mistreat employees and didn't support their development as leaders. But in the end, they still hired the jerks and the company paid the price for it.

Ultimately, I worry that these kinds of stories confuse people. When we see these kinds of leaders being glorified as heroes, even though they are jerks, we become skeptical. You ask yourself: Is this what great leadership is about? Do I need to be a jerk to succeed as a leader? If you look at examples in the media, the answer seems to be yes. But most people I work with want to lead more positively and optimistically. And many get confused when they see jerks rewarded and celebrated to the extent that they are. This practice has to stop.

We can all acknowledge that leaders sometimes need to be harsh, because a positive approach does not always get results. Sometimes you need to hold an underperforming worker accountable. Or you need to bring a sense of urgency to a team that is not delivering. Or you are cleaning up a situation after a major screw-up. In these moments, a glimpse of your harsh side can increase motivation, improve performance, and communicate the severity of the situation. Jerks get people's attention. But there's a difference between selectively being harsh when the situation demands it and being a jerk all the time. One's a tactic; the other is a personality trait.

We Have Promoted Technical Superstars into Leadership Roles

Few leaders set out to become lame or even mediocre. However, something has happened in organizations where we've come to tolerate mediocrity from our leaders. From my work, I have found that part of the problem is that we've promoted strong technical performers into leadership roles. Think about your own career. If you're like most leaders, you were really, really good at what you did—whether it was accounting, marketing, engineering, sales, and so on. In fact, you were one of the best. You were rewarded with a promotion to your first management or leadership role. The thinking was that if you were strong technically, you would obviously be strong in a management or leadership role.

And if you are like most leaders I have talked to, you really didn't have much choice in the matter. Moving up into a leadership role was the only way you could make more money, get more prestige, or have more influence. Up was the only way forward.

But when you took the role, you quickly realized that you needed to start dealing with staff issues and important business decisions. And the longer you were in the role, the further away you were from what got you the job in the first place: the technical stuff.

So you went from being a brilliant individual contributor to being thrown into the leadership deep end without a lot of support from your organization. You needed to figure out all the personnel stuff on your own. You needed to understand how your role changed and the expectations you had to live up to. You either sank or learned to swim. But even if you figured out how to swim, you may have just kept your head above water. To cope, you then relegated the people issues to second place and focused on the more stimulating technical parts of your job. Then you became a leader in title but not in action.

Even if you realize that being a leader isn't your thing and you are tired of disappointing yourself and others, it's really difficult to stop. We haven't made it easy for leaders to put up their hands and say, "I'm not good at this. Help me find another way to add value in this company." It takes a pretty big person to admit his or her weaknesses and give up the perks that come with a leadership role. But until we stop promoting technical stars into leadership roles and stop making it difficult for people to step down, our organizations will continue to be filled with leaders who put their passion for the technical aspects ahead of the leadership demands. In the end, they disappoint us because they don't end up truly leading.

We Have a Quick-Fix View to Developing Leaders

In her book *The End of Leadership*, Harvard professor Barbara Kellerman takes aim at the leadership industry and warns companies to have a "buyer beware" attitude.[5] She argues that this industry hasn't made leaders more effective and ethical—it's done the opposite. She explains that the root of the problem is a set of mistaken assumptions. For one, we have always thought of leadership as being static. We have also assumed leadership is simple and something that can be easily taught and learned by the masses. And we have overemphasized an individualistic view of leadership, ignoring the context in which leaders lead and the impact it has on their effectiveness.

Furthermore, we have been too simplistic about what it really takes to develop leaders. We are always looking for a quick-fix solution to our problems. Companies jump from fad to fad in leadership development, and the leadership industry is more than ready to jump on the latest trend. In addition, in a world driven by social media, where we communicate in short blog posts and 140-character tweets, it's all too easy for leadership advice to become simplistic. We are dumbing down leadership training and trying to make it too quick and easy to become a good leader. The result is too many people in leadership roles simply don't understand what it really means to be a leader.

We Need the Leadership Development Industry to Step Up and Be Accountable

Barbara Kellerman is not the only vocal critic of the leadership development industry; so is Jeffrey Pfeffer, a professor at the Stanford Graduate School of Business. In his book, *Leadership BS: Fixing Workplaces and*

Careers One Truth at a Time, [6] he argues that despite the billions of dollars that companies spend on developing their leaders through training programs, inspirational keynote speeches, conferences, and coaching engagements, leadership isn't any stronger today.

A while back, I was speaking at a conference in California. Also on the agenda was Dr. Pfeffer. Being a big fan of his work, I sat in on his session.

He argued passionately and called out the leadership development industry—the one that I have called home for many years. Pfeffer argued that rather than helping to build better leaders, we had only served to make the situation worse.

Pfeffer noted that most of what the industry proclaims good leadership looks like is exactly the opposite of what leaders need to do in their organizations. Whether it's advice for leaders to be authentic, transparent, vulnerable, or emotionally intelligent, Pfeffer believes that these things are not what make leaders successful in their careers. To succeed in big organizations, you need to be ruthless and narcissistic. He then explained that part of the problem is that anyone can be a self-proclaimed leadership expert in today's world. One doesn't even need any relevant experience.

As evidence, Pfeffer shared an experience he had when he came across a list of the Top 50 leadership and management experts in a business magazine. As he skimmed the list, he quickly realized he didn't recognize many of the names. He then looked at the top 20 people and researched their backgrounds. It turns out that one had no college degree. Only five had terminal degrees in a relevant field. Two had doctorates in religion. There was little to no experience that would suggest they could advise and consult on leadership. What the top 20 had in common was that they all had written leadership books and all did a lot of public speaking.

Now I felt myself start to get a little defensive and I began to squirm in my seat. "I've written leadership books," I thought to myself. "I've done and still do tons of speaking." He went on sharing humorous stories. I laughed, as did the audience, but he delivered what for me was an unsettling speech. He had given me a lot to think about.

As fate would have it, a few weeks after I attended that conference I had a call from a former client. He was an unconventional public-sector leader my team and I had helped to completely overhaul the leadership culture at his organization. After that challenge, he moved to another organization, leading the municipal government of a large city. He wanted me to come in to help him "really shake things up."

When I met him a few days later, he told me that his predecessor had brought in a high-profile leadership expert to provide leadership development training and motivational speeches. He also directly advised the senior leaders in this government.

Thanks to this expert, an extremely complicated leadership structure was put in place. Everything was top-heavy and siloed. Soon, all the leaders became obsessed with building their own empires. The culture became divisive, highly competitive, and toxic. Change was needed.

Eventually, many of the top leaders in this government were ousted and my client was brought in to turn things around. We started to work on a plan to help make that happen.

As I left that meeting, my mind immediately turned to Professor Pfeffer. This was exactly the scenario he was talking about. Now I could see clearly what happens when an organization puts its trust in someone who merely writes and speaks about leadership, but has no real experience actually leading or doing real consulting work with organizations.

His provocations got a reaction in me because I've spent my career in the leadership development industry and believe it can provide real value to organizations and their leaders. But I also acknowledge that it's an industry that attracts far too many imposters and self-proclaimed gurus.

As Pfeffer observed, it seems anyone can set up a blog, write a book, start speaking about leadership, or obtain a coaching certification over a weekend. Some of these people offer real value. Many others simply do not. They dispense advice that is trite, naïve, and at times even harmful for the intended readers.

If you work in the leadership industry as I do, it's time we hold ourselves to a higher standard. We must commit to being the best advisers we can be to our clients. It's time we step up and be accountable.

So do not let the allure of fame or being regarded as a "leadership guru" get to your head. It should never be about you; it should be about your clients and the leaders you serve.

If you are in a company and you need to bring in a leadership expert, don't get mesmerized by the aura (or in some cases the smoke and mirrors) that is presented. Do some real digging into the person's background and work experience. Ask some tough questions. How many years has this person been in the leadership industry? Does he or she have any real business experience or actually worked as a leader before telling others how to lead? Has he or she conducted research or have an academic track record in leadership development?

The costs of getting it wrong can be significant.

It's Time We Stop Settling—and Start Expecting More

When our experience of leadership is routinely disappointing, disconnected, and disgraceful, we begin to lower our expectations. The scandals make the headlines, but the deeper disappointment and even disillusionment happen every day in more mundane ways as we work with empty chair leaders who lack vision, who don't inspire, and who appear to be simply going through the motions.

The longer we live with ineffective and uninspiring leadership, the more disappointed we become. My concern is that we're only becoming increasingly numb to what is truly happening around us. When we experience the isolation of being a leader, we start feeling disconnected. Then we start checking out.

When empty chair leadership disappoints us, we lose hope and give up. We stop aspiring for great leadership from ourselves or others. We settle. As soon as this happens, we stop stepping up as leaders. We become bystanders in our organization. We show up every day and go through the motions. You may have the title of a leader, but you are not fulfilling your obligations. You may not be inspired by the leadership around you. You think to yourself, "What's the point of stepping up and trying to be a great leader?" The second you have that thought, you have lowered your expectations for yourself and others around you. Seth Godin, in his book *Tribes*,[7] has a powerful thought. He says that settling is a malignant habit. It's a slippery slope. One day you wake up and you've become an empty chair leader.

It is time we stop settling.

It is time we start expecting more from ourselves as leaders.

It is time we start demonstrating real leadership accountability.

What does this look like? Based on my research and extensive client work, real leadership accountability is demonstrated when you:

1. Take complete ownership for your entire role—both the technical, people and culture aspects of the job.
2. Lead in a deliberate and decisive manner and always be clear of your obligations.
3. Bring a sense of urgency to tackle tough issues when they arise which helps your organization to move forward and get stronger every single day.

In the rest of this book, we will explore these ideas and more. You will learn how fulfill the four terms of the leadership contract.

The Gut Check for Leaders—What's Wrong with Leadership Today?

As you think about the ideas in this chapter, reflect on your answers to the following gut check questions:

1. What has been your experience with empty chair leadership?
2. Think of your current leadership role and reflect on whether you have settled as a leader.
3. In what ways do you feel disconnected? Why?
4. What has been your experience with disgraceful leadership?
5. Would your employees say that they give you their full discretionary effort?
6. Are your expectations for leadership high enough for yourself and others?

CHAPTER 3

The Leadership Accountability Gap

A while back I met with the head of human resources (HR) for a financial services company. As we sat down to start our discussion, I could tell she was frustrated. She began by saying, "I thought we did all the right things when it came to developing our leaders." She explained that her organization had identified its high-potential leaders and created a development program for them. "We then gave them all promotions, with fancy titles and increased compensation. And now we are waiting— waiting for them to lead," she said.

I asked her to explain further what she meant by "waiting."

"They aren't leading," she said. "They are waiting for permission and direction from the executive team on every issue. Or they're acting like bystanders, watching problems persist or projects derail." She then shared what I thought was her most important insight: "It's like they don't know what it means to be a leader!"

Over the last few years, my team and I have been hearing more and more of this kind of lament from senior executives in all industries. It seems that despite all the investment in leadership development, there is a gap between what we expect of our leaders and how they are performing. As I shared in the introductory chapter, I call this *the leadership accountability gap.*

And since publishing the first edition of this book, it has been surprising to me to see how the ideas have struck a chord with leaders from the C-suite to the front line, from the board to HR. I started to get a sense that leadership accountability was in fact a widespread business issue. I was seeing the same level of frustration with other clients and organizations.

So in the spring of 2015, we decided we needed to conduct more research into the issue. We partnered with Human Resources People + Strategy (HRPS), the executive division of the Society for Human Resources Management (SHRM). Their membership represents the most senior HR executives in business, and we believed members could give us important insights into the state of leadership accountability in companies today.

We conducted a survey using a third-party research firm and reached more than two hundred HRPS members across North America, most of whom were HR leaders and senior executives across a wide variety of industries, representing a number of Fortune 500 companies. It was the first study ever conducted exploring the business issue of leadership accountability and the results were eye-opening:[1]

- The survey found that nearly three-quarters (72 percent) of respondents said that leadership accountability was indeed a "critical business issue" in their organization.
- The survey also found that only 37 percent of respondents were satisfied with the level of leadership accountability in their organizations.

The collective response was loud and clear: The leadership accountability gap is real, pervasive, and a critical business issue that must be addressed.

Discovering the problem to be so widespread, my team and I decided to expand the study globally to companies in North America, South America, Europe, and Asia. A total of 2,084 senior HR and business executives participated in the research.[2] The findings were dramatic—the global data was nearly identical to the findings from our first study, leading to the conclusion that the leadership accountability gap is a global problem.[3]

Understanding the Leadership Accountability Gap: Study Findings

As is shown in Figure 3.1, 72 percent of the global respondents believe that leadership accountability is a critical issue in their organization. Only

72%
Believe leadership
accountability is a
critical business issue

31%
Satisfied with degree of
leadership accountability

Figure 3.1   The Leadership Accountability Gap

31 percent of them were satisfied with the degree of accountability
demonstrated by their leaders.

   The consistency of these survey findings (shown below in Figure 3.2)
is surprising, noteworthy, and ultimately quite telling. Based on the data
we collected in North and South America, Asia, and Europe, it's also
clear that the leadership accountability gap is a critical business challenge
that knows no borders.

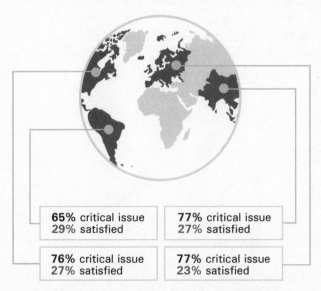

65% critical issue   **77%** critical issue
29% satisfied   **27%** satisfied

76% critical issue   **77%** critical issue
27% satisfied   **23%** satisfied

Figure 3.2   Leadership Accountability: The Global Problem

Take a moment and reflect on your own organization. To what extent do you believe it sees leadership accountability as a critical business issue? How satisfied are you with the degree of leadership accountability demonstrated by leaders in your organization?

Our survey explored other high-level aspects of leadership accountability, including the extent to which companies:

- Have set clear expectations of their leaders
- Believe their leaders are fully committed to their roles as leaders
- Have the courage to address mediocre leadership
- Believe they have a strong leadership culture

The results (see Figure 3.3) show that nearly half of the surveyed companies believe they've set clear expectations. Very few admitted to failing to be deliberate or explicit in setting expectations for their leaders. Based on our client work, we are finding that this is a critical practice for organizations to put in place as it creates the foundation for leadership accountability to take hold. I will come back to this later in the chapter.

One stark finding is that less than half of survey respondents believe their leaders are fully committed to their roles. In my discussions with many senior executives, they believe that many of their leaders are committed to the technical aspects of their roles; however, fewer of them are committed to actual leadership—managing people, inspiring teams, addressing performance issues, and building culture. Using the language that I presented earlier in this book, it's clear we have people in leadership roles who do not own their entire role. Many are part-time leaders and only pay attention to a small part of what they must do in their roles.

49%
Have set clear leadership expectations

45%
Demonstrate a high degree of commitment to their role as leaders

27%
Have a strong leadership culture

20%
Have the courage to address mediocre and unaccountable leaders

Figure 3.3   A Closer Look at Leadership Accountability

One extremely concerning finding for me is that only 27 percent of the respondents believe they have a strong leadership culture in their organizations. This is particularly alarming considering how many organizations need to transform themselves and need strong leadership cultures to help them be successful. This finding suggests that there is a lot of work ahead for companies to build the leadership cultures they need to transform their organizations. I have come to learn through my years of consulting that if a company has a weak leadership culture, this creates risk. The organization will not be able to effectively drive change, achieve long-term sustainable success, or attract the best talent.

A particularly fascinating finding from the study is the meager number of companies (only 20 percent) that believe they have the courage to address mediocrity among their leaders. Respondents openingly acknowledged that they know exactly which leaders are unaccountable and mediocre. However, they also admitted they typically do not deal with these leaders in a proactive manner. The unfortunate impact is that in turn breeds further mediocrity, increases the lack of accountability, and exacerbates the core problem that companies face.

The Satisfaction with Leadership Accountability by Level of Leader

Satisfaction with leadership was explored at three levels: demonstrable accountability from executives, mid-level, and the front-line leaders. Figure 3.4 presents the findings. While the data points to greater satisfaction with executive-level leaders, it's far from an overwhelming

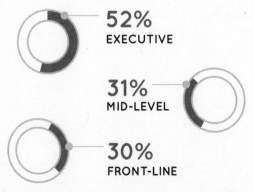

52%
EXECUTIVE

31%
MID-LEVEL

30%
FRONT-LINE

Figure 3.4   Satisfaction with Leadership Accountability by Level

endorsement. Taken collectively, these findings suggest there is quite a lot of work ahead for organizations to develop strong leadership accountability across all levels.

As one senior human resources executive shared with us in France during a customer event, "Senior management must be accountable. If there is an accountability gap there, then there will also be one among their direct reports and other leaders below them. An organization will not be successful."

As you reflect on these particular findings, how would your organization stand up against these results? Will satisfaction by level be stronger than the above or weaker?

The Relationship between Leadership Accountability and Company Performance

My team and I were curious to see if there was any connection between strong leadership accountability and the performance of a company.

We asked survey respondents to self-identify whether their organization was an industry-leading (top quartile) performer, an average/above-average performer, or a poor performer (bottom quartile) relative to competitors in their industry. Twenty-nine percent of respondents self-identified their companies as industry-leading performers; 47 percent were average performers (not industry-leading, but not low performers); and 14 percent self-identified themselves as below-average or low-performing companies.

Although leadership accountability is seen as critical among all respondents regardless of their performance, clear differences arise between industry leaders and the rest (see Figure 3.5). Industry leaders reported a higher overall degree of satisfaction with leadership accountability, invest more time in communicating clear expectations, and report having a higher overall proportion of accountable leaders. It's clear these companies do not become leaders in their field by accident - strong leadership accountability appears to be part of their formula for success.

These findings suggest there is a strong connection between leadership accountability and company performance. This makes perfect sense. If you have a weak leadership culture with unaccountable leaders, you will have a difficult time driving industry-leading performance in your company. Mediocre leaders will never get you to your desired outcomes. They never have, and they never well.

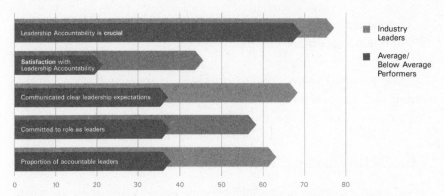

Figure 3.5 The Connection between Leadership Accountability and Company Performance

The Three Dimensions of Leadership Accountability: Behaviors, Organizational Practices, and Culture

Our study also explored three key dimensions of leadership accountability (Figure 3.6):[4]

1. The behaviors that truly accountable leaders demonstrate day to day
2. The organizational practices that help create strong leadership accountability

Figure 3.6 The Three Dimensions of Leadership Accountability

3. The attributes of leadership culture that cultivate and sustain accountability among leaders

The pattern I shared above continued in these findings: industry-
leading companies consistently outpaced the average and low-performing
companies in each of these three dimensions.

The Behaviors of Truly Accountable Leaders

When asked about the leaders in their companies who are truly accountable,
respondents considered the frequency of ten key behaviors. We found a high
degree of consistency among the key behaviors identified, regardless of the
performance of the company. In other words, real leadership accountability
looks the same no matter the performance of a company.

However, as shown in Figure 3.7, there are some very interesting net
differences in frequency of behaviors between the industry-leading
companies, average and below average performing ones.

The most notable net difference among industry leaders and the
average and low-performing companies were revealed in the following
top five behaviors of accountable leaders (Figure 3.8).

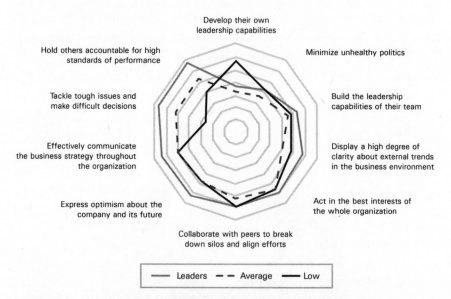

**Figure 3.7 The Behaviors of Accountable Leaders by Company
Performance**

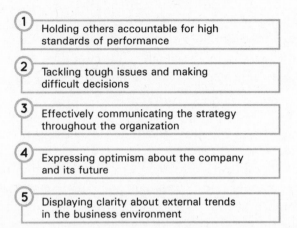

Figure 3.8   The Top Five Behaviors of Truly Accountable Leaders

These five behaviors tell the story about how accountable leaders behave differently than other leaders. During our customer events we also engaged in some meaningful discussions with our clients. Here's a closer look at the findings from those discussions:

- *Holding others accountable for high standards of performance.* Real leadership accountability is built on a foundation of strong standards and clear expectations. Respondents revealed that the leaders in their companies who were truly accountable never settled for merely "good enough." They always challenged their teams and colleagues to aim for higher standards of performance. While in many ways this could be considered an obvious point, the data indicates that it isn't as common a practice as many organizations would like it to be.
- *Tackling tough issues and making difficult decisions.* The largest net difference in the results was in the ability of leaders in industry-leading companies to deal with tough issues and make difficult decisions—a key marker of truly accountable leaders (as discussed in Chapter 7 of this book). In the discussions with our customers, we learned that this was viewed as the most observable and tangible behavior seen in leaders deemed to be truly accountable. At the same time, it was also the behavior most glaringly absent among more mediocre leaders.
- *Effectively communicating the strategy throughout the organization.* Accountable leaders can effectively communicate their company's strategy. This

behavior is important because it helps teams and employees understand how their work contributes to making the company successful, in turn making each task more meaningful and rewarding. A clear vision on strategy that can be expressed by leadership helps every team member "buy in" and stay motivated in their roles.

- *Expressing optimism about the company and its future.* Accountable leaders express optimism about the company and the future. Leaders viewed as unaccountable seem to merely go through the motions in their day-to-day work without personal investment in the direction of the team. Many appear disengaged or unenthusiastic. This undermines the ability of the company to fully engage employees. As one client said, "If leaders are not excited about what we are trying to do as a company, then our employees will never be."

- *Displaying clarity about external trends in the business environment.* The final behavior that revealed a large net difference was in the ability of leaders to be aware of trends in their business environment. We heard many customers at our events lament the fact that many of their leaders seem to lead with their "heads stuck in the sand," or are seen as being too internally focused. In contrast, accountable leaders assess their environment for opportunities or identify threats and risks they can manage. This proactive nature contributes to stronger accountability overall.

The five behaviors described above begin to create a profile of what a truly accountable leader pays attention to and shows which behaviors have the greatest impact. Take a moment to consider whether you consistently demonstrate these five behaviors of truly accountable leaders.

Now let's shift our focus to the other behaviors we explored: collaborating with peers to break down silos and align efforts, acting in the best interest of the whole organization, and building the capabilities of their teams. It was revealed by many of our customers that, increasingly, these behaviors are becoming more important in the culture of many organizations—particularly those with matrix structures. The nature of work in most companies today is horizontal, requiring leaders to collaborate, act in the best interest of the whole organization, and develop their teams to engage effectively with other departments.

Minimizing unhealthy politics was low for all three segments of companies, suggesting that all leaders struggle to address these behaviors within their teams. This reveals a pervasive accountability issue throughout an organization, underscoring the importance of leaders to be accountable and lead by example.

An intriguing finding was that among low-performing organizations, leaders focus a lot of their energy on developing their own leadership capabilities. While conventional wisdom suggests it's important for leaders to invest in their own development, this behavior didn't factor in a significant way in the industry-leading companies.

After a deeper exploration of the findings in discussions with customers and survey respondents, three hypotheses emerged to try to explain the data. The first hypothesis suggested it is possible that unaccountable leaders may spend too much time developing themselves, at the expense of engaging in some of the other behaviors; personal development may become an avoidance strategy employed by some leaders. The second hypothesis was that leaders in low-performing companies know that they are struggling to meet the demands of their role and, as a result, are trying to improve themselves by investing in their development. Finally, some argued that truly accountable leaders develop themselves on the job by engaging in the more difficult leadership behaviors—they challenge themselves to grow every day.

There was no clear consensus to explain the finding; however, it suggests that companies should take a second look at how much time leaders are spending developing themselves and whether this investment is warranted.

The Organizational Practices to Build Strong Leadership Accountability

The study revealed some striking differences between industry leaders and the other companies when it came to the organizational practice put in place to build strong leadership accountability (see Figure 3.9).

Industry-leading organizations considerably outpaced average and low-performing companies across every organizational practice we examined. In two key areas—"ensuring that leaders understand what matters to customers" and "defining leadership expectations"—the gap

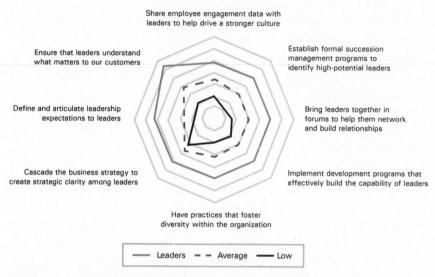

Figure 3.9   The Organizational Practices by Company Performance

was even greater, suggesting these are critical practices that companies must seriously consider addressing in their organizations.

During our discussions with customers and survey respondents, some valuable insights emerged regarding each of the organizational practices.

- *Ensure that leaders understand what matters to our customers.* This practice helps bring clarity to the leaders of the organization. When leaders truly understand the voice of the customers and what matters to them, it creates tremendous focus on key priorities. These then establish a mechanism to drive real accountability.
- *Have practices that foster diversity within the organization.* In many companies, leadership often is molded from a traditional male model. However, industry leaders do not typecast leaders to fit one mold of characteristics; they focus on driving accountability as the primary expectation. Customers shared that this enables a more diverse group of individuals to move into leadership roles.
- *Cascade the business strategy to create strategic clarity among leaders.* Industry leaders spend considerable time ensuring leaders understand the strategic priorities. This also brings clarity to the organization and provides the foundation for accountability.
- *Establish formal succession management programs to identify high-potential leaders.* Industry leaders are continually looking to groom the next

generation of accountable leaders. Demonstrated accountability is a key marker of future leaders.

- *Define and articulate leadership expectations to leaders.* Industry-leading companies make it clear what they expect from their leaders. Often, these messages are presented in a straightforward manner and embedded in the fabric of how the organization operates.
- *Share employee engagement data with leaders to help drive a stronger culture.* We heard that industry-leading companies are very transparent with their employee engagement data. The data is shared broadly so that leaders with highly engaged teams are recognized, while those with low engagement scores are also made apparent. There is essentially no hiding. This helps drive leader accountability for employee engagement.
- *Implement development programs that effectively build the capability of leaders.* Industry leaders put programs in place that do not merely build skills and capabilities, but also foster strategic clarity and drive accountability.
- *Bring leaders together in forums to help them network and build relationships.* Industry leaders understand that building a strong culture is critical to their success, so they find ways to facilitate relationship-building among their leaders through forums and other mechanisms.

As you reviewed this list of organizational practices, which ones are currently strong in your organization? Which need to be strengthened further in order to build strong leadership accountability?

The Attributes of Leadership Culture

As presented earlier in this chapter, only 27 percent of companies surveyed believe they have a strong leadership culture. When looking specifically at culture, stark differences arise among industry leaders, average performers, and low performers in seven of the ten attributes explored in our research (see Figure 3.10).

Ultimately, when an organization has truly accountable leaders that are supported by key organizational practices, then a strong culture of leadership accountability will emerge. One client, an executive VP of business development based in Singapore, really summed up the key point nicely when she said, "The senior leaders create the culture and set

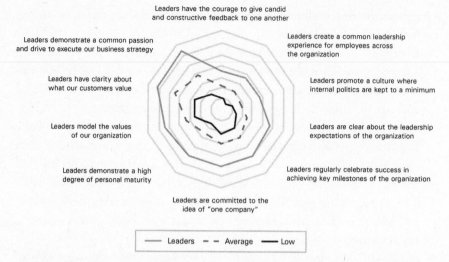

Figure 3.10   The Leadership Culture Attributes by Company Performance

the tone for the organization. It's imperative that they drive the set of behaviors which influence the behaviors of the next line leaders."

This seems to be what many organizations struggle to establish. In our customer events with leaders around the world, the topic of leadership culture generated the most lively and spirited conversations. It is clear to me that leadership culture is a top-of-mind business issue with senior executives globally. Below is a summary of the key themes discussed related to the attributes of leadership culture that we explored in our research. As you read through each one, consider the extent to which these are evident in your own organization's leadership culture:

- *Leaders demonstrate a common passion and drive to execute our business strategy.* This was a highly variable attribute of leadership culture. Most customers wanted it to exist, but few felt confident that it did. In my sense, this is an important area of focus for companies—to create an environment where leaders do feel passionate about the strategy.
- *Leaders demonstrate a high degree of personal maturity.* Personal maturity was seen as a critical cultural element required for real accountability. However, it is lacking in many companies. I had fascinating conversations while exploring why personal maturity is critical to leadership accountability. Many described their desire to have leaders who are "adults." Which meant having individuals who could address difficult

issues objectively, not react emotionally, and take ownership for issues, rather than making excuses or blaming others.

- *Leaders have clarity about what our customers value.* The themes here were similar to the discussion around organizational practices—the voice of the customer is critical to establishing a culture of accountability. To what extent do the leaders in your company have clarity about the voice of your customer and what matters to them?

- *Leaders model the values of our organization.* There was widespread agreement that this is a common expectation in most companies; however, it seems few reinforce this culturally. In other words, they tolerate leaders who do not model the values, largely because they may drive high performance. This pattern needs to change.

- *Leaders are committed to the idea of "one company."* We heard many times about the desire for companies to have leaders who live up to this cultural attribute. While it is an expressed need, current organizational structure and performance metrics reinforce silo behavior among leaders. However, through my own client work, I see more and more CEOs, expecting and wanting this in their organizations. In Chapter 8, we will discuss these ideas in more depth.

- *Leaders are clear about the leadership expectations of the organization.* This attribute falls largely to the organization. If clear expectations are not set, leaders will not know what to be clear about. They will be aimless or begin to lead in a way that is inconsistent with your organization's values.

- *Leaders regularly celebrate success in achieving key milestones of the organization.* This attribute was identified as the largest missed opportunity in many companies. Many do not create a culture in which this is valued. But they believe that if they did this more consistently, it would be a powerful way to reinforce leadership expectations while recognizing the leaders who are stepping up.

- *Leaders promote a culture where internal politics are kept to a minimum.* This attribute generated a lot of interesting discussion. Some shared with us that many of their leaders are consumed by internal politics. Others have addressed this issue head on and promote and hire leaders who put the company first and are largely apolitical.

- *Leaders create a common leadership experience for employees across the organization.* This was an attribute that few customers paid attention to. As a result, they were not surprised that it was rated lower. It's a desire that many executives expressed, but one that seems difficult to drive at present.

- *Leaders have the courage to give candid and constructive feedback to one another.* Peer-to-peer feedback is lacking in almost all organizations. This represents a challenge since many organizations today are matrixed. In many others, work is increasingly done across departments and functional silos. Leaders must work together. Yet, a cultural barrier will limit the ability of leaders to be successful if they can't or won't challenge one another.

Final Thoughts—Building Strong Leadership Accountability: The Road Ahead

The findings from our global study reveal important insights on a critical business issue that companies worldwide are facing—the leadership accountability gap. Not only do the study findings provide a deeper appreciation of what leadership accountability is and what's required to build it, but they also demonstrate the strong connection to company performance, namely that industry-leading companies outpace average and below-average companies regarding their commitment to building leadership accountability.

Collectively, the findings of our global study are extremely relevant today, especially as companies contend with an ever-changing business climate, disruption on all fronts, and the need to transform themselves to remain viable and relevant. One global head of human resources based in the United States summed it up best when he shared with me his perspective: "We are going through quite a bit of change in our company. We need our leaders to be truly accountable if we have any chance of successfully navigating through it all." This is the challenge facing all leaders and their companies today. What is the way forward? I believe it involves understanding the idea of a leadership contract. This is the basis of real leadership accountability, and this is what the rest of the book will be focused on.

We will start by exploring why we need a leadership contract. Then we will examine each of the four terms of the leadership contract and how they apply to leaders at all levels of an organization. Finally, we will conclude the book by looking at how you can live up to the four terms of the leadership contract in your own role and how you can embed the ideas into your organization. Let's begin your personal and organizational journey to creating strong leadership accountability.

The Gut Check for Leaders—Signing The Leadership Contract

As you think about the ideas in this chapter, reflect on your answers to the following gut check questions:

1. Is leadership accountability a critical business issue in your organization?
2. How satisfied are you with the degree of leadership accountability in your organization?
3. To what extent are your leaders fully committed to their roles?
4. Do you believe your organization has a strong leadership culture?

CHAPTER 4

Why We Need a Leadership Contract

It would be hard to imagine a CEO more loved by employees than Arthur T. Demoulas of Market Basket, an iconic 71-store chain of New England grocery stores. In August of 2014, several hundred workers at family-owned Market Basket walked off their jobs in protest after Demoulas was ousted by his cousin, Arthur S. Demoulas, and other family members. Thousands more employees attended rallies and protests to demand Arthur T.'s return to the helm of the chain.

How did Arthur T. Demoulas become so popular? In addition to earning a reputation as a fair-minded CEO, Demoulas insisted his employees be paid 20 to 30 percent more than industry rates. And he spearheaded a 100 percent company-funded profit-sharing retirement program that was the envy of employees in the grocery industry.

When other shareholders demanded a change in management, in large part to ready the company to be bought out by a private equity firm, the board took Arthur T. and his executive team out. This prompted the nonunionized employees to walk off the job. The impasse, which also included a widespread customer boycott, ended with an announcement that Arthur T. had bought out his rival family members for $1.5 billion—a deal that would allow him to resume day-to-day operations of the company.

I have tried to imagine being a leader so beloved that my employees would walk off the job to support me in a time of need. It's a remarkable expression of loyalty and affection. Although "being loved" is not necessarily part of a CEO's job description, there is no doubt that a loyal workforce is a great advantage in any competitive industry. Unfortunately, far too many CEOs are estranged from their workers, either because of their management style or because they are reaping pay and benefits that are completely out of whack with what employees are making.

Demoulas's story is important for all leaders because there was not just one thing that created all that loyalty. He was a CEO who earned the respect of his employees over a long period because of a number of important initiatives and measures. Yes, the profit sharing was a big part of the relationship he had with employees. But many of the workers who walked away from their jobs to protest Demoulas's firing said they were doing it because they loved their company and wanted to protect its unique culture.

Would your employees put their jobs on the line for you?

That's a high bar to set for a CEO or any leader. But it's one of the fundamental truths I have learned about leadership.

As humans, we instinctively hold anyone in a leadership role to a higher standard of behavior. It's hardwired in us as humans to expect more from our leaders.

Think about this for a moment. If you see someone in a leadership role, you automatically expect more from him or her. It doesn't matter what the leadership role is: teacher, pastor, coach, politician, CEO, high-profile athlete, or celebrity. You expect more, and if these people let you down, you then feel a sense of disappointment. If their behavior is really bad, you may even feel disgusted and disillusioned.

This point was really made clear to me during a business trip I had to Brazil in the spring of 2016. I reference this story briefly in Chapter 1. As my flight was landing in São Paolo early Sunday morning, millions of Brazilians were taking to the streets to protest and demand the resignation of President Dilma Rousseff. They were reacting to a corruption scandal that had ravaged the government and caused a serious decline in the country's economy.

What a backdrop for my trip and the many discussions about leadership that I would have over the next three days.

The first of those discussions was actually with the taxi driver who picked me up at the airport and drove me to my hotel. During the ride, he went on and on about the poor state of the country's leadership. By the time we finally got to my hotel, he admitted he was "disgusted" by what was going on.

While the protests were taking part quite some distance from my hotel, I could still hear people yelling and cars honking all afternoon. When it was all said and done, an estimated three million Brazilians participated in the protests. It was a peaceful demonstration involving a wide swath of Brazilian society, including the young and old and families with children.

What would cause so many Brazilians to protest in the streets? Brazil has been gripped by a story of corruption and scandal that has been unraveling over the past several years.

A police investigation—dubbed Operation Car Wash—has revealed that many of President Rousseff's supporters, donors, and members of her government's inner circle were involved in bribery and kickback schemes that may have reached all the way to the president's office.

It appears that key political and business leaders in Brazil twisted or broke rules to help the government win elections and enable high-profile companies to gain exclusive access to government business. In the final analysis, there is much that is rotten in Brazil's government, including Rousseff, who seems to have betrayed the trust of her people.

So I could understand the deeply emotional reactions I would hear in the many conversations I had during my trip. Many Brazilians I spoke to were proud the protests were peaceful and hoped this would encourage the bad leaders to admit their mistakes and either step down voluntarily or face impeachment.

Other people I spoke to were full of anger and disappointment. They were completely disillusioned with senior government officials and business leaders.

I've seen many of these same reactions from employees who worked in companies embroiled in scandal. The emotions in these scenarios can be intense.

In companies, employees rarely protest to show their disgust or disappointment. Instead, they will engage in a silent protest. Some disillusioned employees will simply check out and begin to neglect their work. When they see their senior leaders behave badly and betray their trust, they think to themselves "Why should I even care or bother?"

We expect a lot from our leaders. When they live up to our expectations, they earn our loyalty the way Arthur T. Demoulas did. When they let us down, the disappointment we feel is visceral. And as our world is getting more and more complex, our expectations of leaders are only growing.

So what is a great leader? What makes a leader like Demoulas someone we truly admire and want to work for? I've come to learn that a great leader is, fundamentally, an accountable leader—someone who understands and respects the fact that he or she answers to his or her customers, community, and employees.

An accountable leader demonstrates a bias for getting important work done in the organization. He or she is fully committed to moving things forward. Ultimately, an accountable leader takes personal ownership for his or her role, words, and actions. When this high level of accountability is missing, leadership becomes lame and mediocre—or even corrupt.

Before you move on to read the rest of this chapter, take a moment to answer the following questions: Are you living up to the high standards of behavior we all naturally set for leaders? Do you *own* your entire leadership role?

Do You Know What You've Signed Up For?

A British game retailer, GameStation, revealed in April 2010 that it legally owned the souls of 7,500 online shoppers.[1] As an April Fools' Day joke, the company had added an "immortal soul clause" to its online contract. The contract read:

> By placing an order via this website on the first day of the fourth month of the year 2010 Anno Domini, you agree to grant us a nontransferable option to claim, for now and forever more, your immortal soul. Should we wish to exercise this option, you agree to surrender your immortal soul, and any claim you may have on it, within 5 (five) working days of receiving written notification from gamesation.co.uk or one of its duly authorized minions.

Luckily for inattentive shoppers, the company decided not to enforce that clause. But it made a useful point. With a simple click, you are actually agreeing to quite a lot. You have some sense that you are bound to a contract, but you don't know in what ways. The same is true when it comes to leadership today.

Our organizations are governed by all kinds of contracts. For a generation, our work lives were dominated by the old employment contract. You know the one: You get a job, remain loyal, do as you're told, and the organization will take care of you until you retire. That contract worked for decades, but we know today that it is no longer valid. But what replaced it?

I believe it's what I call the *leadership contract*. It has actually existed for a while, but most leaders still don't understand its terms and conditions, let alone its fine print.

The Leadership Contract and Its Four Terms

A client of mine, a CEO, was about to unveil a new strategy he and his executive team had been working on with the board of directors. It was a departure from the past and would have required a significant step-up in leadership. The CEO and the executive team wanted to make sure that leaders in the organization understood the new strategy and, more important, that they understood what it would now mean to lead in that organization. The CEO said, "I need to know that I have leaders who are fully committed to our strategy and to taking their leadership to new levels. I can't have ambivalent leaders who are just going through the motions. Those days are gone."

I explained to them some of the ideas I had been working on about leadership accountability, and they engaged me to set up a process to help their leaders understand these new expectations and reflect on whether they were ready to accept them. In essence, the board members were being asked to understand and accept a set of new leadership expectations for that organization. A new set of terms was established, and leaders needed to sign up.

We should all go through a process like this when we take on new leadership roles. Our organizations need strong leaders to drive success. When you sign the leadership contract, you enter into an agreement: You commit and promise to be the best possible leader you can be for your organization and for your employees.

But there's more. Since first launching the book in 2013, I've seen more and more companies at critical inflection points. They are working hard to transform themselves to remain relevant in a fast-changing and disruptive world. What this means is that all of us in leadership roles may find ourselves having to sign a new leadership contract because our context has changed. Your company may be launching a new strategy. Your company may have just completed a merger or acquisition. Or maybe your company has been acquired or merged with a competitor. Whatever the trigger, more of us will find ourselves in situations where our business environment has changed. We then need to ask ourselves: Am I committed and prepared to sign up to be an accountable leader in this new context?

Regardless of whether you change your role, or your world changes in front of your eyes, you need to sign the leadership contract. Before you sign up, you need to understand the four terms as presented below (Figure 4.1).

Leadership Is a Decision—Make It

Do you aspire to be a great leader? Or are you just going through the motions? The leadership contract demands that you consciously commit to being the best leader you can be. It's no longer good enough to be a

Figure 4.1 The Four Terms of the Leadership Contract

great technical leader. It's no longer good enough to be an average leader. Your organization needs you to be a truly accountable leader. And it all begins with a decision. Are you ready to make it?

Leadership Is an Obligation—Step Up

Once you make the decision to be an accountable leader, you realize that you must now rise to a new standard of behavior. You have to fulfill your leadership obligation to your customers, employees, shareholders, and community. Are you prepared to step up to the obligations of leadership?

Leadership Is Hard Work—Get Tough

You need to commit to tackling the hard work of leadership. You need to have resilience and a real sense of personal resolve to help your company be successful. You will need to set the pace for others in your organization. You can't be a bystander waiting for things to improve on their own. Are you prepared to get tough and do what is necessary to make your organization a success?

Leadership Is a Community—Connect

It's time to stop being disconnected as a leader. You must reach out and build strong relationships with your fellow leaders. You need to commit to building a community of leaders—it all begins with a commitment to connect. Are you ready for it?

These four terms go a long way toward addressing the problems with leadership accountability today. We can overcome lame and unaccountable leadership in our organizations when leaders truly understand what it means to be a leader and sign up for the right reasons. It's no longer good enough to be a complacent or ambivalent leader. Your organization needs you to be truly accountable. Your employees, customers, shareholders, and stakeholders need you to be at your best.

If you accept a promotion without making a conscious decision to become a leader, you won't get the best possible performance out of your team because you will simply be going through the motions.

If you try to be a leader without considering your obligations to the people around you, you won't be focused on your organization's larger goals. You will be thinking about how to advance your own career instead of how to build long-term success. You will make it all about you rather than the obligations you have to others. This creates risk for you and your organization. You might be tempted to do things that get you in trouble.

If you try to be a leader without digging into the hard work, you won't be prepared for crises. You will be drowning in day-to-day deadlines instead of focusing on where your organization needs to go next. You will find yourself floundering when issues come up on your team because you haven't taken the time to build a collaborative culture. You will leave serious gaps in your team's capabilities because you haven't bothered to tackle the tough issues.

If you try to lead without connecting with other leaders, you will isolate yourself. You will focus on your own narrow little world instead of collaborating with peers from across your organization and your community. You will find yourself blindsided by problems you didn't expect because you didn't connect with anyone who could have helped you prepare. You will end up overstressed and overwhelmed because you don't have anyone supporting you.

Leadership is isolating for many of us. We need to understand that leadership is a community. And we have to stop looking for the quick fix. We need to accept that leadership *is* hard work and that we can't avoid tackling the hard problems.

Does any of this resonate with you?

Accepting this leadership contract will improve our own working lives, but the benefits don't stop there. I believe that leaders who understand their obligations to those around them won't disgrace themselves with scandal. We have seen too many leaders embarrass themselves and their organizations because they were thinking only about their own short-term interests. We need to hold ourselves to a higher standard. The first step is to really understand the obligations that come with leadership. It's about having clarity, knowing what's expected of you as a leader, and then having the commitment to be the best leader you can be.

That's the essence of the leadership contract. It's not a legal or formal contract. It's a personal, even moral contract. It's the personal commitment you make to be an accountable leader—the leader that you must become for yourself and your organization. It's a

commitment to redefine how you lead now and in the future. That's
what you are signing up for.

The Gut Check for Leaders—Why We Need a Leadership Contract

As you think about the ideas in this chapter, reflect on your answers
to the following gut check questions:

1. Did you ever consciously decide to be a leader?
2. Do you lead every day with a sense of clarity regarding your
   obligations?
3. What is the hard work you face? Do you have a tendency to
   tackle it head-on or do you avoid it?
4. Do you strive to build a sense of community with your fellow
   leaders?

CHAPTER 5

Leadership Is a Decision—Make It

Several years ago I worked with a group of senior leaders at a large construction company. We were having a lively conversation about leadership when someone asked me, "Hey, Vince, what is leadership?" I said, "Leadership is a decision." It was the very first time I had said those words out loud. It was an intuitive response in the moment. But right away Earl, one of the participants, snapped, "Well, I never got to make that decision!"

Earl was the senior vice president of engineering services. He had started his career as an engineer, but the organization soon offered him a supervisory role and a series of promotions. Earl said that he accepted each of these promotions without thinking about whether he truly wanted a new role or whether he was really ready to commit to it.

I looked around the room. Everyone was listening intently. It seemed like Earl's story was striking a chord with the other leaders.

Earl explained that he thought taking on those leadership roles was the logical thing to do. From a practical perspective, it was the only way he could make more money and get more prestige within the company. But he said that every time he took on a more senior leadership role, he moved further and further away from what he really loved to do: engineering.

I have told Earl's story many times, and I have been surprised by how many leaders say they've done the same thing.

Although making more money, expanding your skills, and having more impact are all somewhat valid reasons to be a leader, they are no longer enough in today's world of business.

Every day you have opportunities to make a leadership decision. But do you answer that call? Many times making the decision to lead isn't easy—it's easier to stay put and play it safe. But staying put makes you an empty chair leader and keeps your organization stuck.

Why Doesn't Anyone Want to Be a Leader Anymore?

I have met a lot of people who relate to Earl's experience, and most of them are about Earl's age. I have also noticed that the younger generation isn't as willing to take on a leadership role just for perks or prestige.

My team and I worked with a software company a while back to design and deliver a two-day leadership program aimed at 30 people they had identified as high-potential (hi-po) leaders. To begin the project, we interviewed these hi-po leaders. What we found was quite surprising. The majority of them didn't want the label of a high-potential leader. In fact, leadership had a negative connotation for most of them. They thought being a high-potential leader would just mean doing more work. They felt busy enough already, and being saddled with more leadership tasks (including dealing with difficult employee performance issues) certainly didn't appeal to them. They did the math and figured out that all the extra work wouldn't really be reflected in their salaries. And they didn't want to take time away from their families to put in those extra hours. That wasn't a sacrifice they wanted to make.

The executive team was surprised—and frustrated—to hear this news. They had assumed everyone would want to be a leader. They thought these employees would be proud to be tagged with the hi-po label. But the more we talked to the hi-pos to figure out why they had such negative views of leadership, the more we realized the executive team was the problem. Executives were the model for leadership in that company. They all worked 60 to 80 hours per week. They were always on planes traveling the world. When you saw the current executives from afar, as the hi-pos did, all you saw was hard work and personal sacrifice.

The executive team soon realized that they needed to do a better job of demonstrating to the hi-pos all the rewards associated with leadership roles—the gratification that comes from serving customers, building great teams, and creating a successful business.

So we changed the focus of the two-day leadership development program. Instead of a launch program, we created a process to help those would-be leaders better understand what a leadership role is really all about—the good, the bad, and the ugly. The participants loved this approach. They were grateful for the chance to decide for themselves whether to step into these new roles. They started to realize they had been focusing only on the downside of leadership. After that two-day event, all but five of our potential leaders decided to continue. Those who opted out did so mainly for personal family reasons but asked to be considered again once their young children were older.

Something is changing in our organizations. Younger employees understand that leadership is a decision and that it needs to be deliberately made. I saw this recently with one of my own team members—a smart, personable guy who had been an informal leader for a while. When his manager and I offered him a formal leadership role, he said, "Wow, I'm really flattered. Thank you so much. Do you mind if I take a couple of weeks to think about it?"

Both his manager and I were a little surprised to hear this. I remember thinking to myself, "Listen, buddy, in my day when someone gave you a leadership opportunity, you just took it. No ifs, ands, or buts!" Even I am having a hard time letting go of this outdated perspective on leadership.

We met with him again after the two weeks were up, and this time he said, "Thanks for giving me the time to reflect on this big decision. I needed to think carefully about this. Both my wife and I have big jobs, and we also have a young family. I needed to know before committing whether this was the right thing to do for my family. I have thought it through, and I'm in."

I thought to myself, "This guy is much smarter than I was at his age." He knows what it means to be a leader. He appreciates the demands and the pressure. That's why he wanted to make sure he could really commit to doing the work and becoming a great leader. He took his time to reflect and then made his leadership decision.

Why You Need to Make the Leadership Decision

The first term of the leadership contract (see Figure 5.1) begins with the idea that leadership is a decision. There isn't much point in discussing

Figure 5.1   The First Term of the Leadership Contract

anything else about leadership until we get this clear. Too many theories about leadership just assume that everyone wants to be a leader. But this is a faulty assumption—one that we often don't realize we are making.

We need to replace this faulty assumption with the idea that everyone needs to decide whether he or she wants to be a leader. If we do that, we will end up with leaders who truly want the role and are prepared to be accountable and do what is necessary to help their organizations succeed. We also help those who don't want the role find other ways to add value in their organizations.

One of the reasons you need to be more deliberate in making leadership decisions is that organizations have changed. In the past, companies were much larger than they are today, with many levels of managerial roles throughout the hierarchy. The good thing was that all those roles acted as effective stepping-stones, enabling individuals to progress nicely from one leadership role to another. Because you could see the stepping-stones ahead of you, each move seemed like a natural and logical step to take, and you really didn't have to do too much thinking about the roles you were taking on.

However, companies today are leaner and flatter. The stepping-stones are gone and have been replaced by giant leaps. So when you take on a leadership role in today's world, you don't see the next steps at all. What you see is a big chasm between your current role and the role ahead of you. This is one of the primary reasons why there is such a high incidence of failure among leaders assuming new roles.

Much of the research has shown—whether it's at the front line, in the middle, or at the executive ranks—that a significant percentage of leaders derail within a year or two of accepting new roles. I believe it's because they don't deliberately make leadership decisions. They don't fully understand what they are taking on and instead make the leap blindly, underestimating the demands and expectations. You may get seduced by the new title, the status, the money, and the perks. You may make assumptions about what leading will be like, but your assumptions may be wrong.

To me, it is a lot like being a first-time parent. No matter how many parenting books you read or how many stories you hear from your friends and family, you can't truly understand it until it's happening to you. And then it hits you—during the 3 AM feedings or after your fourth straight sleepless night. Then you know how challenging being a parent really is.

The other reason you need to be more deliberate in making leadership decisions is that we've always assumed that everyone wanted to be the leader, and we have ended up glorifying leadership roles above others in our organizations. We give leaders more money, more perks, and more prestige. But in reality, we've never let people decide whether they want to take on a leadership role. As a result, I've seen many leaders who don't make the conscious decision to lead. Instead, they just accept the roles they're given. Over time, they become ambivalent or reluctant leaders like Earl. Or they end up always questioning and second-guessing themselves.

Well, guess what? If this is you, you aren't fooling anybody. We can smell the indecision, the tentativeness, and the uncertainty you project.

It's important to note that in the past we may have been able to get away with weak leadership because our world was less complex than it is today. We could get by with individuals who didn't make the real decision to be leaders. But things are very different today. Ambivalent or tentative leaders just aren't strong enough to take us through this complex environment. There's too much at stake today. We need to make sure that all leaders consciously and deliberately make the decision to lead and make it for the right reasons. This is the starting point for real leadership accountability.

The Two Kinds of Leadership Decisions

Athletes have to make lots of decisions on the field (or on the court or on the ice). In the midst of the action, they have to be able to decide again and again how to move their team closer to victory. Coaches and players can also call a time-out when they believe there is a particularly important decision to make, one they can't make in an instant.

Like athletes, leaders also make dozens of real-time decisions in the middle of the action. These "small d" leadership decisions come up many times in a typical day. And then there are the time-out moments. These Big D leadership decisions are the critical moments in your career when you have to pause and be more deliberate about the choice you are about to make.

Both types of decisions are important (see Figure 5.2). Big D leadership decisions come at critical times in your career and force you to reflect on who you are as a leader and whether you are ready to take on a new leadership role. Small d leadership decisions are made in the moment and may seem minor, but over time, they can also have a considerable impact on your effectiveness as a leader.

It is important to clarify one point. Leaders make all kinds of decisions, such as where to invest for growth, which suppliers to use, and how to manage customer issues. These are typical business decisions, and there is a lot written about effective decision-making for leaders out there.

What I'm talking about here is something more specific. It's those decisions you have to make about your role as a leader both at critical times (Big D leadership decisions) and in the day-to-day experience of leading (small d decisions). These leadership decisions shape how you ultimately show up as a leader. They dictate how others judge your effectiveness as a leader.

Figure 5.2   The Two Types of Leadership Decisions

Big D Leadership Decisions

In December of 1968, the astronauts on *Apollo 8* were the first humans placed in a lunar orbit. Their primary task was to take photographs of the moon and identify possible landing sites for future missions.

As their spacecraft drifted from behind the moon, they saw the earth rising above the lunar horizon. Astronaut William Anders quickly took a picture of the amazing scene.

That photograph gave humanity its first chance to look at Earth from space. Up to that point in time, our view of Earth came from maps and globes—images of countries divided by lines and colors. Anders' photograph showed us the planet as it really is—a sphere. Many believe this was a turning point in human history because it fundamentally changed how we viewed ourselves and our planet.

Historians have used the term "turning point" to identify key moments in history, such as the *Apollo 8* story, that change the flow of history significantly.

Leaders also experience these moments in their careers when they are about to assume a more senior leadership role. It is important at these critical times that leaders pause and reflect on what they are signing up for.

As leaders, our careers evolve over time. If we are successful, we gain roles of increasing responsibility. Along this journey, there are four critical times that are particularly important for leaders.

These four leadership turning points demand that you take some time to think about what has changed in your leadership role and, more important, how you must change to be successful as a leader. At each of these four leadership turning points, you must pause and deliberately make a Big D leadership decision.

- The first turning point occurs when those in your organization tell you that they see you as someone with leadership potential. This happened to me when Zinta first told me I had leadership potential. While I had a role as an individual contributor, I realized I immediately had to pause to understand what her words meant to me and what I needed to do to become a leader.
- The second critical turning point occurs when you take on your first supervisory or front-line management role. When this happened to

me, I quickly realized that from that moment on I was responsible for others. My focus changed from everything being about me and my performance to everything being about supporting the performance of others.

- The third critical leadership turning point is when you assume a mid-level or senior management role. The demands of leadership change considerably, and how you see yourself also must change. When I had one of these roles, I realized that I needed to change my approach to leadership from driving the performance of my team to working across the organization with my peers to drive the success of our entire organization.

- The final critical turning point of leadership occurs when you assume an executive role. I remember when I took on my first executive role. I felt the weight of my obligation to my board and shareholders. My responsibility to my team and colleagues across the company also increased dramatically.

Each of these moments is a turning point in your career. Each represents a significant shift in what is expected of you as a leader. Not only does your role change, but you also must change. You must be clear about what is expected of you and how you need to change the way you lead to succeed. You can't just jump into the role full of naïve enthusiasm or assume it's just another career move.

Instead, you need to pause and make sure that you are clear about the changing demands of your role. You must be certain you are truly prepared to live up to these demands to ensure that you will succeed when you take the leap. And that is ultimately what a Big D leadership decision is all about. If you don't take a time-out to deliberately make these Big D leadership decisions, you may sign up for something you are not prepared for, and you won't succeed in your new role.

Small d Leadership Decisions

As a leader, you also make many small d leadership decisions every day. Although these decisions may appear tiny and even innocuous compared with Big D leadership decisions, they in fact play an important role in shaping who you are as a leader. I find, however, that many leaders don't appreciate the importance of these small d leadership decisions.

Consider, for example, Curt, a controller in his organization. His days are constantly filled with too much to do, putting out fire after fire. In these moments when a small d leadership decision has to be made, Curt knows what he should really do as a leader, but he's too busy to pause and be deliberate. He thinks, "I'll let this one go by this time. I'll make this small compromise just this once." Before he knows it, compromise after compromise has become his regular pattern. He never fully appreciates how his personal leadership effectiveness is eroding and how he is inadvertently letting his team and organization down.

It's in those small moments, when you are under pressure and feeling overworked, that you still have to make the right small d leadership decisions.

Consider a few of the following typical situations that you find yourself in regularly:

- You are in a meeting and an important issue arises that you disagree with. What do you do? Do you challenge it, or do you let it go?
- A colleague is demonstrating bad leadership behavior that is inconsistent with your company's values. What do you do? Do you provide feedback now, or do you wait for the next opportunity?
- A project in another area of the company is off the rails. No one seems to care. What do you do? Do you confront the issue, or do you ignore it because it's none of your business?

In the course of a day, you may find yourself in many of these situations. In isolation from one another, they may not seem that important. It might seem to make sense to compromise and let the issue go. But when you stand back and think about it, these situations are not isolated. They are all connected and shape the kind of leader you are. All the small d decisions you face add up to something truly significant: your identity as a leader. How you handle them affects your credibility. They tell your colleagues whether they can trust you—or not.

Now here's what many leaders do not fully appreciate. We are all doing this. We are all failing to be deliberate about how we manage small d decisions. Think for a moment about the collective impact that this may have on your organization. Consider the business impact of all the leaders in your company showing up every day and compromising on these small d decisions. Can you see why organizations struggle to drive sustained high performance and innovation?

It's time you start taking these small d decisions seriously. It's time you become more deliberate in your leadership decisions.

So how can we become better at this? The next time you find yourself in that moment when a small d decision needs to be made, ask yourself:

- How must I show up as a leader in this moment?
- What is my obligation as a leader?
- What do my organization's core values dictate that I do in this situation?

Once you begin to internalize these questions into your day-to-day leadership, you'll find yourself being more deliberate and consistent as a leader. You will provide the leadership that your organization and your team need from you. You will begin to forge a strong reputation as a credible and deliberate leader.

Big D and small d Leadership Decisions—Clarity and Commitment

As the interim CEO of Target Corporation, John Mulligan had a simple message for his senior executives: It's time to lead. Mulligan had been tasked to pick up the pieces after the company's former CEO, Gregg Steinhafel, left the retail giant reeling from failed ventures and a massive breach of customer data from its online operation. In addition to moving Steinhafel out, investors and proxy advisors had declared all-out war on Target's board of directors. The proxy firms recommended that shareholders use the annual general meeting to vote out seven of the company's 10 directors. They were all reelected, but the message from investors was pretty clear: Get your act together. Reacting to that signal, Mulligan started taking bold steps to reinvent the leadership culture at Target.

Mulligan moved all the company's top executives into offices that shared the same floor of its headquarters in Minneapolis. The former *executive committee* of the company was renamed the *leadership team*. Internal executive committees were disbanded to streamline decision-making.

"All across Target, we need more 'leadership' and less 'committee,'" Mulligan told executives in a letter obtained by *the Wall Street Journal*.[1]

Mulligan believed Target had become bogged down in high-level "bureaucracy." I believe it would be safe to say that Target had built a company where administrators and paper pushers occupied roles that real leaders should have filled.

In this scenario, nobody has the intestinal fortitude to stand up and put his or her own opinions on the record. People sit quietly by as they watch others make mistakes. Everyone is afraid to offer his or her own ideas in case they fail. Nobody is making the big or small leadership decisions that need to be made.

I've seen this story play out too many times. When a company is in trouble and not performing, we try to find some significant thing that is a cause of all the problems. We often fail to appreciate how a lack of leadership accountability day to day can lead a company into a downward spiral. This is why it is important to be deliberate as a leader every single day. Your accountability as a leader starts with your leadership decision.

Ultimately, Big D and small d leadership decisions both require clarity and commitment on your part. You need clarity about what you're taking on when assuming a leadership role. You need to be clear on the following:

- What's the role really about?
- What are the expectations?
- What will success look like?
- What value must I bring as a leader?
- What impact must I have every day?

You will also need a strong degree of personal commitment. Ask yourself:

- Am I up for this? Am I all-in as a leader?
- Am I fully committed to doing what I need to do to make my team and company succeed?
- Am I able to handle the heat that I will be exposed to?
- Am I prepared for the hardships that will come my way?
- Am I committing for the right reasons, or am I doing this only to feed my ego?

Too many leaders lack this kind of commitment. In a recent global survey we conducted, we found that most organizations believe just under half of their leaders are fully committed to their leadership roles. That means we have people in leadership roles who don't own their entire role. They may be focused on the technical aspects of their jobs, but when it comes to the people leadership aspects, they aren't as committed.

If you aren't committed to your entire leadership role, then you need to have a career discussion with your manager. Find a technical role that allows you to do those things that enable you to be successful without having to take on the burden of being a leader.

It's important to pause and reflect on these questions, especially when you are at a critical turning point in leadership. Why? Because many aspects of your leadership role change.

For example, you will find that at each turning point the amount of complexity you deal with increases. You have to be able to tolerate ambiguity and the pressure it will put on you. If you are lucky, you'll be in an organization that will help you through this. But most leaders will need to face this challenge on their own.

You will also face considerable scrutiny, which just keeps on increasing across the four turning points. You must be open to it, yet develop a thick skin so it doesn't undermine your confidence. I believe that the increased scrutiny is a function of the fact that leadership really matters today. There's a lot riding on you—so you'd better not screw up! First, your peers are scrutinizing you to see whether you really are high-potential material. Then your employees analyze your every word and action. Colleagues across the organization weigh in with their own views of your performance. Finally, board members, customers, analysts, and shareholders will scrutinize your every decision and every move. The spotlight keeps getting brighter.

You can also experience the realization that you are accountable. There is no room for excuses as a leader. In fact, the more senior the leadership role, the greater the degree of accountability you must assume.

You will also come to realize that you must demonstrate increasing levels of professional and personal maturity. As an emerging leader, you'll find that those around you will want to see you show up as a leader. As a front-line manager, you will need to rise above the noise and drama of the people issues and bring a leadership presence. At the middle level, you will need to be an ambassador of your organization. This requires you to be levelheaded and have a strong sense of poise. At the executive or C-suite level, your professional maturity (or lack of it) sets the tone for your entire organization. You will need to have a real executive presence because your personal reputation is tied so closely to your organization's reputation.

Finally, you will also come to understand that the degree of impact you must deliver increases dramatically at each turning point. As you become a more senior-level leader, the impact you're having is easier to see. The flip side is that so are your mistakes. You will feel a self-imposed sense of urgency to have real impact (or at least you should feel it). You will come face-to-face with your core obligations as a leader, and you will need to take them seriously.

The reason you need clarity and commitment in making Big D and small d leadership decisions is that at each turning point, the heat and pressure rise. This is why you can't take on a leadership role simply because it feels like the next logical step. This is why you can't jump at an opportunity because it's going to pay you more, give you more perks, or offer a better title on your LinkedIn profile. This is why you can't simply click Agree without understanding what the fine print of the leadership contract is about. You need to pause and truly understand what you are signing up for.

A Real Leadership Decision Is Visceral

I spoke about leadership as a decision at a conference, and the CEO of the company I was working with had an interesting response. He said, "I found the idea of leadership as a decision to be really interesting. As I thought about it, I can tell you the leaders in my own company who have made the leadership decision and those who haven't."

I believe anyone can tell who's made the decision to lead—most of us just aren't thinking about it in these terms yet. But when you make the decision to lead, I think you'll find that the change in you will be visceral—you'll feel it and know it, and so will those around you. Leadership accountability will ooze out of every single pore of your body. And when you make both the Big D and the small d leadership decisions deliberately and with clarity and commitment, your game will go to another level.

I believe you'll find that once you truly make your own leadership decision and commit to being an accountable leader, something will change inside of you.

Take the example of Lucia. She is based in South America and reached out to me on LinkedIn. She wanted to thank me for writing *The Leadership Contract* because the ideas were truly helpful to her. In our exchange, she shared that she'd always been the kind of person who played it safe in her career. But now there was a director position available in her company. Her first instinct was not to pursue the job because she felt she didn't have what it would take to be successful. She wrote, "But after reading your book, I decided to put my name forward, and I got the job!" I was excited for her. Lucia continued by saying it was the best decision she ever made. She would never have anticipated all the opportunities that opened up to her because of that one leadership decision. Lucia's story is a powerful one.

Deciding Not to Lead Is an Important Leadership Decision

People often ask me, "What if you decide not to be a leader?" I believe this is also an important leadership decision to make. Big D leadership decisions are important because what you do as a leader matters. But if you make those decisions lightly, if you feel pressured to take on those roles, if you do it only for the money or the perks, then you run the risk of becoming an empty chair leader. You can fake it for a while, but eventually your lack of clarity and commitment will start to show. So the question comes back to you: Do you know yourself well enough to decide whether leadership is for you? Do you have the maturity and courage to say no? I believe we need more people to have the self-awareness and personal maturity to make good leadership decisions, including the decision to turn down a role that is not right.

Steve Wozniak had the courage to say no. Long before he appeared on reality TV, Wozniak was the engineer who invented the first Apple computer. He was a programmer at Hewlett-Packard (HP) when he was approached about the job at Apple. He knew he didn't want to be a corporate leader, so he was worried about joining a new company. But

Apple promised him that he wouldn't have to go into management—he could stay at the bottom of the organization chart as an engineer. Apple turned to Mike Markkula, Jr., a successful investor, to run the company, and it let Wozniak keep doing what he did best. Although Wozniak didn't have the title, he was still an important technical leader in the company.

Another good example comes from Phil Libin of Evernote. In June of 2015, he revealed he was stepping down from his role as CEO. I'm a big fan of Evernote and its online note-keeping service, so this story caught my attention.

Libin was remarkably candid about his decision. He said the company he'd led since 2007 would end up in the hands of "someone who is going to be better than me at it." "I'm a product person," Libin said. I'm sure you would agree with me—this isn't the kind of behavior we typically see from CEOs and senior executives.

When you track the ups and downs of business leaders, you're more likely to see leaders hanging on at all costs—even if the company suffers as a result. In contrast, Libin seems to be a pretty humble guy who understood what his company needed next. To me, the key part of this story is not, however, the fact that Libin is stepping down. It's that he knows he's more of a product guy, and his company needs a "professional CEO." That is a powerful leadership decision. Did Libin's actions suggest that he no longer has what it takes to be a strong leader? Are his actions an admission of failure? No!

In my opinion, this story is about a leader who had the self-awareness and maturity to know where he added his greatest value, coupled with the self-confidence to admit where he did not.

Unfortunately, I've seen many leaders struggle in the same situation. Some let their ego get in the way—admitting they are not good at something just isn't possible for them. For others, their self-identity is so wrapped up in their title that they can't envision themselves in any other role. I've also seen leaders be so stubborn, digging in their heels to stick around, only to be humiliated when someone else decides it's time for them to leave.

The stories of Wozniak and Libin demonstrate the self-awareness that is necessary to make a leadership decision. Wozniak knew how he was wired, what he liked and didn't like to do, and where he could add

value. Libin knew his company needed a different kind of leader for a
new era.

When You Are At a Crossroad and Feel You No Longer Fit

Recently, I was approached by a middle-level leader in a large engineering company. I had just finished delivering a closing keynote speech to
600 managers at all levels where I shared the ideas from this book. This
fellow lingered around for a while after the presentation. He eventually
approached me. I could tell he needed to talk.

We sat down and he immediately said he was at a personal
crossroads. He had been with his organization for some time but
was personally feeling down on the company. He was checked out
and his team could sense it. I asked him to share an example, and he said
that he was not filtering messages from the executives to his own
department effectively. He would always add his own cynical spin. He
was essentially bad-mouthing the company. He knew it wasn't right for
him to behave this way because he was a leader. But he couldn't stop
himself.

On the one hand, I was struck by this individual's level of personal
insight. He knew what he was doing was wrong. But on the other hand,
he couldn't get himself to just stop his negativity.

He also shared that all of this was eroding his personal reputation
within the company. He was worried that any hope he had of moving up
in the organization was dwindling.

I asked him, "Why don't you leave?" He explained that he felt
trapped. He had been with the company a while and had invested in his
pension. He also had kids to put through school. At a personal level, he
feared making the jump to another company.

This is something I've seen time and time again—so many leaders
become misfits in their organizations. It can happen for many reasons.
Your company may be acquired. A new CEO or executive comes in
with a goal of turning the company around with a new strategy. Maybe
you see the culture begin to change and you are no longer aligned with
your company's values. Maybe you disagree with the strategic direction
of the company. Or you get a growing sense in the pit of your stomach
that you just don't fit like you used to. You then start checking out. This

is a time when you need to pause and make a Big D leadership decision. If you don't, and you stick around, you may find that you quickly become irrelevant in the eyes of fellow employees.

If this describes you as a leader, you need to ask yourself: What am I doing here? You know you are in this state when you've lost your passion for your role. You begin to look at everything through a negative lens. Or you start to let things slide, and your performance and that of your team decline. If this is happening to you, there's a really good chance that you aren't happy. And guess what? Your family knows it as well.

Staying in your role because you need a paycheck, or because you don't want to lose whatever perks you may have, isn't good enough. I've seen some misfit leaders who know they don't fit and are miserable in their jobs but choose to wait it out, hoping that the organization terminates them so they can get severance. That's not real leadership accountability in action.

So how do you manage when you find yourself in this situation? First, you need to appreciate that all leaders go through rough patches— periods when they question their role, the direction of their company, or whether they still fit. Your challenge is to make sure this rough patch doesn't become your permanent condition.

You need to also confront the downside of your behavior. Negativity, especially from leaders, can have a detrimental effect on your own health and the health and morale of your employees.

Finally, give yourself a time limit to reach your final decision—to leave or to stay. If you decide to stay, then you must commit to improving your behavior. Be the leader! If you leave, do it on the best terms possible. Don't let your negativity undermine your chances of securing a future leadership role elsewhere.

What If You Change Your Mind?

It's also important to keep in mind that your leadership decision can change, and an initial no can become a yes. I recently worked with a client named Barb, the chief human resources officer (CHRO) of a global energy company. One day, we were talking about some high-potential leaders in her company. She shared a story about one of her direct reports, Marcela.

In their development discussions, Marcela said to Barb, "I have been observing you in your role. I have seen you interact with our CEO, other senior executives, board members, and the unions, and I can see how much pressure you are under. You know, I don't think I'm ready for this right now."

This is a great example of the work leaders need to do to gain personal clarity. Once she was identified as a hi-po, Marcela went to work. She studied the demands of the role she was being groomed for, and she had enough self-awareness to know that she wasn't ready for it. That takes maturity and humility. Every organization needs more leaders like Marcela.

Marcela then spent the next year reflecting on what she wanted to do. Like a great leader, Barb continued exposing Marcela to broader opportunities that gave her more information and insight. After 12 months, Marcela decided she was ready. She had both the clarity and the commitment required to become a great leader. Barb was also confident that Marcela was ready for the right reasons.

David was another client of mine who changed his mind about a leadership decision. He was the chief operating officer (COO) of his company. The CEO decided to retire and David was encouraged to apply for the open position. David was an introvert by nature and didn't feel he'd be good as a CEO. He wasn't sure he could do all those market-facing activities. However, once he saw the candidates the board was considering, he thought hard about his original decision. He felt he could learn to be more extroverted. He also realized that his company needed continuity at the top. He came to realize he could do the role—and decided he was the best candidate. He spoke to the chair of the board, and the chair gladly invited him into the search process. David got the job and went on to become one of the most successful CEOs his company ever had.

Both Marcela and David demonstrate tremendous self-insight and personal maturity. Unfortunately, a lot of leaders do not possess these qualities. I've worked with plenty of leaders who have wanted to take on senior roles so desperately that they jump at the chance, not really understanding the demands of the role, only to falter months later. You must be self-aware enough to know whether you are ready. You also need to have the maturity to make this decision. You have to take this decision seriously—it's your accountability to your organization and ultimately to yourself.

The Gut Check for Leaders—Leadership Is a Decision

As you think about the ideas in this chapter, reflect on your answers to the following gut check questions:

1. Can you think of a time when you jumped into a leadership opportunity without really appreciating what you were getting into?
2. What are the major complexities and pressures of your role? Who is legitimately scrutinizing you?
3. When have you been in a situation that forced you to make a Big D leadership decision?
4. Think about the small d leadership decisions you find yourself confronted with. What guides you when making these small d decisions?

CHAPTER 6

Leadership Is an Obligation—Step Up

I n 1907, an American engineer named Theodore Cooper was leading a project to build the Québec Bridge spanning the St. Lawrence River. Once complete, it would be one of the largest and longest structures ever built. It would provide an economic boost to the region, enabling goods to be shipped more easily by rail between the American New England states and the Canadian province of Québec.

Cooper was chosen because of his stellar reputation, illustrious career, and expertise in bridge building. His 1884 book *General Specifications for Iron Railroad Bridges and Viaducts* was the definitive textbook for other bridge design engineers at the time.

But on a hot summer's day in late August of that year, tragedy struck. Near the end of the workday, a worker was driving rivets into the southern span of the bridge. He noticed that the rivets he had driven in an hour before had snapped in two. As he was about to report his concerns to his foreman, the air was suddenly filled with the deafening sound of grinding metal.

The worker looked up and saw the bridge begin to fall into the water, creating a force like nothing he had ever felt before. The sound carried for miles. People in nearby Québec City felt an earthquake-like tremor.

Most of the 85 men working on the bridge were immediately catapulted hundreds of feet into the air as the bridge fell beneath their feet. They died the second they hit the water. Other workers were crushed or dragged underwater by the falling bridge. Some died onshore because rescuers couldn't free them from the twisted metal debris before the tide came in that night. The community watched helplessly as these workers drowned. Seventy-five men lost their lives that day.

A Royal Commission investigating the tragic event found that the bridge had collapsed under its own weight. Design errors and miscalculations of the load that the structure could bear were the root of the problem. But the issues went far beyond technical errors. The commission criticized Cooper and the bridge company for putting profit before the safety of the public.

Cooper came under fire because, although he was an expert in bridge design, he had never personally designed a bridge as large as the Québec Bridge. The commission also concluded that political and economic pressure had influenced his judgment. Finally, Cooper's arrogance kept him from heeding the many warning signs that emerged during construction regarding the weight of the bridge and the quality of the materials. As author Kip Wedel chronicles in the book *The Obligation: A History of the Order of the Engineer,* "He had ignored too many warnings, shrugged off too many doubts, and as investment mounted and construction advanced, it only grew harder and harder for him to contemplate his errors. Perhaps by the time the massive project fell, he had decided it could not fall because he had designed it."[1] Cooper's reputation collapsed when the bridge did.

It would take a full two years for all the metal debris to be cleared from the river. But even then, the story of the Québec Bridge wasn't over. In 1916, a second attempt at building the bridge ended in another collapse. Thirteen more lives were lost. The two tragedies clearly showed that the engineering profession needed to change.

In 1918, reforms put the profession on a stronger foundation. Professional engineers would have to be licensed, and designs for public infrastructure projects would need to be approved by a licensed engineer. Then in 1925, a group of Canadian engineers established a ceremony called the Ritual of the Calling of an Engineer. They aimed to make graduating engineers aware of the obligations of their profession.

The Iron Ring Ceremony

Since that time, this ritual now known as the Iron Ring Ceremony, has been conducted in universities across Canada. The secret ceremony highlights the obligations that engineers accept as they enter the profession.

Older engineers retell the story of the Québec Bridge disaster so that the new graduates understand what can happen when their work is not done properly.

An iron ring is placed on the little finger of the dominant hand to act as a symbol and a reminder of the obligations that come from being an engineer. Because engineers wear the ring on their dominant hand, it rubs against every design they create, a constant reminder of their obligation to public safety and to the strong moral tenets that characterize professional engineers.

The design of the iron ring is also symbolic. New rings are made with rough edges to symbolize that a young engineer is rough and inexperienced. This instills a personal sense of humility and acts as a reminder of how much the engineer still has to learn. Over time, the rough edges begin to smooth out as the engineer creates design plans and gains experience, age, and wisdom. The ring is given to the young engineer by an older professional who will mentor the candidate.

During the ceremony, young engineers are reminded never to lose their moral center in the face of external pressures. They must understand that what they do has a broader impact on the public. They are reminded that they will need to make ethical choices during their careers, and when they do so, they must not simply try to stay out of trouble; they must make decisions from a desire to maintain the highest possible standard for the engineering profession. The ceremony also stresses the need for a sense of camaraderie among professional engineers to support one another's development and growth.

Over my career, I have worked with a lot of technical organizations and engineers. I truly respect and admire the care and concern engineers have for safety in the work that they do. They seem to carry the weight of their obligations front and center in their minds every single day.

I believe too many leaders today lack this sense of obligation. When people first take on leadership roles, nobody teaches them that leadership is an obligation. Look at the leaders at the center of scandals and corporate corruption. It's clear that many leaders have lost their way. They either have forgotten (or were never aware of) the obligations that come with being a leader.

This is why obligation is the second term of the leadership contract (see Figure 6.1). As a leader, you need to step up and recognize that when you take on a leadership role, it's not all about you.

Figure 6.1   The Second Term of the Leadership Contract

The ideas in this chapter may feel heavy to you. They should. As a leader, you need to feel the weight of your leadership obligations. If you don't, you run the risk of not living up to them, and we have seen what happens then. The consequences will go beyond you and end up affecting your customers, your organization, your employees, and your communities.

I'm sure you have worked with leaders who were driven primarily by personal gain. For them, their leadership role was all about the money, the titles, the stock options, the company cars, the perks, and the power. Working with them, you had a sense that they missed something along the way. They just did not get it, or maybe they lost their way.

I believe this partly explains why there is such a low level of trust and confidence in senior leadership. Employees look to the upper echelons of their organizations and see leaders primarily motivated by personal gain. I suspect that if you asked, employees would say, "I see what's in it for you, but I don't see what's in it for the rest of us."

This is where we need to begin our reflection on the obligations of leadership. If you make it all about you, you won't be truly successful because you will be leading for the wrong reasons. You will be letting down everyone who is counting on you. More important, your true colors will shine through when your leadership is really tested.

We need to understand what it is truly going to take, and gain a clearer sense of the core obligations of leadership.

What's It Going to Take?

Take a moment to reflect on your own leadership experience. Think about the first time you took on a leadership role. Did you ever really stop to think about the obligations you were assuming as you took on that role? I would go further and suggest that your boss or organization probably didn't sit you down to say, "Listen, here's what your obligations are as a leader." I'm sure that rarely happens. If you are like most leaders I work with, you probably had to figure it out on your own. Now, most leaders are pretty smart people, and eventually they might get it on their own. But what if they never do? I don't believe we can just rely on happenstance. We need to be more deliberate and be clear on our obligations as leaders.

I'll also let you in on a secret so that you don't have to figure it out all on your own: To be effective, sometimes you will need to separate your personal feelings from your obligations as a leader. Let me explain. You need an ability to separate you as a person from you as the leader. It takes a strong person to be able to have this level of personal insight, but it's going to be crucial to your success as a leader, especially as you move into more senior-level roles.

A great example of this comes from an episode of the old television program *The West Wing*. Jed Bartlet, played by actor Martin Sheen, is the president of the United States. He's dealing with one of his biggest dilemmas as president. There is an inmate on death row, and Bartlet is under great pressure to intervene and give a stay of execution. He reaches out to many people to get advice. He asks an old personal friend—a priest, played by actor Karl Malden—to visit him. When the priest arrives, he is in awe of the Oval Office. After some small chitchat, the priest asks President Bartlet, "What do you want me to call you, Jed or Mr. President?" The president pauses and replies, "Mr. President." He feels compelled to explain his reasons. He insists that it is not about ego. Instead, as a president he has to make very important decisions: which disease gets funding or which troops are sent into battle. He continues by saying that when confronted with these kinds of decisions, it is important for him to think of the office rather than the man. It's a brilliant moment in the episode and a brilliant line. It demonstrates a leader who never loses sight of his broader professional obligations. He realizes it's not about him; it's about the role he has, and he needs a way to separate the man from the office so that he can effectively fulfill his obligations.

I have personally found this idea helpful in my own leadership role. I remember a shift I had in my own mind during one team meeting. We were debating a strategy we were working on. My team is filled with smart and passionate consultants who vigorously position their ideas. In this discussion, we were reaching a bit of an impasse. As I listened to the discussion, I realized that I was pushing hard to get my own idea across. Then I stopped myself and asked, "What's my obligation right now as a leader?" The answer immediately came to me. My obligation was not to sell or push my own idea on my team. In fact, as the leader I could have easily dictated what I wanted and everyone would have accepted it. They would not have been happy, but they would have followed my orders. But I knew that wasn't what was best for our business. My obligation in that moment was to create the best possible conditions for my management team to think through our strategy. That was my obligation as the leader. It was my obligation to my CEO, my board, my clients, and my shareholders. This ability to separate the person (what you are personally vested in) from your professional leadership obligation is critical for you to master.

To master this ability, you must also have clarity about the core obligations you must live up to as a leader. That's what we are going to explore next.

The Five Core Obligations of Leadership

"Who is the company?" That's what one of my clients recently asked his colleagues. We were in the middle of a session on leadership, and this senior vice president was trying to explain his idea of what it means to be a leader. He said that when he first became a manager, he was thrilled to have the opportunity. He got completely wrapped up in the title, the extra money, and the power that his role provided. He finally felt like the big man on campus.

But the longer he stayed in the job, the more frustrated he became. As a manager, he now had a closer view of how the company operated than he had in his previous role. He could see bigger challenges and more serious dysfunctions than he had ever seen before. And he kept complaining, saying to himself, "This 'company' has got to get its act together!"

For a long time, he believed the company was a thing—an external entity separate from himself. He kept blaming the company's senior leaders for the problems he was experiencing.

Then he said, "When I took on this senior leadership role, I soon realized 'the company' wasn't a 'thing' after all—the company was me. I was the company." He said at that moment he shifted his focus as a leader. "I soon learned that it wasn't all about me. I had to live up to higher expectations."

With that realization, he stopped being a self-centered manager and started being a real leader, one who was aware of his obligations to the success of the organization.

He stopped looking at his role through the lens of what was in it for him. He started to understand and accept the broader obligations of leadership—that a leader is someone who takes accountability for the company and its customers, its employees, and the communities in which it does business. He began to feel the weight of being a real leader and realized that a lot rested on him now. He developed a real commitment to his leadership role and the obligations it demanded.

All leaders have obligations. Some are legal, some are financial, and some are moral and social in nature. In the end, your obligations as a leader are about a sense of duty or a promise to those you work with and those affected by what you do. Your leadership obligations should compel you to lead for the common good.

There are five core obligations that all leaders must understand, internalize, and live up to (see Figure 6.2). I will outline them next.

Your Obligation to Yourself

When you take on a leadership role for the right reasons, you should feel the weight of being a real leader—the realization that a lot is resting on you and that a lot is expected of you. You must realize that you have an obligation to yourself to be the best leader you can possibly be. When you understand that core obligation, you will find it actually feels good to live up to your potential—to grow, not to stagnate or become an empty chair leader.

Figure 6.2   The Five Core Obligations of Leadership

Unfortunately, too many leaders fail to live up to even this first obligation. Too many leaders stop working on themselves. They reach a level of performance and stop growing. They stop challenging themselves. As a result, many derail. Others fail to live up to their potential. In the end, they don't live up to their personal obligations—their commitment to being the best possible leader.

I work with leaders like this all the time. We come into their organizations to deliver leadership programs, and they assume the development opportunities are for other leaders, not for them. They think they are exempt because they don't believe they need the development.

But your obligations to yourself go even deeper than developing your skills. You need to have the self-awareness and honesty to understand where you may get yourself into trouble as a leader. Too many leaders assume leadership roles with arrogance instead of humility. When you start from a position of humility, you recognize that you work in a complex world. At any moment, something could happen in your operating environment to test your leadership.

You must also recognize that leadership brings temptations: power, money, greed, success, and fame. Many leaders who fail to live up to their personal obligations don't effectively manage these temptations. And there are other temptations to look out for as well: sex, alcohol, and drugs.

Many business leaders have the power, influence, and money to engage in all kinds of vices. But if you don't anticipate and manage your temptations, they will end up controlling you. There's research now that supports this fundamental idea.

A recent study published in the May 2015 issue of *Personality and Social Psychology Bulletin* suggests that otherwise good people can do some pretty bad things if they are not prepared for the temptations that they can face. Researchers Oliver Sheldon and Ayelet Fishbach found that when someone anticipates temptation, and is reminded of the moral and ethical implications of doing a bad thing, he or she is much less likely to succumb. The study asked 200 business school students to participate in a mock real estate transaction involving historical properties. One group of students was put through a series of exercises to remind them of the need to preserve the historical properties and the importance of not succumbing to unethical behavior. The other group was told it was representing a client who wanted to acquire the heritage property with the express purpose of demolishing it to build something new.

The results were clear. More than two-thirds of the students who underwent no preparation lied about the real purpose behind the purchase of the heritage property; less than half of those who had been reminded about the moral and ethical imperatives of preserving the property lied.

The study's authors concluded that in the absence of specific warnings about the perils of temptation, human nature leads us to believe that it is okay to break the rules. "Unethical behavior may not be experienced as something that needs to be resisted if people think it's socially acceptable or does not reflect on their moral self-image," the report stated.[2]

What does this mean for leaders? Anytime you accept a leadership position, you need to cultivate the self-awareness and self-honesty that will help you anticipate those moments when you might get yourself into trouble. You need to know what might tempt you.

Start by accepting that you will face temptation in your leadership role. You will be afforded access to certain resources and the power to make certain decisions, all of which could be opportunities for you to put your self-interest ahead of everything else. If you know these temptations exist at the outset, you may be better prepared to make the right decisions when you eventually are tempted.

What temptations could undermine your leadership?

It is also important to understand that your obligations to yourself as a leader also mean you need to strengthen your personal health through regular exercise, by building a strong family life and a personal support network, and by maintaining a sense of personal balance. A participant in one of our Leadership Contract workshops shared that her single most important obligation was to take care of her health: "If I am not healthy, I won't be able to lead effectively."

Being able to be your best self is crucial, because no matter how tough or challenging a situation may be at work, no matter how difficult the conflict, as a leader you have the obligation to be the leader. That's the higher standard you are being held to. It's the pace you need to set.

A question I'm often asked is: "Vince, this is easy when you have a great boss, but what if your boss is a jerk or is completely uninspiring?" I know this is difficult, but you must still keep to a higher standard of leadership. A client of mine shared a great quote with me about this issue: "Don't lead as you are led, but lead as you know you must." That's what sets the great leaders apart from the rest. They maintain their obligations as leaders even when surrounded by lame and ineffective leadership.

What is the obligation you have to yourself as a leader?

Your Obligation to Your Customers

There's a line that I share with my team all time: "In our business, nothing happens until a customer decides to buy something." Too many leaders take their customers for granted. Sure, we talk a lot about being customer focused or exceeding customer expectations, but the reality is that few leaders lead with the obligation to the customers at the front of their minds. When I work with new clients, I listen carefully to the way they speak during meetings. It's surprising to me how often senior leaders can spend days talking about strategy and never once say the word *customer*.

Your obligation as a leader is to lead in a way that is focused on delivering value to your customers. That's the promise that every organization ultimately makes. As a leader, you need to be clear about your customers' needs and expectations. This will help you ensure that business decisions and priorities are focused on delivering value. You need to make sure that your organization's products and services are designed to meet or exceed your customers' expectations.

You have an obligation to treat your customers fairly. If you drop the ball in the course of doing business with them, you need to take accountability and respond quickly to make things better. You also need to act as their advocate in your own organization so that everyone inside understands the needs of your customers.

When you get your obligation to your customers right, you get their loyalty. But it doesn't last forever. The pressure is always on, and you can never forget your obligation to them. In my experience, I find there is one simple way to keep this obligation front and center in your mind as a leader, and it comes down to one word: *gratitude*.

When you are grateful for your customers, you recognize that your business wouldn't exist without them. I have talked to owner-operators of construction companies, retail stores, and other small businesses, and these self-employed individuals always seem to have a genuine sense of gratitude because they know their customers have plenty of choices when it comes to where to spend their money.

In our competitive world, all customers have choices. And when they choose you and your organization, you need to be grateful. You need to make sure that this sense of gratitude is in the front of your mind when you work with them so that they actually feel it.

How would you define your obligation to your customers?

Your Obligation to Your Organization

Sam Palmisano, the former CEO of IBM, was once asked in an interview about his key obligation as a leader. He saw his obligation as being a temporary steward of the enterprise. It wasn't about him and his own ego. Instead, he was clear that his core obligation was *to leave IBM stronger than when he took it over*. And in his 11 years as CEO, he did just that. For example, the company's return on capital increased from 4.7 percent when he first started his role to 15.1 percent when he left. But he also balanced strong financial results with an unrelenting focus on developing future leaders. Geoff Colvin of *Fortune* magazine wrote that Palmisano left a legacy of leadership at IBM[3] and this is what made him a truly rare leader. How rare? Bill George from Harvard Business School defined him as the best CEO of the twenty-first century—an individual able to blend humility and openness with directness and pragmatism.[4]

Always focus on having a long-term view of success. This is a characteristic of strong leaders I've witnessed over the years. They understand that the old model of heroic leaders is archaic. They see themselves as part of a community of peers. Not only are they clear on their obligations from a financial standpoint, but they also understand their broader obligations to the health and sustainability of their organizations.

As a leader, you have a core obligation to ensure the future success and long-term sustainability of your organization. Unfortunately, I see too many leaders acting as bystanders in their organizations: standing around watching projects derail or seeing problems but not jumping in to fix them. Just going through the motions and thinking that it is someone else's responsibility is simply not good enough. Other leaders squander financial resources without thinking about the impact on the business. Many fail to manage poor performers actively, not realizing they are undermining the success of the organization. This also isn't good enough anymore.

I worked with a company that had distinct lines of business. One leader, Wayne, led a business that was doing well. However, there were early warning signs that his market was shifting in ways that could put his business at risk. These warning signs seemed like they were in the far distance. He didn't need to pay attention to them because his business was doing so well in the present. But then growth began to stall. Before Wayne knew it, all those warning signs came together to disrupt his market in ways he never imagined. In executive meetings, he shared his surprise, claiming that these market forces emerged almost overnight. They didn't. Although he was meeting his obligation by driving short-term growth of his organization, he failed to pay attention to his long-term obligation to the success of his organization. By the time he realized he had to act, he had missed his chance.

You must step up to your obligation to your organization. You must make things better every single day—in ways that position your organization for both short- and long-term success. That's the obligation you have taken on, whether you are aware of it or not. When you show up each day, you work in the interest of the whole enterprise. You don't focus only on your own department or functional area or your own self-interests. You need to anticipate threats in your operating environment that can put your organization at risk. You must create a sustainable business strategy that will drive competitive advantage over the long-term.

You must build strong relationships with other stakeholders, such as suppliers, regulators, and unions. In too many organizations, these relationships are adversarial, strained, and unproductive. You must work to improve them to live up to your obligation to your organization.

In the end, I find that leaders who truly understand their obligation to their organization see it as a living thing—something that has to be cared for to ensure its long-term survival and success.

How would you define your obligation to your organization?

Your Obligation to Your Employees

As a leader, you have an obligation to your employees. This means committing to creating a positive leadership experience for them by establishing a compelling culture—a work environment based on respect and dignity that encourages a positive working relationship, celebrates success, and makes employees feel valued.

When you create a compelling culture, your employees will be fully engaged and your customers will feel that engagement. I have learned that a positive leadership experience translates into a positive employee experience, which in turn creates a strong customer experience. In other words, you can't have strong employee engagement without strong leader engagement.

As a leader, you also have an obligation to make sure your employees understand the company's strategy so that they understand how their work contributes to the overall success of your organization. This is what makes work meaningful.

Once you ensure that employees have clarity, you then must support them in their ability to get work done. This means you need to remove obstacles that impede their performance, and you need to support their ongoing development and growth. In the end, you need to love helping people grow by challenging and stretching them. You can't own the success or engagement of your employees—they have their part to play. But you certainly do own creating the conditions for employees to thrive. You must pay attention to their career development by having career discussions. Think of the times when you've been at your best as an employee. Chances are you had a leader who took his or her obligation to employees as seriously as every other obligation he or she had. He or she focused on your personal growth and career development.

Since publishing the first edition of this book, I've thought more about a leader's obligation to his or her employees. What I've come to realize is that the best gift you can provide to an employee is the opportunity to lead and to do meaningful work.

I actually learned this lesson when I found my very first part-time job as a teenager. I was 16 years old and I really wanted a job at a men's clothing retailer at a mall near my home. I had no experience but lots of optimism. Gary, the store manager, struggled with the idea of hiring me. He told me that I was too young because the store focused on an older, more mature clientele. I told him that age had nothing to do with it. I promised I would succeed in the role. I kept following up and following up. He finally decided to give me a chance.

I knew he was taking a risk on me, so I worked extra hard to impress him. In the end, everything worked out fine. I was effective in the role. But what I took away from my experience with Gary was that he was always looking for opportunities to help me grow and learn about the business. He made what was simply a part-time job much more meaningful than I could ever have hoped. That was his leadership gift to me.

Gary's gift has stayed with me my whole career. And as a leader, I'm always looking to share the gift of leadership—giving others on my team the opportunity to lead, to grow, and to have greater impact on our business. I strive to create meaningful roles for people on my team. I also say to new people joining my team that I'm personally motivated to make their time with our company one of the top career experiences they'll ever have. The great leaders I worked with over the years did that for me, and I feel compelled to pay it forward to others.

In today's world, leaders must be actively focused on creating opportunities for others to lead, in particular for young people, women, and minority groups. When we do so, we create a rich diversity of thinking, experiences, and capabilities that will help our organizations succeed in a time of change, ambiguity, and disruption.

Think of your current role and ask yourself, "Am I providing opportunities for others to lead? Am I paving the way for women?

Am I creating meaningful work experiences for the young people in my company?"

Your Obligation to Your Communities

In 2014, CVS announced it would become the first major pharmacy chain in the United States to ban tobacco products. At a time when fewer and fewer people are smoking, you might not think that's newsworthy. But consider that this decision was estimated to cost the company $2 billion in lost sales for its 7,600 stores across the United States.

The strategy behind the move was fairly simple. With the *Affordable Care Act* formally in place, and tens of millions of additional Americans gaining health insurance, CVS wanted to be a primary provider of health care. Like Wal-Mart and other big retailers, CVS started opening up mini-clinics in its stores to provide basic care and health advice.

Clearly, CVS realized that selling a toxic product such as tobacco just didn't align with its health-conscious corporate profile and its core purpose of helping people on their path to better health.

The stakes were very high with this decision. CVS was wagering that its new activity around health care services would offset the loss in tobacco sales. Although many industry pundits applauded the move, it wasn't completely without risk.

Many leaders cower from making the tough decisions, even if it's the right thing to do. Let's face it; we live in a world where doing the right thing is often ignored in the name of profit. As CVS demonstrated, tough decisions can mean loss of revenue in the short term. Many retail analysts believe, however, that CVS will benefit in the long run by confronting this issue now.

More important, if you have the strength to do the right thing, you need to embrace risk and accept the possibility that your decisions may not work out. Think of your own company or industry. What key issue is calling out for you to step up and do the right thing for your customers, your shareholders, and for society?

Charles Garfield was a pioneering researcher in the area of personal and organizational peak performance. He recognized decades ago that we can't create successful organizations in the midst of a decaying society. He believed, and I agree, that organizations and the communities in which they do business are deeply connected.

This obligation means you pay attention to the obvious things. You pay your taxes. You behave like a good corporate citizen. You take responsibility for the environment. You support local groups, schools, and charities. You understand that creating a successful organization is important to the communities in which you do business. Successful organizations create economic value. They create jobs. They become multipliers for a host of local businesses that depend on you. These ideas are not new, but it's time that we remind ourselves of them.

But it's also important to understand that these obligations are now common expectations for all leaders and their companies. Millennials expect to work with organizations seen as being great companies that drive strong financial performance and live up to their broader obligations to the communities in which they do business. The good news is that a growing number of organizations are doing this as we speak. They are doing well by also doing good—the two are not mutually exclusive. Together, they add up to a powerful legacy we can all leave as leaders.

The Five Core Obligations in Action

When a leader truly understands his or her core obligations, it's obvious. Mark Bertolini, chairman and CEO of health care insurer Aetna Inc., recently confirmed that his company had raised all employees' hourly wages to a base of $16. The pay and benefit hikes Aetna introduced will help about 5,700 employees, most of whom were making $13 to $14 an hour.

Aetna found that most of its lowest-paid employees were single mothers, and their wages were not enough for them to make ends meet. Bertolini said he could no longer justify poverty-inducing wages when his company was doing so well. "Here we are a Fortune 50 company and we're about to put these people into poverty, and I just didn't think it was fair," he said.

Aetna's decision to voluntarily reach above mandated minimum wages is part of a growing movement among the CEOs at successful companies to restore some dignity to hourly pay. Costco cofounder and former CEO Jim Sinegal has not only increased wages and benefits for his employees to sector-leading levels, but also lobbied government to increase minimum wages.

These great leaders do what's right for their company, their employees, and the key stakeholders they serve. Truly accountable leaders go one step further and ensure their organizations do right by society.

This isn't always easy to do. Many of us tend to be pretty narrowly focused on the events of our own lives. When something catastrophic happens in another part of the world—an earthquake, a tsunami, or another tragic event with many lives lost—the story is all over the news. Yet when you show up to work on Monday, it's business as usual.

You and your colleagues may talk about the events, but only briefly. The people you work with are more interested in talking about their kids, where they're going for vacation, or what's going wrong at work. So you put your head down and keep working away.

Why are we so preoccupied with the mundane details of our lives? Why are we not more concerned about the profound events around us?

One explanation may be that our leaders are not all that interested in the world outside their own organizations. If leaders do not seem to care about suffering, injustice, or tragedy, why should we?

Of course, not all leaders are like that. More and more I see business leaders stepping up to their obligation to society as a whole. They leverage their position of power and influence to put a spotlight on important social issues. Here are a few examples:

- Apple CEO Tim Cook has built a reputation for being outspoken on social issues. A dramatic example occurred at the company's 2014 annual meeting. Cook was involved in a very public argument with a climate change denier who criticized Apple for investing too much in sustainability and environmental initiatives. Cook angrily rebuffed the shareholder, telling him, "If you want me to do things only for ROI reasons, you should get out of this stock."
- Sheryl Sandberg, the chief financial officer (CFO) of Facebook, made the topic of women in leadership front and center through her book *Lean In*. But she didn't stop there. She also went public with her personal story of grief after her husband, Dave Goldberg, the CEO of Survey Monkey, died unexpectedly on his 50th birthday. By bringing the issue of grief in the workplace to the attention of the public and media, she is helping millions of people.
- In June 2013, when Ed Clark was the CEO of TD Bank, North America's sixth-largest bank, he gave a speech at the WorldPride

Human Rights Conference in Toronto about how the corporate world needs to embrace and respect the needs of lesbian, gay, bisexual, and transgender (LGBT) people. TD Bank officially began to publicly support the Pride movement in the early 1990s and in 1994 offered full benefits to the partners of same-sex married employees. However, no senior executive at the bank had ever expressed his or her views as strongly and in such a public forum in support of LGBT issues.

- Arianna Huffington, co-founder and editor in chief of *The Huffington Post*, has been outspoken on the issue of health and, in particular, sleep. She's brought much needed attention to the chronic sleep deprivation faced by our society. This attention is turning to positive action.
- In 2010, Bell Canada, a leading telecommunications and media company, launched a "Let's Talk" initiative to raise awareness and begin an open dialogue about mental health issues facing millions of Canadians. Company CEO George Cope lived his own experience with this issue as his mother struggled with depression throughout her life. Under his leadership, the company developed a multiyear strategy designed to fight the stigma associated with mental illness, improve access to care, support research, and ensure Bell leads by example in workplace mental health. Over $85 million has been raised to date, with a goal of driving that number to well over $100 million by 2020.
- Howard Schultz, former CEO of Starbucks, has never been a leader to ignore the world around him. In December of 2014, he wrote a heartfelt letter to his employees on the issue of racism. He also convened an impromptu open forum at the Starbucks head office in Seattle for 400 staff and partners. In Schultz's words, he had become very concerned about the violence and unrest that was erupting across the United States, from Ferguson, Missouri, to Oakland, California. Schultz asked: "What are our individual and collective responsibilities to our country as well as to our own company?"

These business leaders recognize that their companies are not separate from the world. They also are a growing number of enlightened leaders who believe we all benefit when our CEOs, senior executives, and their companies demonstrate an understanding and sensitivity about social issues and events.

Leaders who shut their eyes and stick their fingers in their ears will ultimately lose credibility with their employees who do not have the luxury to ignore these problems. Conversely, nothing builds loyalty, trust, and engagement like a leader who takes steps to show employees that he or she sees the same problems they do. This is what it means to live up to your obligations as a leader—to focus on the whole picture of yourself, your customers, your employees, your organization, and your community.

Revisiting the Iron Ring Ceremony and What It Means for Leaders

I believe that we as leaders need a version of the Iron Ring Ceremony to help us understand our leadership obligations.

What I especially like about the Iron Ring Ceremony is that it instills early on the ideas of humility, obligation, and deliberateness. At the core of the ceremony—and the meaning behind the symbolic iron ring—is the idea that engineers must be humble. They understand that what they do has a broader impact on the public and society as a whole. They are told that, like the ring, they are rough and inexperienced and must grow and develop over time. And they are promised that a mentor will support them.

Let's contrast this experience with what happens to most new leaders. First, there isn't a ceremony like the Iron Ring Ceremony that helps you understand the obligations of leadership. Second, if you're lucky, you may get a mentor or a coach to help you integrate in your first 100 days, but for most people the experience of leadership is pretty isolating. There is little support and guidance. You feel like you've been thrown in the deep end of a pool, and you must sink or swim. Finally, and more important, most people who take on leadership roles do it with a sense of bravado and arrogance instead of humility. You feel like you can't admit that you have rough edges because you can't show your weaknesses or vulnerabilities. You also feel intense pressure to prove yourself at all costs. Maybe this is why up to 40 percent of leaders fail after assuming new leadership roles.

Rosabeth Moss Kanter from the Harvard Business School says that leaders today need a healthy dose of humility.[5] They need a deep desire to serve others with an emphasis on values and a sense of purpose, a sense of the long-term consequences of one's actions, and personal knowledge of one's strengths and limitations. Ultimately, she says that as a leader you must have a desire to do what's right for the common good, not just what's good for you.

Final Thoughts—Leadership Is an Obligation

It's important to understand that living up to each of the five obligations of leadership isn't easy. At times, they will be in conflict with one another. Inherent tensions will arise that you need to manage. Trade-offs will have to be made. In these cases, you need to recognize there will be no easy answer that will resolve things for you. Leadership is never that easy, as much as we might want it to be.

If you are truly aware of what your obligations as a leader are and never lose sight of them while you lead, you will be better able to manage the inherent tensions that will arise. It's not enough that only you become aware of your core obligations at a personal level; every leader in your organization must do the same. When we do this, we can start a dialogue where our obligations become clear. We'll become more aware of what we truly believe in and what we may merely be paying lip service to. In the end, this process will help all leaders step up.

The Gut Check for Leaders—Leadership Is an Obligation

As you think about the ideas in this chapter, reflect on your answers to the following gut check questions:

1. What do you define as your primary obligation as a leader? To what extent do you lead every day with this obligation front and center in your mind?
2. Consider the five core obligations of leadership described in this chapter. What insights did you gain regarding your obligation to:
   a. Yourself as a leader?
   b. Your customers?
   c. Your organization?
   d. Your employees?
   e. The communities in which your organization does business?
3. What do you believe is your formula to drive the success of your organization or your team?
4. What actions will you take to live up to your core obligations as a leader?

CHAPTER 7

Leadership Is Hard Work—Get Tough

True leadership courage is hard to find. The headlines are rife with tales of leaders—both in business and politics—taking the easy way out of problems. These are leaders who cut and run instead of staying and confronting their challenges.

That is what makes Lisa Su so special. The CEO of Advanced Micro Devices (AMD) is the very definition of leadership courage.

In 2014, the MIT-educated Su took over the helm at AMD at a time when it seemed the company was on the verge of collapse. Today, AMD is a huge player in the semiconductor sector again and the company's stock has more than quadrupled. How could Su engineer such a dramatic turnaround?

In an interview in *Fortune* magazine, Su said that rather than fear the challenge of rebuilding AMD, she welcomed it with open arms. This attitude, Su said in the article, was forged during her days working at IBM when a manager gave her a piece of advice that changed her outlook on business and life: "Lisa, run toward problems."

And run she did. In just over two years, Su was able to completely change the business strategy at AMD. The company had become wholly focused on semiconductors for the PC market; as consumers turned to other devices to do the majority of their computing, AMD suffered.

Su immediately shifted focus and ramped up innovation at AMD. Today, less than half of AMD's business is devoted to PCs. The rest is focused on gaming, mobile devices, and immersive technology.

"I have to say being CEO of AMD was my dream job," Su told *Fortune*. "Running one of the largest semiconductor companies in the United States was my dream job. Now, yes, we had a lot of challenges, but I didn't focus necessarily on how hard life would be. I focused on the incredible opportunity in front of me."

Su is credited as being a game-changer who helped transform AMD. She was rightly acknowledged by *Fortune* magazine as one of the top 100 global leaders in 2016.

It's always gratifying when I see a successful leader who embodies something as important as courage. It gives me hope that others will see the same story and start applying what they see in their own leadership challenges.

I can say with certainty that there are a lot of leaders who require a booster shot of courage. When I talk to my clients about what separates truly accountable leaders from the mediocre ones, personal courage always rises to the top of the list. The global research I shared in Chapter 3 provides clear evidence that supports this point.

Yet, in my daily work with some of the world's largest organizations, I hear stories about leaders whose default setting is to wilt in the face of adversity. These are leaders who never take responsibility for things that go wrong, preferring instead to throw some of the people they lead under the bus to make the problem go away. These are the leaders who sit quietly in meetings, refusing to share their ideas because they are afraid of conflict.

These leaders may actually believe that what they are doing is a benefit to their organizations. In fact, they are not only hurting their own careers, but they are limiting the effectiveness and success of their organizations. When you run away from problems, you weaken yourself, your team, and your company.

So it is important to understand that being a leader isn't easy. Let's face it: Leadership is hard work, and it's getting harder. To truly excel, to truly be a great leader over the long-term, you must have the courage and persistence to do the hard work of leadership. Delivering consistent financial results, attaining high team performance, executing strategy, managing multiple and often conflicting priorities, and driving innovation aren't easy. You must realize that there is hard work that you alone as a leader can and must do, and if you don't do it, you'll set yourself and your organization back.

Alibaba CEO Jack Ma couldn't agree more with this term of the leadership contract. He spoke recently to a group of leaders packed into a large meeting room to hear him dispense the leadership wisdom that made him a billionaire as he built one of the world's most successful e-commerce companies. His message was clear and to the point: *If you want your life to be simple, you shouldn't take on a leadership role.* In other words, leadership brings hard work, and if you aren't up for it, then don't take on the job. Do something simpler.

Unfortunately, too many leaders take on the job but then are reluctant to dig in, choosing instead to avoid the hard work. Others act as bystanders, watching things happen. And then there are those leaders who simply look for the easy way out, thinking that some quick-fix idea will make everything better, only to be surprised when these quick fixes don't fix anything. We need to stop underestimating what it takes to be a consistently great leader. Sure, leadership can be easy if you're satisfied with mediocrity. But that's not what the leadership contract is all about.

It's time that we as leaders understand that the real work of leadership isn't easy. We also need to understand that we'll need resilience, determination, and a deep sense of personal resolve to be effective. This is what the third term of the leadership contract is all about (see Figure 7.1).

Figure 7.1   The Third Term of the Leadership Contract

Do We Have Wimps or Leaders in Our Organizations?

A few years ago, I was leading a strategic talent planning session with the executive team of a large organization. We were brought in because the executive team could not agree on a strategy to keep their talent pipeline full. They just kept going around in circles, unable to hit on the right approach.

So we came up with a new plan. We created a visual with four categories: those identified as superstars and high-potential leaders; the solid performers, the questionable leaders on the cusp; and those who were so bad at their jobs that they needed to exit the organization. Being confronted by these numbers forced some very awkward conversations.

The most interesting moment came when the executive team started talking about the weakest leaders–the people who needed to be let go. Many of the executives spoke passionately about not giving up on those individuals, pleading that they just needed more time to help bring their overall performance up. In the end, it was pretty clear that the executives were very reluctant to make some hard leadership decisions.

Through all this debate, the CEO remained silent. Then he took a red and green marker, went to the wall where we had the poster up, and circled a number of names in green. He said to his team, "We have to do whatever we can to retain these individuals and grow them."

Then he took the red marker and put an "X" across several names. As he did this, he said, "I don't care what we do with these individuals. We've been babysitting them for too long. I've written them off and no longer have confidence in them!"

The CEO's team was surprised by some of the individuals he marked off. When they asked for his rationale, he said, "I've seen enough to conclude they will never be valuable leaders in the organization." It was almost as if, at that moment, the CEO realized he had privately written those people off for quite some time but had learned to tolerate and overlook their poor performance.

Those red X's may have seemed harsh, but they exposed the fact that the entire executive team was enabling mediocrity because they weren't prepared to have the tough conversations needed to deal with these poor performers. Maybe if they were truly accountable as a team and had the courage to have these talent discussions earlier, they could have helped some of those weaker leaders get stronger. But they didn't.

Far too many organizations suffer from the same problem. A lot of my clients talk about how their leaders don't seem willing to take on the hard work that comes with their roles. I often hear comments like, "Our leaders avoid managing poor performers," "Our leaders don't give candid feedback," or "Our leaders really struggle in making difficult decisions."

Hearing the same themes over and over again, from client after client, I can't help but ask myself: *Are there any real leaders in our organizations, or are we just surrounded by wimps?* It seems like there are a lot of wimps out there—people who don't have the courage to take on the hard work of leadership.

I've seen what this looks like firsthand. At a recent client event, I talked to some supervisors and managers who told me they actually leave all the hard work of people leadership to their HR department. Let's think about that for a moment.

These leaders are actually "outsourcing" a key part of their jobs to someone else. At first, I was a little shocked. But the more I thought about it, the more it started to make sense. These leaders aren't really committed to their roles. So why not let someone else manage all the tough people issues—providing difficult feedback to employees, having the challenging performance conversations, and addressing poor performers?

Holding people accountable isn't easy. Managing poor performers isn't easy. Accepting candid feedback about how you need to grow as a leader isn't easy. Confronting your personal gaps takes courage. But instead of getting tough, too many leaders choose to wimp out.

You must accept this third term of the leadership contract. You can't take the easy way out. It's no longer good enough for you to be a bystander. You have to get tough. Everyone, including your team, your department, your boss, and your organization, is counting on you to be a leader and not to wimp out. This will also mean being tough with yourself.

The Hard Rule of Leadership

If you are ready to be a true leader, then it's time to learn a rule that few leaders understand. I call it the hard rule of leadership: *If you avoid the hard work of leadership, you will become a weak leader. If you tackle the hard work of leadership, you'll become a strong leader.*

When I talk about the leadership contract with clients, the moment I introduce this rule is when the room really gets silent. This is the moment when we start calling out the stuff that we all carry around with us but never get a chance to talk about openly and nondefensively. This is the moment when we start digging into what's really going on in our day-to-day lives, when we confront the reasons we haven't been living up to our obligations as leaders.

Let's explore this rule further.

Avoid the Hard Work of Leadership, and You Become Weak

Take a moment to be honest with yourself and think about the hard rule of leadership as it applies to you. What hard work are you avoiding in your role? Maybe there's a difficult decision that you alone need to make. Maybe there's some straight-up feedback you need to deliver to a colleague. Maybe there's a chronic underperformer you know you need to deal with but haven't. Maybe you've been putting off doing a 360-degree assessment on yourself for fear of the feedback you'll receive.

Many leaders don't realize that when you avoid the hard work of leadership, you actually end up making yourself weak. And it goes beyond you. You also end up weakening your team, your division, and your entire organization. The hard work will always be there, and if you keep putting it off, you'll spend your days dealing with the same issues over and over again. You'll never truly advance or make progress. You, your team, and your organization will be stuck. Does this sound familiar?

Let's consider the story of Margaret. She was a senior leader in a struggling information technology professional services firm. The company brought in a new chief operating officer (COO), and he engaged me to help him and his senior team create a new strategy for the future. We set up regular forums for the top leaders to come together, and Margaret was one of those leaders. By the third session, I noticed Margaret was really getting frustrated.

I said, "Margaret, what's going on? You don't look like a happy camper."

She paused and then said, "I'm getting sick and tired of these meetings. You know, I've come to all of them with this list of things I need to get done, and every time I walk away my list remains untouched."

I said, "Okay, Margaret, thanks for sharing your reactions. Why don't you take a minute and review this list right now and ask yourself how many items could have been tackled before coming to this meeting?" As she was looking at her list, I said, "Margaret, I want you to be honest with me."

She looked up sheepishly and said, "All of them."

I said, "What do you think has been holding you back?"

She paused and then explained, "Because they involve a lot of really tough conversations with the people in this room."

I reminded Margaret and the entire group that the purpose of the meetings was to explore the future strategy of the organization. They couldn't afford to get bogged down in day-to-day operational issues. It was their job as leaders to tackle those operational issues head-on, no matter how difficult they might be. I challenged the group to come to the meetings with as many items checked off their lists as possible so that they would have the freedom to think about the future. During the rest of the day, I saw Margaret meeting with her colleagues, booking times to address the hard things she was avoiding. It was clear she had learned the hard rule of leadership.

Many leaders don't understand that it is their job to get tough and tackle the hard stuff. Like Margaret, many never check a single thing off that list we all carry with us. Maybe confronting our peers is too difficult. Maybe it never seems like it's the right time to do it.

Unfortunately, a failure of nerve is a failure of leadership. Failing to have these conversations keeps you and your company from moving forward. It keeps you distracted by unresolved issues. It keeps you stuck.

The 10 Ways Leaders Make the Hard Work Harder

Through my own leadership experience and my work with hundreds of leaders at all levels, I've learned that not only is leadership hard work, but also a lot of us inadvertently make the hard work harder. How? By doing certain things that actually keep us avoiding the hard work (see Figure 7.2). As leaders, we need to be aware of how we do this so that we can become stronger as leaders and develop the confidence to tackle the hard work.

As you read this next section, reflect on your own leadership role and identify the ways you make the hard work of leadership even harder for yourself. I encourage you to be honest.

1. Getting in Over Your Head. Sometimes a situation changes and you're no longer equipped to manage it. Maybe you don't have the skills you need to be successful. Maybe your ego gets in the way and keeps you from asking for help. Maybe you are feeling inadequate and working hard to prove yourself to your colleagues and your organization. Maybe you lack self-confidence and everyone knows it. Your team can smell it,

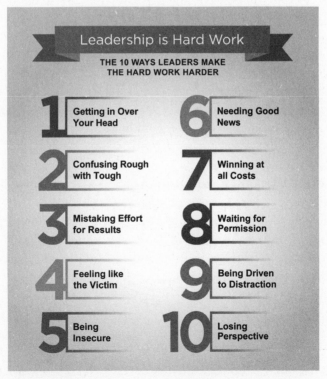

Figure 7.2   The 10 Ways Leaders Make the Hard Work Harder

and it undermines your credibility. You start playing it safe and become an empty chair leader. If this sounds familiar, you may be in over your head.

I once worked with a struggling leader whose performance began to decline. He was well liked, but pretty soon that didn't matter because his poor performance started to frustrate his team members. He knew he wasn't cut out for the role he was in. But instead of admitting it and addressing it directly, he let his performance slide to a point where his manager had to terminate him. If you find yourself in so far over your head that there's a real risk that your projects will have bad outcomes, then you need to have the courage to ask for help. Otherwise, you'll keep yourself and everyone around you stuck at the level of your incompetence.

We create risk for our organizations when we lack the courage to admit that we're in over our heads. Asking for help isn't easy. Your ego gets in the way. You probably feel tremendous pressure to prove yourself to others. But in today's complex world, you need to continually monitor your own performance and make sure you aren't putting yourself and your company at risk.

It is important to note that at times getting in over your head is a great way to grow as a leader. If you are successful in managing the situation, it can take you to a higher level of performance. But what I'm talking about here is those situations when you are unable to take your performance to a higher level. You are in so far over your head that you are now creating risk for yourself and your organization.

Do you find yourself getting in over your head as a leader?

2. Confusing Tough with Rough. There aren't many really tough leaders out there. There are a lot of leaders who think they are *tough*, but they're actually *rough*. They're holding on to old ideas of leadership that tell them you need to be a jerk to show how tough you are. Many of these leaders regularly mistreat, disrespect, and insult others. They frequently tear a strip off their direct reports, even in public. Yelling at people is easy. Being genuinely tough is much harder.

A recent *Washington Post* article entitled "Is Your Boss Making You Sick?" lists a number of seminal studies showing that abusive leadership can, over time, contribute to higher rates of heart disease, heart attack, and angina among employees. These studies also show links to sleep problems, high blood pressure, and a wide range of mental health problems, including depression.

If you are one of these rough leaders who are prone to temper tantrums, emotional outbursts, or chronic moodiness, I have two words for you: Grow up! This behavior is understandable for toddlers but not for leaders. Your lack of professional maturity makes things harder for you. Your inability to keep your emotions in check puts everyone on edge. You're creating a climate of fear, and you'll never get the best out of your team and colleagues as a result.

A generation ago it was probably okay to mistreat people. Leaders could do it because they had power and the Boomers would put up with it. But if you take the rough approach today, you'll become a lonely leader pretty fast. The bottom line is that if you are a jerk as a leader, no one is going to want to work with you. It's that simple. Why? Because Millennials won't put up with you; they'll just leave. To make matters worse, Boomers are following their younger colleagues' lead and becoming less willing to put up with a rough leader.

As a leader, do you confuse tough with rough?

3. Mistaking Effort for Results. Vic was pretty angry when he left his annual performance review. He couldn't believe his boss, the company's chief information officer (CIO), had given him an unsatisfactory performance rating. Didn't she know how hard he had been working?

As the director of information technology, Vic's big project for the year was implementing a new cloud-based customer relationship management (CRM) system. He had run into problems right from the start. The first vendor he chose wasn't really up to the task. They gave him bad advice, and by the time he realized it, months had gone by and the project's costs had escalated. Now he was under pressure to get the system out, so he skimped on internal education. When the CRM hit the sales force, he got a lot of complaints.

Vic thought he had given the project everything he could. It had been a hard year. He had put in countless hours. He was often on call 24/7. And he felt like hiccups were common enough when implementing a new system.

His manager saw things differently. She knew how many hours Vic had put in, but in the end, he just didn't deliver. So although Vic rated himself as "meeting expectations" for the year, his manager gave him that dreaded rating of "unsatisfactory."

During the meeting, the CIO explained that, as a leader, Vic shouldn't confuse effort with results. "It's one of the first ground rules of leadership," she said. She also reminded him that as a leader, he needed to be able to take an objective view of his own performance, even when it fell short.

I've run into leaders like Vic many times. They're so focused on how hard they're working that they can't see the actual results they've accomplished—or failed to accomplish. This keeps them from seeing their own performance objectively and ultimately makes things more difficult. Many leaders think working hard is the same thing as doing the hard work of leadership. It isn't. Keeping yourself busy by toiling away at drudgery is hard and wears on you over time. But that's very different from tackling the real hard work of leadership.

Do you have a tendency to mistake effort for results?

4. Feeling Like the Victim. I once had a phone call that really bothered me with a leader I was working with. This woman spent 30 minutes complaining about her company and her role. The more she went on, the more frustrated I became.

It's never fun to get an earful of someone else's negativity, but this call really stuck with me. I was still thinking about it later that afternoon. Eventually I realized why: This woman was a senior leader in her company, but she didn't show up as a leader. Her complaining made her sound like an employee.

Everybody gets frustrated at work. That's normal. But leaders need to be able to move through the frustration. I'll cut an employee who's complaining some slack because he or she probably can't change his or her day-to-day circumstances that much. But a leader can.

I called this leader back and had a frank talk with her. I told her that although I understood the reasons for her frustration, she needed to step up and move forward. She needed to stop believing she was the victim and get busy tackling the hard things in her leadership role. If there's a problem, don't whine about it—fix it!

Do you show up as a victim at times? How does this set you back?

5. Being Insecure. When you are insecure as a leader, you come across as wishy-washy, unwilling to take a stand on any issue. Maybe you don't have the courage or stomach to be a leader, and you take the easy way out on important decisions. If you're really insecure, you don't trust others and you end up micromanaging. You never let go of anything. You keep doing work you shouldn't be doing, and others around you don't grow. You may also hire weak talent for fear that stronger people will surpass you.

Other insecure leaders need to be liked by everyone. So they are agreeable—too agreeable. They never tackle the hard stuff for fear that they won't be liked. Being a leader isn't about winning a popularity contest. In fact, being liked as a leader is often overrated. You are going to be obligated to do some things that won't make everyone happy. You can't let insecurity stop you from doing what needs to be done.

It's important to acknowledge that most of us as leaders have moments when we feel insecure. Maybe you're facing a big challenge that has you questioning your ability to succeed. Maybe intense scrutiny is making you second-guess yourself. Whatever the reason, most leaders get that sense of insecurity from time to time. When it's momentary or fleeting, it's usually not a big deal. But when it lingers and starts getting the best of you, it can undermine your success.

Traditionally, we have demanded that our leaders act and appear at all times like invulnerable, infallible superheroes. That discourages many leaders from confronting their insecurities. Unfortunately, when we duck and run from our insecurities, we rarely master and overcome them. When insecurity is not addressed, drama usually ensues. Many leaders build up their egos to compensate for a low sense of self-worth.

The key to overcoming insecurities begins by admitting that you have them. It's not a sign of weakness—it's a sign of strength as a leader.

Do you let your insecurity get the best of you?

6. Needing Good News. Many leaders want to hear only good news. They make their own lives harder because everyone who works with them spins information, and they never hear the real truth. If you avoid bad news, you keep yourself in a state of delusion, never confronting what's really going on. It's like being at a carnival and going to the House of Mirrors. Everything you look at is distorted. This distorted view keeps you disconnected from what's going on. You run the risk of missing things. Problems get worse, and your work gets more difficult.

Remember, your job as a leader is not to avoid, ignore, or deny bad news; it's to find out the bad news as early as you can so you can act before the problem becomes more complicated.

Do you want to hear only good news as a leader?

7. Winning at All Costs. Competition is a great motivator, but some leaders take it to an absurd extreme. They see everyone as an adversary or an enemy—even within their own organizations. Everything is a win-lose proposition. That extends to relationships, too; they eliminate anyone who doesn't support what they're trying to accomplish. If you're overly competitive, you won't tolerate dissenters or differing points of view. You'll most likely come across as pompous, conceited, and totally absorbed in your own personal agenda.

Excessive competition creates poor working relationships with team members and keeps you from engaging stakeholders genuinely. If you can't bring people along with you, you'll make your life much harder. In today's world, you need to be a savvy influencer and collaborator. You can't just intimidate people into going along with you. You need to be able to create win-win outcomes, instead of trying to win at all costs for selfish reasons.

As a leader, are you always driven to win at all costs? Do you appreciate how this strategy may be making things harder for you as a leader?

8. Waiting for Permission. I've seen many leaders who always seem apprehensive because they are waiting for permission to lead. This is a huge source of frustration for senior-level leaders. I've often heard CEOs exclaim, "What are they waiting for?" Many leaders mistakenly assume they can't act without approval from senior leaders. You need to understand that you have been put in a leadership role to act and tackle the hard work of leading. You haven't been given a leadership role to be a bystander.

Social psychologists have discovered a behavioral pattern called the *bystander effect*. People don't offer to help a victim in an emergency situation if other people are present. In fact, the more people present, the less likely it is that someone in need will get help. The mere presence of other bystanders diffuses the responsibility to act.

Is this happening to you? Are you waiting around for permission or acting like a bystander?

9. Being Driven to Distraction. I once worked for a manager who was a train wreck. She was a nice enough person, but she was completely disorganized. You could never count on her for anything. Meetings would be canceled at the last minute. Priorities were always shifting. We'd commit to a plan of action on a project, only to have the timelines change or have everything pushed to the back burner because we just couldn't get our ducks in a row. Her poor executive assistant spent all her time booking and rebooking meetings. As a result, this manager would go through a new assistant every six months.

It was clear she lacked discipline, and it was completely undermining her ability to lead us. A lack of discipline creates tremendous uncertainty for the people you lead. Your lack of preparation creates an environment in which crisis reigns supreme. A colleague of mine who suffered under a disorganized manager once said: "I simply show up every day waiting for the next urgent matter to tackle. Whatever!"

In what ways might you be undisciplined and driven to distraction as a leader?

10. Losing Perspective. During a recent leadership development program, I watched three senior public-sector leaders have a heated discussion. I could tell they were talking about a pretty serious issue, so I let them get into it.

But after a while, something started to bug me about the conversation. I called a time-out and said, "I've been following along pretty well, but now I'm getting confused. When did this issue happen?" In unison, they said, "Ten years ago!" And here I thought they were talking about a current issue that they needed to work out. "We've spent 25 minutes talking about this. Can anyone tell me how this is relevant to your leadership roles today?" I asked. Silence. I continued, "I don't understand how you can still be this emotionally invested in something that happened so long ago. It's clear you have all lost perspective as leaders."

Unfortunately, I've been delivering that speech a lot recently. It's all too easy for people in an organization to get into the habit of rehashing old issues. But holding on to the past doesn't help. It acts as an anchor holding you back. You have to let it go.

Sure, leaders need to learn from the past, but if you're repeatedly discussing the same old events, you have lost perspective.

Do you find yourself getting stuck because you often lose perspective?

Tackle the Hard Work of Leadership and You Become Strong

The hard rule of leadership also says that if you tackle the hard work of leadership, you become strong. Moreover, it's not just you who becomes

Figure 7.3   The Three Ways to Get Tough

strong; it's also your team, your division, and your entire organization. Why? Because you don't get stuck. You keep things moving forward, progressing all the time, instead of letting the same issues and problems continue to dominate your life.

There are three things (see Figure 7.3) you need to understand to make this rule truly work in your role as a leader:

1. You need to shift how you view the hard work of leadership.
2. You need to develop a mindset of resilience.
3. You need to build a strong sense of personal resolve.

Shift Your View

How you view the world in which you lead can have a significant impact on how you show up as a leader. For example, many of our leadership development programs include an activity called the Future Environment Map. During the activity, participants identify key trends in their emerging business environment. They identify a host of trends in technology, the regulatory environment, customer dynamics, their competitors, and so on. We capture the ideas on large sheets of sticky notes and put them on a massive poster. As leaders look at the hundreds of ideas, they immediately grasp the complexity of their operating environment. They also start to appreciate how driving growth will be a challenge. Finally, they start to internalize the challenges they will face as leaders.

I then ask the leaders one final question: "As you look at this emerging environment, do you feel like this is the best time to be a leader in your company or the worst time?" It's an important and provocative question. Many leaders look at their emerging operating environment negatively—all they see is the hard work ahead. For them, it's the worst time to be a leader, and many question whether they are up for it.

Other leaders are more optimistic. They see opportunity. They acknowledge the complexity, the risks, and the hard work, but they react with excitement.

Stephen Covey once said, "The way we see the problem is the problem." You need to start looking at the hard work of leadership in a different way. Instead of looking at it as something to avoid, start looking at it as a sign of progress. You need to be able to look at your role and your emerging environment and see all the hard work ahead of you with a sense of optimism, not pessimism.

When you shift your view in this way, you start to anticipate problems. You become more active in seeking problems out earlier, before they can impede your success. You want to hear bad news as early as you can get it so you are in a better position to mitigate risk, as well as tackle and solve an issue before it gets out of control or gets bigger than it needs to be.

So how do you sort through all the numerous challenges and figure out what hard work you must tackle? Ask yourself: "Are the results that I am accountable to deliver at risk?" If your sense is that they are, you'd better start addressing the issue. Then ask yourself: "Is the way the work is being done inconsistent with my organization's values?" This can create other issues that will require your attention if you don't deal with the challenge head-on. Finally, consider your stakeholders: "Could the issue jeopardize my obligation to my key stakeholders?" If you sense that it might, you need to get involved and resolve the issue.

We all need to recognize that it's our job to tackle the hard work of leadership. Stop avoiding it. You are the only one who can do it. Many of your direct reports can't do it, so don't wait for them—get tough.

Build Resilience

On a business trip, I had the opportunity to watch the movie *Chef* on my flight home. It's the story of Carl Casper, a chef played by actor Jon

Favreau, who crosses swords with influential food critic Ramsey Michel, played by Oliver Platt.

The film follows Casper as he struggles to deal with a very negative review Michel wrote. Casper is so deeply hurt by the review that he eventually confronts the critic face-to-face and has a complete meltdown, which is captured on video and posted online. It goes viral, and because of the subsequent publicity, Casper loses his job and begins the painful process of rebuilding his life.

The most moving part of the film for me is Casper's repeated claims during his confrontation with the food critic that he doesn't care about the bad review at all, while it's absolutely clear that it's eating him up inside. He was deeply hurt by the review and expresses it emphatically. When the film was over, I couldn't stop thinking about how much Casper became obsessed with the negative review. It was clear he didn't have a thick enough skin to handle the feedback.

It made me think about a lot of leaders I have worked with—from the senior-most levels of the C-suite all the way down to line managers—who at times completely wilt in the face of criticism and negative scrutiny.

The moral of the film is a life lesson for leaders: Whatever people are saying about you, however you're being criticized, you need to have a thick skin. Criticism comes with the territory of being a leader, and if you aren't ready for it, then you may need to think twice about becoming a leader in the first place.

Criticism is hard to take, especially when you put your heart and soul into your job as a leader. That passion and commitment are what make great leaders great. And when we are negatively scrutinized, it can hurt. But we can't let criticism get the better of us. The only way we can carry on with our duties is to have a thick skin and accept that criticism as part of the job.

If you can't weather it, you may find that it begins to undermine your entire performance as a leader. You may be seen as being too sensitive and defensive. And it can go further. If you can't handle negative feedback, it might lead you to pander to your various stakeholders. You then start leading to make everyone happy rather than leading to drive organizational success. Instead of trying to find ways of making everyone better, you are obsessed with what people are saying about you and how you can make them like you.

On the flip side of this equation are the leaders who deal with criticism by completely insulating themselves. They reject or deny criticism outright. They sometimes react angrily toward the people uttering the nasty remarks. These people have forgotten that criticism can, in some instances, provide us valuable feedback that makes us better leaders.

It's a very difficult balancing act. You can't ignore negative feedback. But you can't let it completely distract you from your duties as a leader. You have to learn to accept it and move on. You have to be able to bounce back.

I recently met with a client to discuss his company's leadership development needs. This company was undergoing a transformational change, and its leaders were under tremendous pressure. My client explained that a key focus for development was to help the company's leaders be more resilient.

Given the challenges and pressures that leaders face, it's easy to see why resilience is so important. Organizations need leaders who can recover quickly from setbacks and difficulties. They need leaders who can handle changes in their work environments and manage not only their own personal reactions to stress, but also their direct reports' reactions.

However, I'm afraid that traditional views of resilience may be outdated today. The old view sees resilience like those inflatable Bozo the Clown punching bag toys, the ones you can punch repeatedly, and they just keep bouncing back up for more. I believe many leaders think this is what resilience is about: You keep taking the punches, and you bounce back up for more. However, this approach isn't sustainable. You'll eventually wear yourself down.

How resilient are you? Reflect on the following questions:

- Do I remain optimistic in the face of adversity?
- Do I tend to have a thick skin that helps me deal with scrutiny and criticism?
- Do I manage my emotions and reactions to stressful events?
- Do I get myself back on my feet after a setback or disappointment?

You need to be aware of your own level of resilience in the face of obstacles, because how you respond affects the way you lead—and the people you lead. You can imagine how a group will respond when its leader always sees the negative first, has a tendency to catastrophize events, or loses it in the face of adversity. Your response will make the hard things even more difficult.

Resilience isn't just about taking punches. True resilience begins with a balanced perspective. Responding in an extreme way can undermine your effectiveness. Strive to maintain a healthy viewpoint on events while you weigh the pros and cons and seek a positive way forward. The good news is that resilience is not an inborn trait. It's a muscle that can be exercised and strengthened. The more you tackle the hard work of leadership, the stronger you become and the more your resilience increases.

Develop Personal Resolve

Resilience is your ability to bounce back. Resolve is your ability to dig deep and push forward in the face of adversity. It comes from having a strong sense of inner purpose, drive, and tenacity that helps you rise above the pressures of leadership. It means you are able to succeed despite any obstacles, even failure.

You must call upon your personal resolve to tackle the hard work of leadership. You use it to help you do the hard things you know are right when easier options present themselves. Resolve enables you to have that tough conversation today instead of putting it off until tomorrow or walk out of a frustrating meeting and not be distracted for the rest of the day. It's not letting whatever has happened to you define you. Learn from it and move on!

Leaders with sound resolve can find strength in the midst of a challenging situation. They find a way to generate positive energy from adversity and convert it into forward momentum. Leaders with resolve also glean lessons from their experiences that in turn help them more effectively deal with future pressures. Essentially, they stay strong because they tackle the hard parts of leadership. That's what being tough is really about.

So how do you build your sense of personal resolve? Here are a few ideas I've learned in working with thousands of leaders through our leadership development programs:

- First, it helps to have a compelling leadership obligation that helps anchor your leadership. It pulls you forward when you are struggling.
- Second, recall past experiences when you have successfully demonstrated resolve. Uncover what led to your success in the past and how you can apply the same lessons in your current situation.

- Third, manage your personal energy to maintain your optimal level of performance. This includes all the stuff you already know: regular exercise, eating well, sleep, relaxation or meditation, and having a sense of balance in your life.
- Fourth, draw on your community of leaders for support and encouragement. There is nothing that undermines your resolve more than feeling isolated and disconnected from others. Do you have a colleague you can trust to go to when you need to vent?
- Finally, it helps to have what I call a good *reset button*—one that enables you to reframe, refocus, and move on in any given situation. So the next time something happens during your day that tests your resolve, observe how you respond. Do you let the event disrupt your entire day? Do you take it for what it is, learn from it, and move on to the next thing? It's helpful in these moments to do a mental and emotional reset:
  - *Calm yourself.* Take a deep breath and get in touch with your reactions to the situation. Don't act immediately.
  - *Reframe the situation.* What's the hidden opportunity that has now emerged? In what ways can you creatively turn the situation around?
  - *Learn from it.* Ask yourself what you can learn from the situation. How might you approach it differently next time?
  - *Inspire yourself.* Based on what you have learned, leverage the energy to propel yourself forward. Use the lessons as inspiration.

Final Thoughts—Leadership Is Hard Work

The CEO of a large financial institution recently convened a meeting to review the results of a major strategic initiative. As the executive team presented on their work, the CEO noticed a major gap in their plan—a gap significant enough that it would have easily scuttled the entire initiative.

The CEO was noticeably frustrated when he called out the entire team for this misstep. "We have had dozens of our leaders working on this plan over the past few months," the CEO said, "and I can't understand how no one caught this problem. That is hard to believe, given the fact that we have some pretty smart leaders here. Why was it left to me to call this out?"

Maybe the team members all thought it was someone else's job to speak up about the gap. Maybe everyone felt they would do more damage to their personal brands by pointing out the gap, and it was safer and easier to stay quiet. We've all seen people get punished for speaking out about something controversial.

But no matter what their excuses were, this team knew all along about the gap but decided to "let it slide" in the hope that someone else would address it at a later date. To me, this represents one of the most powerful examples of unaccountable leadership that I've seen or heard about.

I've certainly experienced the "let-it-slide" phenomenon over my own career. You see a lot of people working hard on a priority project. Some may see problems and gaps, but do nothing about it. They know things are off track or have a sense that the quality of work is poor. Yet, they just let it go, let things get worse, and hope that someone else fixes it.

This is a perfect example of what it means to avoid the hard work of leadership—and what the consequences are. When you put off those tough conversations, when you let things slide, you put your organization, and your own career, at risk.

Baseball player Sam Ewing once said, "Hard work spotlights the character of people: Some turn up their sleeves, some turn up their noses, and some don't turn up at all."

I began this chapter by saying that leadership involves hard work and, based on my discussions with leaders, it seems that things are going to get even harder. By now it should be clear to you that if you wimp out and avoid the hard work of leadership, you will weaken yourself and your organization. You will start a deadly spiral that will make you weaker and weaker. Instead, you need to build a sense of resilience and personal resolve that will help you do the hard work of leadership. Only then will you find that you are stronger and more able to tackle future challenges. It's time to get tough.

The Gut Check for Leaders—Leadership Is Hard Work

As you think about the ideas in this chapter, reflect on your answers to the following gut check questions:

1. What is the hard work of leadership that you must tackle in your role? What hard work are you avoiding? Why are you avoiding it?

2. In what ways might you make the hard work harder for yourself?
3. What is your mindset regarding the hard work of leadership? Do you see it all in a positive way or negative way?
4. How might you be able to strengthen your resilience and personal resolve?

CHAPTER 8

Leadership Is a Community—Connect

A while back I went with one of my sons to his indoor rock climbing competition. I've attended many of these events, and I've always been struck by the special vibe that accompanies them.

The rock climbing gym was buzzing with the energy of athletes of all ages, as they prepared for some really intense competition. The buzz is not unlike what you would find at most weekend athletic tournaments that parents bring their children to, but I have found that rock climbing competitions have a unique culture and atmosphere.

Whenever someone takes on a climb, the whole gym yells with encouragement and cheers him or her on. And by everyone, I mean everyone: coaches, parents, and competitors from different climbing gyms.

It goes further. After my son completed his first attempt at a particular climb, he was approached by an opponent from a different gym. He gave my son a few pointers on how to tackle the climb differently on his next try.

Imagine that—opponents not only cheering for one another but also coaching each other to perform at their personal best.

Then it hit me: In indoor rock climbing, the competition isn't between the climbers. The competition is the climb itself. It's the obstacle that everyone is trying to defeat. There are still winners and losers, but that's based on skill and talent, and not necessarily vanquishing an opponent.

A lot of the organizations I work with could use a little more of this spirit. I've seen a lot of organizations in which the cultures are really focused on fierce internal competition. Sometimes the internal competition is fiercer than the competition in the marketplace.

We've forgotten who we're really competing against.

What if we operated more like athletes competing in an indoor climbing event? Can you imagine showing up to work to find your fellow leaders ready to support you? Ready to provide you with coaching to make you better? Ready to encourage you, rather than try to break you down?

You would be a completely different leader. In fact, you would be a completely different human being.

I believe this is the biggest missed opportunity in leadership today. More and more of the leaders I work with today are expressing a yearning for something different in their experience of leadership. I can understand why. For most of us, the experience has been mediocre.

Think of your own experience. There's a good chance you and your fellow leaders haven't been on the same page and have worked at cross-purposes because strategic clarity has been low. Or maybe the primary focus is on protecting turf and competing internally, silo against silo. Conflict runs rampant. Frustration is high, and getting anything done feels next to impossible.

Or your experience may be one of sheer apathy where there is little energy or vitality. You and your fellow leaders seem to be going through the motions—bystanders cloaked with fancy leadership titles. It's exhausting and even demoralizing.

Whatever the experience, you may end up questioning why you ever became a leader in the first place. You also know deep down that there has to be a better way.

There is.

What if, instead, you worked with a group of leaders who were all truly aligned to the vision and strategy of your organization? What if there were a real sense of collaboration that enabled innovation to flourish? What if all the leaders in your organization showed up every day fully committed to being the best leaders they could possibly be? What if leaders supported one another to achieve higher levels of personal and collective performance?

This is what a genuine community of leaders feels like. It's the fourth term of the leadership contract (see Figure 8.1). It's also the foundation

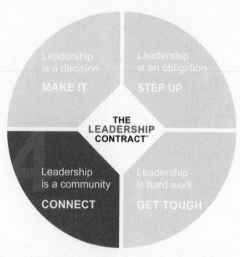

Figure 8.1 The Fourth Term of the Leadership Contract

to building a strong leadership culture that will be your ultimate differentiator.

This idea may seem like some distant dream. But the truth is that it isn't a dream; it's what you need to create excellence and opportunity in your organization.

The Missed Opportunity

I believe a community of leaders is the real missed opportunity in organizations today. If there's one thing I've learned over the past 25 years in the leadership business, it's this: *If you can create a strong community of leaders in your organization, it will become your ultimate differentiator.* As one CEO client of mine put it recently, "If I can figure out how to get our top three layers of leadership truly aligned and engaged to our strategy— fully committed to be the best leaders possible—it will be our secret sauce, our edge in the market." He is not alone in this thinking. More and more senior leaders I work with are starting to understand the power of building a strong community of leaders. That's what the final term of the leadership contract is all about and what we will focus on in this chapter.

This has been the most important theme that has emerged for me since writing the first edition of this book. Of all the ideas I shared from

The Leadership Contract, this one about building a community of leaders has resonated the most with leaders and organizations everywhere.

All my conversations have validated that as leaders we are disconnected. We are tired of working at cross-purposes. We want to feel a greater sense of connection with our fellow leaders. And organizations also know they aren't doing enough to build strong communities of leaders. They know how much more successful they would be if they could.

As I explained in Chapter 2, the challenge we have is that our old models of leadership have always been about individuals—the one single hero at the top of the organization. This model may have been sufficient in a simpler time. It is becoming clear, however, that this model won't work in a more complex world. No one leader can have all the answers today. And when you think about it, it's pretty risky to put all your faith in one individual.

We Are Wired for Community

If the old model of leadership has always been about individuals, then the model for the future is about a community of leaders. The good news is we are ready for it, because as humans we're wired for community.

Seth Godin in his book *Tribes* says that for millions of years, humans have been part of one tribe or another. We can't seem to help it. Our need to belong is one of the most powerful survival mechanisms that we have. Whether it is through the small villages in which we live, or the clubs and groups that we form, we seem to have an internal need to connect and interact with others.

Neuroscience validates this theory and shows that feeling connected is intrinsically rewarding for each of us at the cellular level.[1] Health research also shows that the social support that comes from being part of strong communities is good for our health.[2] We don't need to look further than the proliferation of social media sites. Online communities have the same effect on us, tapping into our need to belong and to be connected.

If we extend this thinking to leadership, I believe the individuals who are able to build and sustain a strong community of leaders will thrive in the future. But this is a new idea, and we need to acknowledge that most of us don't live in strong communities of leaders at all. Because we've had such a focus on individual leaders, we've never taken the time to understand how to leverage leadership more broadly in organizations. Sure, some companies invest a lot in leadership development, but in the end, these development models are built to produce individual leaders. Very little focus is on helping build collective leadership. Few organizations are able to truly create and sustain a strong leadership culture. As a result, the kinds of leadership cultures that exist in most organizations today aren't that effective, and in some cases, they are downright dysfunctional. Let's look at a few examples.

A Rotting of Zombies

In this organization, leaders show up every day merely going through the motions. They are zombies—the walking dead. The leadership culture they create lacks vitality, focus, and positive energy. The atmosphere feels dull and mundane. Leaders don't have clarity about what they are there to do, and there is little commitment to doing the work. It can be a pretty dreadful place to be. This is what existed in the beige organization where I worked with Zinta.

This environment is typical of many heavily bureaucratic organizations. Performance is not strong, and trying to get anything done is next to impossible. At the individual level, it can feel stifling. You can smell the stale air of mediocrity. It's like living at a Department of Motor Vehicles where they've locked the doors, and you have no way out.

You know you are part of a rotting of zombies when your day-to-day environment lacks a real sense of urgency. There's no unifying force that brings your leaders together. There is no clear set of expectations for leaders about how they should behave and act.

Zombie leaders have no sense of connection to one another or to a greater compelling vision. Instead, they're connected by their collective misery. They are like crabs in a bucket. If one tries to escape, the others will grab him and pull him back down, thereby always preserving the same sorry state of affairs. Real leaders who try to change things for the better ultimately give up because of the huge amount of inertia. My colleague Zinta tried to change this kind of organization 25 years ago. She faced resistance at every turn. As we know, she may have paid the price with her life—the stress of working in a leadership culture that was a rotting of zombies eventually and sadly took its toll.

I was asked to deliver the closing keynote speech on The Leadership Contract for a Conference Board event a while back. At the end of that talk, I challenged the audience to build a community of leaders in their workplace by reaching out and strengthening one relationship with a fellow leader—a very small step. At the end of my presentation, one woman approached me and said, "You know, Vince, I thought hard about your challenge to us, and I can't think of a colleague I care enough about to strengthen the relationship." She could sense my disappointment. She then proceeded to describe her day-to-day environment. She didn't know it, but she was describing a rotting of zombies. It was wearing her down. The leadership culture was weak. There was no emotional connection among the leaders in that organization. I asked if she'd gained any insights from my presentation. She said, "It's clear that I have a choice to make: either to leave this place or start building community nonetheless." I don't know what she decided to do, but my hope is that she didn't just go back to being a zombie.

A League of Heroes

Many organizations have leadership cultures that can be described as a league of heroes that is often rooted in the charismatic personality of one leader—usually the founder or CEO. It's ultimately based on the old model of leadership that glorifies one hero. At times, this organization can have some positive aspects if the glorified leader at the top is a person of integrity. When the glorified leader is highly narcissistic, however, the work environment goes bad fast and can become dysfunctional.

The real risk with a league of heroes is that too much rests on one individual leader. When that leader leaves, nothing sustainable is left behind. The organization dies.

I worked with an organization led by one of these glorified leaders. Greg was the founder and CEO of his company. He was a terrific individual who was extremely charismatic and very good at what he did. He was also adored by his employees. And when I say adored, I mean truly adored. It wasn't uncommon for employees located at offices around the world to have Greg's photo framed at their workstations. How many of you as leaders can say that your employees have your photo on their desks? That's the level of connection that this organization's employees felt with Greg. His impact on the company was significant. However, there was little room for other leaders to exert influence on the organization. The leadership culture was not as strong as it needed to be. Too much was on Greg because other leaders didn't step up.

Unfortunately, Greg died in a tragic accident. The company was distraught and became lost without him. Performance plummeted. A huge hole was left, and the other leaders who were thrust into senior leadership roles struggled. It took some time for the organization to get back on track, and it did so only after a lot of pain. Eventually, the company was sold to a competitor. It was the only way to carry on the legacy that Greg started when he created the company.

This story shows the risk taken when a leadership culture is anchored to one leader who is the hero. When it's all rooted in one leader, even if that person is great, it can turn a company upside down when that leader leaves because nothing sustainable beyond that leader's work has been created.

A Stable of Thoroughbreds

Take a moment and picture in your mind horses at a track getting ready to race. They're in their starting gates, pawing the ground, snorting, full of restrained energy. The starting bell rings and the horses are off, each determined to reach the finish line first.

Many organizations have leadership cultures that can be described as a stable of thoroughbreds. Leaders behave like those horses. Each is in his or her own starting gate, representing his or her department or function. They all have blinders on and are completely focused on their own objectives and priorities. As the starting bell rings, the gates open and they are off, each trying to win and cross the finish line first. The competition is fierce; it's all internally focused and highly dysfunctional.

I worked with the top 80 leaders of an organization during a leader forum event. The purpose of the meeting was to tackle many of the dysfunctional ways in which the top leaders were working with one another. A hot issue surfaced on day two of the program, and all hell broke loose. I let it go for a while to see whether anyone would notice. Sometimes you have to do that to make leaders aware of the dysfunction they have created. After several minutes, the CEO finally did notice. She turned to me with complete frustration and exasperation and said, "Why can't we operate as one company?" She'd seen the light and understood the extent of the problems she was facing. The company's leadership culture was not sustainable. She would not be able to change the company until the leadership culture was changed. She needed to create a *one-company* mindset.

I let the discussion continue even further until I began to notice the frustration peak among the leaders. I then stood on a table and yelled out to get their attention. "Ladies and gentleman, what's going on here?" I asked. "Let me remind you that the competition isn't in here; it's out there [I pointed to the windows], and they are beating you because you choose to spend your days fighting with one another in here."

Silence filled the room. Slowly people started to speak up, reflecting on what had happened in the room and how it was exactly like their day-to-day experiences. We began an important discussion that slowly started to lead this group of leaders to a place of heightened awareness. The fact was that they needed to change or they would be out of business. That imperative allowed them to refocus on what they needed to do to survive.

I have found this idea of building a one-company mindset a big opportunity for organizations. More and more CEOs desperately want it to take hold because they know it's what will drive long-term success. However, making it a reality isn't easy, especially when you work with thoroughbreds every day.

You know your leadership culture is like a stable of thoroughbreds when senior leaders behave as heads of their functional areas rather than as true leaders of the whole organization. One or two functional areas will typically dominate the organization, and those leaders end up competing with each other, trying to be the one who is really running the company. You will typically see classic departmental structures and silos that are deeply entrenched, preventing any real collaboration, innovation, or drive.

I find the real challenge with a stable of thoroughbreds is that internal competition becomes the ultimate driving force. That's what leaders get obsessed about, consumed by, and rewarded for. Politics, posturing, and game playing rule the day. You win when the other guy or gal loses— even when the other guy or gal is a colleague. You'll never build a one-company mindset in this leadership culture.

A client I worked with had two strong executives: One led marketing and the other led research and development (R&D). Those in marketing saw themselves as the leaders of the company because they were the owners of the sales strategy. The people in R&D saw themselves as the leaders because they developed new products for customers. Both senior vice presidents were very capable, but they had created a false competition between the two parts of the organization. The internal competition was wasting considerable energy and derailing the overall success of the company.

Whether it be sales versus marketing, head office versus the field, corporate versus lines of business—whenever this kind of internal competition exists, in the long-term it works against a company. It keeps leaders internally focused. Worse, it keeps them focused only on their own success rather than on the collective success of the entire organization. And you see it play out in many obvious and subtle ways—departments that don't share resources, succession planning efforts that get stalled because leaders don't share talent across the organization, or lines of business that are unable to drive innovation and change aggressively.

At the extreme, getting anything done in this type of organization is absolutely painful. Everything feels like a fight, and a vision of building a one-company identity is naïve at best.

It's Time to Build a Community of Leaders

Now is the time to become deliberate and build a genuine community of leaders. That's what the fourth term of the leadership contract demands from you.

Having a community of leaders means recognizing that leadership is not about individual leaders but rather the entire cadre of leaders. When you get it right, it can be your ultimate differentiator—your truly sustainable source of competitive advantage—and it all begins with you. You can decide to start creating a community of leaders where you live every day as a leader. You don't have to be a CEO to start.

You also don't need any special knowledge or insight. You already know what a strong community of leaders is like. One question I always ask leaders is: *What kind of climate would you need to be at your best and make your fullest contribution as a leader?*

It's remarkable to me how consistent the answer is when I ask this question. Leaders don't describe a rotting of zombies. They don't describe a league of heroes. They don't describe a stable of thoroughbreds. They never say, "I will be at my best in a climate of apathy, low trust, or low alignment." They always say the same thing. "I will be at my best in a climate where leaders have real clarity about the value they must bring. There's a deep commitment to the organization and to being the best possible leaders. There's high trust and mutual support among leaders, and this extends into relationships with employees. Everyone is part of one company, fully committed to drive its success."

After years of asking the question over and over again and getting the same answer from leaders in all sectors, at all levels, and in different countries, it seems to me we already know what we need to do. We're hardwired for it. We crave the kind of one-company mindset that we know is possible. Yet we struggle to create real leadership communities, remaining trapped instead within ineffective and even dysfunctional leadership cultures. It's time we bring about what we already intuitively know we need.

A Strong Community of Leaders—Clarity and Commitment

Every strong community of leaders that I've experienced or witnessed shares two critical characteristics: a high degree of clarity and a high degree of commitment.

First, all leaders are clear in their understanding that the community of leaders is built upon a shared aspiration for great leadership. Everyone understands that leadership will be the ultimate differentiator. A client of mine is the CEO of a financial services company, and he believes that every employee deserves a great leader. He's completely focused on making it happen. This simple idea sets the tone for the rest of the organization.

The community is not created merely to establish a better way for leaders to work together, although that does happen. Instead, the goal is to make your company more successful and drive sustainable business achievement. It's about that one-company mindset I described earlier. The community of leaders is also based on the reality that no one leader will have all the answers. Leadership is more distributed today and we must leverage the capability, ingenuity, and commitment of all leaders and employees.

Second, there is a high degree of clarity about the kind of leadership required for success. As a leader, you have a clear understanding of the leadership expectations. You know what you must do to make the organization successful, and you know how you need to lead. You don't settle for lame or bad leadership. In fact, a strong community of leaders removes those individuals who consistently fail to live up to their leadership expectations and obligations. These organizations know that a few bad leaders can undermine the overall leadership culture. So they don't tolerate lame or bad leadership. Neither should you.

You will also find that leaders demonstrate a high degree of commitment, first to the idea of a community of leaders and also to the work that needs to happen to make it so. You demonstrate your collective accountability and commitment by setting the pace and committing to being the best possible leader you can be. This is part of your decision and obligation as a leader, and it's part of your role in fulfilling the first two terms of the leadership contract. Be the leader everyone else wants to emulate.

You and your fellow leaders also demonstrate your commitment by doing the hard work of leadership. No one is a bystander or spectator. Everyone participates fully. You have the courage to call out bad leadership behavior. You challenge the community if leaders are not living up to the aspiration of great leadership. At first, this will be difficult; but once you create your community of leaders, everyone will come to expect it. They will look to you for feedback, and you will look to them for feedback. You will have a deep sense of personal commitment to your fellow leaders. You will support their growth and development.

In fact, if *you* aren't living up to the level of leadership that has been set, you can count on someone in the community of leaders to reach out to you and say, "Hey, you aren't doing your job. We need you to be better. So step up!" No one is afraid to challenge another person. You will also know that everyone will have your back. You know they will be there for you to support you, even when you are vulnerable.

For this community to work, you will need to show your commitment over the long term. A strong community of leaders isn't a destination to arrive at. It requires constant work. You must continuously create ways to connect with your fellow leaders, to build and strengthen relationships, and to drive even more clarity and commitment. The good news today is that social media tools can help you build that sense of connection and community among your leaders. Many companies are leveraging social media to help their businesses connect with customers and other stakeholders. Ultimately, social media tools are about creating connections and exchanging ideas. They will help you enable your leaders to connect with one another and build a sense of clarity and commitment.

You will know when you have it right because it will be a visceral feeling. You will feel the high level of clarity and commitment. You will be blown away by the level of trust and mutual support. You will feel that you are a part of something great, something special, and something rare.

If you've never experienced a strong community of leaders, at first you may not trust it because you won't believe it's going to work. But give it time. It will be hard work, but it will be extremely rewarding. As a leader, you'll feel liberated because you'll have a sense of confidence, knowing that others have your back and are acting in your best interests and in the best interests of the organization.

I experienced this visceral feeling back in August 2011. It was days after Hurricane Irene hit the Caribbean, the U.S. East Coast, and parts of eastern Canada, and I was flying home after a business trip. My seat on the plane placed me in the middle of a group of eight young men. They were talking loudly, joking around, full of excitement and energy.

I chatted with them as we took off. The most talkative member of the group, Daryl, reminded me a bit of the lead singer in a band, brimming with charisma and effortlessly able to connect with people. He introduced the rest of the group to me and explained they were a line crew for a contract utility company. They were headed to Toronto to pick up some trucks and then drive to Connecticut to repair electrical lines damaged by the hurricane.

This big mission explained why they were so excited, but as the flight continued I noticed something else about this group. They were constantly teasing one another. They shifted easily from talking about their personal lives to talking about the job they were going to do in Connecticut. It was obvious that they shared a deep connection. They weren't just friendly co-workers; they had a true bond.

I said to the group, "You guys seem really tight. Why is that?" As soon as I asked the question, I could see Daryl's demeanor change. He became still and thoughtful. He said, "Doing the kind of work we do, we're taking our lives into our hands every single day. We're like a band of brothers. We have to have each other's backs—one mistake and you can lose somebody forever."

That's what it feels like when you share a deep connection with your colleagues. That's what is possible when you are part of a strong community of leaders. But I don't think it should take a hurricane to build that powerful sense of connection and trust. Your life doesn't have to be on the line. Rather, it simply requires a common aspiration, clarity, and commitment on the part of all the leaders in your organization.

As you read this section, you might be saying to yourself, "Vince, this is all sounding pretty idealistic, soft, and fuzzy. Isn't it?" Here's the surprise—it's actually really difficult to do. We sometimes use the soft excuse to avoid doing the really difficult things needed to build a strong community of leaders.

But imagine the difference to your employees, your customers, and your shareholders. Imagine the collaboration, innovation, and productivity that will result from having that community in place. It will be staggering.

Has Everyone Noticed the Change in the Room?

Rob was the CEO of a large utility company. He had been in his role for about 18 months. During that time, he had rebuilt his executive team. Even though he had a strong team, he knew it alone couldn't lead the company. He needed all his leaders aligned and on board, so he established the first leadership forum meeting for his top 200 leaders. It was a one-day event to bring the top leaders together to learn about the strategy of the company.

As he entered the meeting room that day, he was stunned by how quiet everything was. As he was getting his cup of coffee, he saw that 200 leaders were all sitting alone quietly. Very little discussion was happening. He led the day, but it was a painful experience. The leaders just sat there, listening but not engaged in other ways. Rob said, "It was like pulling teeth."

When Rob discussed the day with his executive team, they all realized that they had a lot of strong technical leaders who were very inwardly focused. The team also realized that these leaders would not be equipped to deal with a more complex operating environment requiring them to be more nimble, competitive, and customer centered in the face of deregulation. The experience of the leader forum confirmed that Rob and the team had work to do to strengthen their group of leaders.

We created a leadership development program with the goal of starting to build a community of leaders in the organization. At first, the program met with considerable resistance. In the past, other leadership programs had been seen as a waste of time.

However, as the cohorts began to go through the program, they began to realize its value, and perceptions began to change. About a year after running a series of the intensive leadership programs, Rob held another leadership forum event for the top 200 leaders. This time when he entered the meeting room, Rob was struck by a very different vibe. As he went to pour himself a cup of coffee, he noticed that this time there was a positive energy in the room that hadn't existed a year before. He could see leaders talking and laughing with one another. He could tangibly feel that something profound had changed. He began his opening remarks by saying, "Good morning, everyone. Have you noticed the change in the room today?" He began to explain what he observed, what he felt, and how it differed from a year ago.

The leaders in the room agreed, and an impromptu open discussion took place. It became clear that things hadn't changed just in the meeting room; things had changed on the job, too. Leaders talked about how they felt more optimism, more clarity, a greater receptivity to change, and a deep sense of trust and support.

One leader, Brian, shared a story to validate everyone's observations. He said he had taken part in the leadership program back in the spring, and during the program built some strong relationships with a few leaders whom he hadn't really known before.

A few months after attending the program, Brian had a major crisis at work—one that he had never dealt with before. A lineman in his area died on the job. Brian had to manage the entire situation. He had to inform his people and the family of the employee. He had to manage his own grief and that of his team. Brian shared with the group that in the past he would have just tried to figure it out on his own and that there was a good chance he would have stumbled. This time he immediately reached out to his colleagues from the program and explained, "I was completely taken aback when the four of them immediately came back to me. Within half an hour, two of them were in my office and the other two on a conference call line. And after a 20-minute discussion, they helped me figure out how to effectively handle the crisis, which I did." Brian concluded by thanking his colleagues and saying that he had never felt that kind of support before in any organization he had worked for.

That's what a true community of leaders is all about. It's important to note that you don't need to be a CEO to create one. As I said earlier, that's the beauty of communities: Anyone can start them. Just look to social media. There are thousands of vibrant online communities that all began with one person who started it and gathered a following. It's the same idea in starting a community of leaders. Any leader at any level can do it. You can start wherever you are—by staying in your department or by bringing together a few leaders at your own level. As you share the idea of a community of leaders, you will find many like-minded individuals—those like you who yearn for a different and much more positive experience of leadership. So don't wait. Start today.

Do You Have What It Takes to Be a Community Builder?

I was chatting with a senior executive at a large organization that had just seen a new CEO arrive on the scene. I asked how it was going, and she said that the striking thing about the new CEO was that he was very "self-effacing."

She said this was a big change from the former CEO who was very smart but brash and lacking in modesty. She said, "He would suck all the oxygen out of any room because the attention always had to be on him."

She then proceeded to explain how things already were different with the new CEO. First off, the daily drama the previous CEO had created was eliminated. Other leaders in the company began to step up as more space was created for them. There was a great sense of collaboration among the senior leaders because the new CEO was acknowledging the impact and contribution of others. Essentially, the oxygen was being shared, and everyone could see and feel the difference.

We all know leaders out there who are overconfident and self-centered. However, the propensity to be brash and consumed with one's own personal agenda can come at the expense of a company's agenda. Acting like the lone hero can undermine other leaders and the entire organization. It also keeps you isolated and disconnected. This is an approach to leadership that many of us know too well and one that gets in the way of building a true community of leaders.

Now imagine a different approach—one that is more self-effacing. In fact, you can see the business world starting to celebrate examples of self-effacing leaders. For example, Wall Street cannot say enough good things about leaders like Citigroup CEO Michael L. Corbat.

Wall Street isn't typically known for its quiet and humble leaders. Yet within that world, Corbat has not only helped stabilize Citigroup, but he also has done it without making himself the central focus of stories about the bank's efforts to settle lawsuits and investigations, and return to profitability.

This stands in stark contrast to other Wall Street CEOs who had either become synonymous with, or in some cases eclipsed by the brand of the companies they led. They were continually being quoted in the media and were darlings of the social elite circuits. Many of those leaders later found themselves the poster children for the greed and excess behind the U.S. mortgage crisis.

In the end, this kind of behavior is rooted in selfishness. I was reminded of this point when a client asked me to lead a pointed discussion about the kind of leadership their organization needed to build for the future.

I asked the group of leaders to identify the characteristics of the great leaders they personally admired. The typical things emerged: vision, courage, and a drive for results. As the discussion continued, one leader said that the greatest leaders are *selfless*. It was a term that caught everyone's attention. Then one by one, people started to agree. Great leaders rarely put themselves or their personal agendas first. They lead for a greater purpose that goes beyond self-interest. They lead for the whole enterprise. It's at the cornerstone of building a community of leaders, and in reflecting on whether you have what it takes. Reflect on the questions below to determine whether you are a selfish or selfless leader.

- Is it all about you? It's been my experience that far too many leaders have self-interest as their primary motivator. They are always asking themselves, "What's in it for me?" Everyone who works for them knows it, and it erodes trust. This doesn't build community.
- Do you abuse your power for personal gain? A clear sign of a selfish leader is the propensity to use your power not only to promote your

own career but also to hold others down. Do you take advantage of
your position to make decisions and orchestrate outcomes because you
will personally gain in the end? This behavior doesn't build
community.

- Do you spend all your energy protecting your turf? If you do, then
  you're making every decision through a personal lens rather than doing
  what's best for your entire company. If you're worried only about your
  own department, budget, and resources, a genuine sense of community
  will never happen.

If you answered yes to even one of these questions, then you may be
seen as a selfish leader, and you need to address this before you even
contemplate trying to build a community of leaders in your organization.

So, we all need to learn how to become community builders. We
need to fight the drive to be selfish. We need to fight the tendency to be
isolated from one another. We need to break down silos. We need to
build relationships with one another. My colleague and I were working
with a research and development organization filled with scientists. We
were working with the top leaders and sharing the ideas in *The Leadership
Contract*. During a large group debriefing, two of the participants shared
with the larger group that both had been with the company for seven
years and this was the first time they had ever had a face-to-face
conversation. What made the story stand out for me was that both
leaders worked in the same building and were just separated by one floor
from each other. I said to the large group, "How is something like this
even possible? How can you be senior leaders in this company and you
don't even know the people in this room?"

They all recognized how silly the situation was and how it held their
organization back. We then discussed strategies for them to become true
community builders. More on that later in the book.

Final Thoughts—Leadership Is a Community

During my graduate degree program, I took a course on organizational
development. My professor, Dave, was in his 70s. He was a wise and
mild-mannered individual. In one class we were talking about organizational culture. I asked Dave what one key question he would ask in an
organization to gauge its culture quickly. He said, "All you need to ask

yourself is, 'How is asking for help viewed in this organization?'" It was a brilliant response.

Dave explained that if you are in an organization where asking for help is seen as a weakness, you can already predict many aspects of the culture. People work hard to prove themselves. Issues are never truly addressed. A sense of internal competition emerges. No one dares to be vulnerable. It's a stable of thoroughbreds.

I've used this question hundreds of times over the years, and the responses I get are always quite telling.

I have found that being able to ask for help and being confident in getting a positive response is a core characteristic of a strong community of leaders. In these leadership cultures, leaders ask for help. There is no reservation, hesitation, or concern about having to look good. In a strong community of leaders, asking for help is expected for very practical reasons. Everyone understands that there is a lot of work that needs to get done and the organization can't be slowed down. When you don't ask for help, you keep your organization stuck. Issues and problems are allowed to fester, distract you, and suck the energy from your organization.

Ask yourself: How is asking for help viewed in my organization? Your answer will immediately tell you whether you are in an organization where a community of leaders exists or is possible.

The Gut Check for Leaders—Leadership Is a Community

As you think about the ideas in this chapter, reflect on your answers to the following gut check questions:

1. Think of times in your career when you may have worked in organizations with cultures described as a rotting of zombies, a league of heroes, or a stable of thoroughbreds. What was the impact on you?
2. Have you experienced a genuine community of leaders? What was the impact on you?
3. How will you build a community of leaders within your organization?

CHAPTER 9

Sign the Leadership Contract

E arlier in the book, I defined a truly accountable leader as one who demonstrates a bias for getting important work done. An accountable leader is fully committed to moving things forward in the organization and takes full and personal ownership for his or her leadership role. When a company's leaders lack this kind of accountability, you end up with lame leadership.

This is why the leadership contract is important. By now you know what it means and what it entails. It all begins with holding yourself accountable as a leader. When you do, you commit to setting the pace for others as you strive to be the best leader you can be.

This means defining who you are as a leader, not solely as a technical expert. It means refusing to settle for mediocrity and no longer tolerating lame leadership in yourself and those around you.

Up to this point, you might have been a leader who just clicked Agree without truly understanding what you'd signed. Maybe you let the lure of a new title, new status, more money, and potential perks cloud your judgment. Maybe you were swept away by the opportunity and ended up underestimating what it takes to be effective. Whatever the situation, if you clicked Agree without truly understanding the four terms of the leadership contract, you can't be as effective as you need to be.

By now, you know that *leadership is a decision you have to consciously make*. You understand there are times when you have to pause, take a time-out, and make a Big D leadership decision. You recognize that in the daily act of leading, you will also make many small d leadership decisions. Both types of decisions will shape who you are as a leader. You'll notice a visceral difference when you make these decisions more deliberately. You'll feel it, and so will those around you.

Second, you know that *leadership is an obligation and you need to step up.* You understand that it's not all about you—it's about your customers, your employees, your organization, and the communities in which you do business.

Third, you know that *leadership is hard work and you need to get tough.* You recognize that there is a lot of hard work that you as a leader must do. It's *your* work—no one else will do it, and if you don't tackle it, you will make yourself and your organization weaker. The first person you need to get tough with is yourself. You must hold yourself accountable before you have any hope of holding others accountable.

Finally, you know that *leadership is a community and you need to connect.* No matter where you are in your organization, no matter what level of leadership role you have, you must work to build a strong community of leaders—one in which there is a deep sense of alignment, mutual support, respect, and trust. You know that if you can get this right, the community of leaders will set your organization apart. It will be your ultimate differentiator.

So that's the fine print of what it means to be an accountable leader. All that remains is for you to sign the leadership contract.

It's Time to Sign the Leadership Contract

In the blockbuster movie *The Hobbit*, Bilbo Baggins is enjoying the simple life. Then he's approached by a group of dwarves who inform him that they are on a quest to reclaim their lost kingdom and secure a treasure.

Before they start out, the dwarves present Bilbo with a contract to sign, describing his role and the contribution he'll need to make as a burglar. It looks pretty straightforward at first: out-of-pocket expenses, time required for the task, and remuneration. It explains Bilbo will be given one-fourteenth of any total profit, which sounds reasonable. Then one of the dwarves mentions terms regarding funeral arrangements. And Bilbo reads that they aren't liable for any lacerations, eviscerations, or incinerations sustained during the journey. By now, this contract is making the nature of the upcoming journey seem pretty clear. Thinking about the possible risks, Bilbo actually faints.

Despite his original enthusiasm, Bilbo doesn't sign the contract right away. But if he didn't sign it eventually, there would be no journey. All that talk about reclaiming a lost kingdom and treasure would be moot. It's only after he signs the contract that the journey begins. This journey will involve great challenges and even hardships, but in the end Bilbo and the dwarves succeed in their quest.

Right now, you might be feeling a little like Bilbo, reading over all that fine print about evisceration. Up to this point in the book, we have been reviewing what the leadership contract is, what the four terms mean, and how you must put them into action. You can see how the four terms will make you a better and more accountable leader. You might be inspired and motivated to put them into action. You may have also considered the implications of the four terms for your own leadership role. But the reality is that until you commit and sign the leadership contract, this is all moot.

Remember, the leadership contract isn't a legal document. I once did a one-day leadership forum with the top 150 leaders of an organization, and the agenda went out ahead of time with the title of my presentation ("The Leadership Contract") and a brief description. The leaders all came to the event anxious, expecting they would actually have to sign a legal contract. Once they understood what the leadership contract is really about, they settled down a bit. But in retrospect, I don't think their self-imposed anxiety was such a bad thing. It made those leaders pause and really think about this thing called leadership and whether in fact they were prepared to sign the leadership contract.

In the end, the leadership contract is an agreement you make with yourself—it's a personal and even moral obligation you alone decide to take on. I will never know whether you've actually signed it. People you work with won't know unless you tell them. But in another sense, we will all know based on how we see you show up each and every day as a leader. If you are only going through the motions as a leader, there's a good chance you haven't signed. If you have signed, everyone will sense your commitment to being the best leader you can be. This won't make you the perfect leader—there is no perfect person—but it will definitely make you one whom others want to emulate.

Once you sign the leadership contract, everything changes. You will find there is no going back. Your organization expects a lot from you, whether you are an emerging leader, a front-line manager, a mid-level manager, or an executive or C-suite leader. Your organization needs you to step up. You need to be as strong a leader as possible so that you can make your organization strong. Your employees, customers, stakeholders, and communities are all counting on you. And when you sign the leadership contract, you make a promise to be accountable to all of them.

It's a lot like when a couple decides to get married. After all the preparations and plans, it all comes down to the moment when the bride and groom hear these words: "I now pronounce you husband and wife." As soon as the officiant says those words, they truly become a married couple. Everything changes, but the two individuals don't change. They are the same people. But something fundamental has taken place. What has changed may not be apparent immediately, but over time it becomes obvious as the couple continues to live together and learn what it truly means to be married and fulfill the terms of that relationship.

The same is true with the leadership contract. I won't know whether you actually ever signed it, but I will know as soon as I see you in action as a leader that you have made the personal commitment to be an accountable leader.

So it is up to *you* now—are you ready to sign the leadership contract?

The One Thing You *Cannot* Do

Before you answer, I must be clear with you on one important point: *You cannot stay in your role without signing the leadership contract.* If you do, you'll end up leading in a mediocre way. You will do a disservice to your organization and the people you lead. You will also do a disservice to yourself. So let me repeat: *You can't stay unless you sign.*

Right now, I'd like you to take a moment and reflect on the four terms of the leadership contract. Consider all the ideas we've explored together in this book so far. Review the questions that I had you reflect on at the end of each chapter. Now read the leadership contract that follows and carefully consider the words and the implications to you.

THE LEADERSHIP CONTRACT™

I understand that The Leadership Contract™ represents a deep and personal commitment to being the best leader that I can be—the leader my organization needs me to be. By signing The Leadership Contract™, I am making a personal commitment to myself. In turn, I will no longer settle for mediocrity. I will not simply go through the motions as a leader. I will be an accountable leader. I understand that I can choose to share my commitment with others, or I can keep it to myself. Either way, those around me will know that I've signed up for The Leadership Contract™ based on the way I show up each and every day as a leader.

1. Leadership Is a Decision—**Make It**
I understand that leadership is a decision, and by signing below, I decide to be a leader. This means that I will be aware of when I need to make Big D leadership decisions. I also will bring this clarity to my role each and every day as I make effective small d leadership decisions.

2. Leadership Is an Obligation—**Step Up**
I understand that I am obligated to be the best leader I can be. I have an obligation to my customers, my employees, my organization, and the communities in which we do business. I will lead in an ethical manner. I will live up to the position of responsibility that my organization has given me.

3. Leadership Is Hard Work—**Get Tough**
I understand that as a leader there is hard work that I must do to make my organization successful. I also understand that if I avoid the hard work, I will make myself, my team, and my organization weaker. I commit to not being a bystander or a spectator. I will demonstrate resilience and personal resolve to tackle the hard work.

4. Leadership Is a Community—**Connect**
I will work to create a strong community of leaders in my organization. I will aspire to great leadership in myself and encourage it in others. I will set the tone for other leaders. I will strive to be the leader whom others want to emulate. I will build relationships based on trust, respect, and mutual support. I will work to drive greater clarity and commitment among our leaders so that we can effectively execute our strategy and help make our organization successful.

I agree to the Four Terms of The Leadership Contract™ set out above and will demonstrate my commitment by signing below.

X _____   Date: _____

Signing the Document

By signing the leadership contract, you are making a leadership decision. You are committing to becoming the best leader you can be for your organization and those you lead. You are consciously saying you will step up to your obligations as a leader. You will commit to tackling the hard work of leadership. You will also build a strong community of leaders within your organization. If you can agree with these terms and have the conviction to be the best leader you can be, sign and date the contract.

Really, I mean it. Sign on the dotted line.

So what just happened? Did you sign? Did you do it halfheartedly or with real conviction? Did you put the book down because you thought it was a silly exercise? Remember that, whatever happened, I'll never know. The important thing is that you know, and that's what being a real leader is all about. The commitment you make to yourself is your first obligation as a leader.

There are a few scenarios worth addressing at this point in the process.

You Realize You Don't Want to Lead

Maybe you were about to sign and then you pulled back. Maybe you realized something about yourself: *I don't really want to be a leader.* Maybe you never have wanted to be one.

Congratulations. This is an important insight. Please note that there is nothing to feel bad about. It's better to be honest with yourself one way or another. As my team and I have shared the idea of the leadership contract with clients, we have encountered people in leadership roles who end up realizing they shouldn't be leading. It's something they never wanted to do, and it's something they shouldn't do. In many cases, they ended up taking on other roles in their organizations where they continued to add value and everything worked out fine. However, some of those reluctant leaders decided to leave their organizations. That's good news, too, because those people are finally pursuing what they truly want to do in their lives. These are definitely *not* easy decisions. But you do need to be honest with yourself and your organization!

You Want to Sign but You Don't Feel Ready

Maybe you found that you couldn't sign the leadership contract because you don't feel ready to take on a leadership role and fulfill its terms. You may have other priorities in your life that are more important, such as a young family who needs your attention. That is perfectly fine. What's important is that you are making a deliberate decision not to lead—and that is actually an important leadership decision. Keep adding value as an individual contributor or by sharing your specific expertise. When you feel ready, reread this book and then sign up.

You Have Confirmed a Decision You Already Made

Some leaders I work with say that signing the leadership contract is a confirmation of a decision they have already made in the past, just not so explicitly. You might be one of these leaders. You have fully committed to being the best leader you can be, but you've done it unconsciously. In my experience, once you consciously commit to signing and putting the leadership contract into action, it immediately takes you to another level as a leader. Your commitment grows stronger. You feel even more conviction about being a great leader than ever before.

Final Thoughts—Signing the Leadership Contract

This book is based on the idea that many of us have signed up for leadership roles without understanding what it truly means to be a leader. When we take on a leadership role, we know we're signing up for something important, but most of us aren't fully clear what's involved. Like all those online contracts, you've clicked Agree without ever reading the terms and conditions. You show up every day trying your best, but you're never 100 percent sure you are doing what you need to do as a leader.

The leadership contract gives you the clarity you need to do what is expected of you as a leader. As you review it, it creates in you a sense of personal commitment to be the best leader you can possibly be. You will find that this experience will change you as an individual. You will feel it. It's visceral. As I said earlier in this book, not only will you feel it, but so will those around you. You might be approached by a colleague who stops you in the hallway and asks, "Hey, did you lose weight? Did you do something with your hair? There's something about you that's different." That difference is simply the fact that you have now signed the leadership contract and have made the commitment to be an accountable leader and make your organization as successful as it can be.

With this in place, we now need to look at how to put the leadership contract into action. We will do this by exploring how the leadership contract applies to the four turning points of leadership I described earlier in the book. We will explore how you can put the leadership contract into action at a personal level and at an organizational level.

The Gut Check for Leaders—Sign the Leadership Contract

As you think about the ideas in this chapter, reflect on your answers to the following gut check questions:

1. How do you feel now that you have signed the leadership contract?
2. How do you feel if you were not able to sign the leadership contract?
3. Has anything changed in how you view yourself?
4. How will you behave differently as a leader?

CHAPTER 10

The Turning Points of Leadership

A t this point, I'm assuming you've signed the leadership contract. If so, congratulations. I applaud you, and you should give yourself a small pat on the back, too.

You might be thinking to yourself, "Now what?" It's a really good question and the topic of this chapter. We are going to explore the implications of the leadership contract for you as a leader, whether you are an emerging leader, front-line leader, mid-level leader, or an executive. They're not that much different than those you agree to when signing any other kind of contract. The act of signing is one step. The next is enacting the terms of the leadership contract in your own leadership role.

Let's get to work.

Whether you are new to your leadership role or have been in it for a while, the ideas in this chapter will give you the clarity you need to make sure you are living up to the demands and expectations of your position. Armed with these insights, you'll make better personal leadership decisions and improve the way you manage your leadership career and lead yourself during challenging times.

To help you get a clear sense of what the leadership contract will mean to you, we will return to the leadership turning points that I first introduced in Chapter 5.

Revisiting the Turning Points of Leadership

There is a quote that I've always liked from the Spanish philosopher José Ortega y Gasset. He said, "Tell me what you pay attention to, and I'll tell you who you are." If you extend this idea to leadership, it simply means that you can tell a lot about leaders based on what they pay attention to. The four terms of the leadership contract help you pay attention to the fine print of great leadership. In the process, you become more deliberate as a leader because you have both the clarity and the commitment you need to become a great leader.

As you will recall from Chapter 5, a turning point is an event that causes a significant change to occur. For us as leaders, there are four critical turning points where we need to pay special attention, pause, and reflect on our leadership roles (see Figure 10.1).

The reason this is important is that the stepping-stones we traditionally relied on are now gone. Every leadership role you take on today and in the future will involve making a significant leap, and not all individuals will make successful transitions. Studies have consistently shown that the failure rate for leaders—whether they are managers, mid-level leaders, or executives—is high. Many fail within 18 to 24 months of starting a new role.

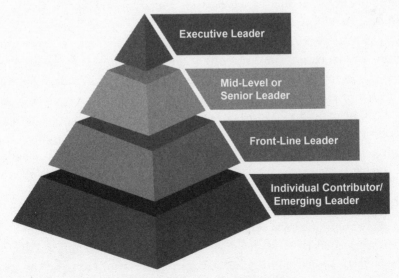

Figure 10.1 The Four Turning Points of Leadership

These individuals never intended to fail. They were like you: bright, ambitious, and committed to success. But it seems those qualities aren't enough to guarantee success for leaders today. That's why you need to pause, be clear on what you are taking on, and ensure you are doing everything you can to succeed in your leadership role. This is where the four terms of the leadership contract become very valuable.

They provide a useful way to help you reflect on your role and give you clarity on what you specifically need to pay attention to at each turning point. This reflection will position you for success and help you avoid the failure that plagues so many leaders.

Turning Point 1: Individual Contributors and Emerging Leaders

The first time you even consider being a leader is a critical moment. As I described in my own personal leadership story in Chapter 1, when Zinta told me, "You need to be in management," that was the first time anyone said those words to me. What surprised me was how something immediately changed in me. Those words forced me to see myself differently. And that's what happens when you are tapped on the shoulder and told you are seen as an emerging leader. All of a sudden, you start a personal discovery process of understanding what leadership is and what it will mean to you.

Take the experience of Tariq. He was a leader in a transportation company specializing in distribution and warehousing. He was taking part in a leadership development program for emerging leaders. He told us that after attending the program he gained a whole new appreciation for how he would need to behave as a leader. He quickly realized he couldn't be seen as a complainer or whiner any longer. He had to evolve from being an employee to becoming a leader. He realized that he had to set the bar higher for himself. It would no longer be appropriate for him to behave as one of the gang on the construction crew.

This insight troubled Tariq because he had already started to feel the separation building between him and those he worked with as peers. All emerging leaders face this challenge. The good news for Tariq was that he was open to understanding the realities of his future role, and the four terms of the leadership contract helped him.

As I described in Chapter 4, many individuals in important individual contributor roles are also being tapped on the shoulder and asked by their organizations to step up as leaders. The individual contributor is often confused. "I'm not a leader," they think to themselves. "I don't manage a team, or run a department. I'm just doing my job." Yes, you may not be managing a team or running a department, but you do have an important leadership role for your company. Chances are you bring a high level of expertise. Or you possess a set of critical stakeholder relationships important to your company's success. Or perhaps you have an important market-facing role that helps build the brand of your company. Whatever it may be for you, when you're asked to step up, you need to start thinking of yourself as a leader. Like all emerging leaders, individual contributors in key roles must redefine themselves as leaders.

Take the example of Beth. She worked in the health care industry with a local community agency. Her role was to put health promotion programs in place within the city in which she lived and worked. She didn't have a team to manage. But she brought years of expertise in health care and a host of important relationships with all levels of government, nonprofit agencies, and companies in the private sector. When her manager first talked to her about needing to step up as a leader, Beth was confused. But her manager helped her see how important her role was to the organization and the community. She had a really unique role within the organization, and her success was ultimately based on her well-developed leadership capabilities. Over time, Beth began to see herself as a leader. As she did, she realized she needed to step up in even more significant ways to drive the health promotion mandate she led.

As an emerging leader or individual contributor, it's often your organization that makes the first leadership decision. Someone in the company will see you as a potential leader and will let you know it. This recognition becomes an invitation for you to start learning about what leadership is really about and whether you are suited for it.

Don't fall into the trap that many emerging leaders and individual contributors do: Don't refuse the invitation because you think leadership will just be about more work. Yes, there is a lot of extra work and effort required when you are a leader. But there is also greater opportunity to affect your organization and your team. So your goal at this point should be to remain open and learn as much as you can about what being a leader is going to be like. It's also important to be honest with yourself. If you don't feel you are up to being a leader, then wait until you are ready.

It's also a good time to start paying attention to your core obligation as a leader at this level: getting yourself ready to be a leader. This readiness starts with shifting your mindset from thinking like an employee to thinking like a leader. Start looking for ways to show up and demonstrate your ability to lead. Don't limit yourself with traditional definitions of leadership like the idea that you are only a leader if you have direct reports. You still must step up to your leadership obligations.

One of the critical obligations you will have is to ensure you develop strong soft skills. This was reinforced to me recently when I worked with a client. The CEO of a mid-size technology company was addressing a group of high-potential leaders in her company.

She said to them: "Your technical skills generally get you your first management or leadership role, but a large part of your success after that will be based on the strength of your soft skills."

Her comments struck a chord with me. The best leaders are often those who demonstrate a capacity to work closely with people and build teams, all while demonstrating a healthy capacity for self-awareness.

It's hardly a new idea. After working with thousands of leaders over the years, I've come to the undeniable conclusion that it's the strength of your soft skills that will make or break you as a leader.

However, soft skills are proving to be even more critical today and certainly will be into the future. The Adecco Group recently released a white paper entitled "The Soft Skills Imperative." They argue that although technology is quickly taking over all aspects of the world of work, the ability to understand people—largely through soft skills—is a huge competitive advantage.

The Adecco Group report includes things such as the ability to express empathy, communicate persuasively, seek common ground with stakeholders, and engage people so they feel invested in the company.

A recent LinkedIn study conducted by economist Guy Berger also identified the top ten soft skills that companies were seeking in their job candidates: communication, organization, teamwork, consistent punctuality, critical thinking, social skills, creativity, interpersonal communication, adaptability, and a friendly personality as the ten soft skills most in demand among employers.

The study also found that close to 60 percent of companies in the United States cannot find talent with strong soft skills. In my experience, this isn't just an American issue. It's an issue everywhere.

You have an obligation to yourself to make a sincere commitment to develop strong soft skills to accompany the technical acumen you probably already possess. If you ignore the soft skills necessary for effective leadership, you run the risk of becoming irrelevant and, ultimately, unwanted. Alain Dehaze, CEO of The Adecco Group, takes this issue even further when he states that in years to come, leaders will be measured more for their ability to cultivate soft skills rather than technical expertise. Will you be one of these leaders?

A lot of the hard work that you must do will be personal in nature. Once you are given the label of emerging leader, it's hard not to let it go to your head. However, if you do, everyone will know it, and it will affect your relationships with your colleagues. So it's important to remain humble.

It's also important that you start building your personal resilience and resolve by deliberately stretching yourself beyond your comfort zone. And it's a great time to pay attention to all the core people skills that you will need to excel at. Develop your ability to manage conflict, give feedback, and hold people accountable. Let me tell you from personal experience and the experience of hundreds of leaders I've worked with, it's best to learn these skills now, because if you don't, your personal gaps in these areas will come back to haunt you later.

You can also start paying attention to building a sense of community with fellow leaders. The best way to do this is by connecting with other emerging leaders in your organization. You may also find it helpful to build a small group outside your organization, either through a professional network or your own contacts. That's what I did when I was an emerging leader in my first job. I struggled to find like-minded individuals inside my organization, so I gathered a few colleagues and friends and set up a network myself. We would get together four to six times a year to talk about leadership and our careers. I found it helped me cope with the challenges I faced within my own organization.

Start looking for ways to bring forward your ideas and start showing up as a leader, even if you don't have the title or the role yet. You need to start building your resilience to be able to deal with the increased demands and adversity that will come from having your first leadership role. Take advantage of whatever development opportunities your organization may offer. Look for ways to expand your skills on the job through special assignments and projects. And begin to observe other leaders in action. See what works for them and what gets in their way. Over time you will gain clarity on how you want to show up as a leader.

Finally, I hope that you never lose sight of this reality: *Your organization is going to need a constant supply of strong leaders for the future.* If you decide to be one, the future is yours for the taking. But you must first get clear about what it means to be a leader and have the commitment to make it happen. Your key action at this turning point is to be honest with yourself.

Turning Point 2: Front-Line Leaders

If you are a front-line leader, you have one of the most critical leadership roles in your organization. I know you may not believe it, but it's true. You are the closest person to the employees and customers of your organization. You have the proverbial finger on the pulse of what is happening. You can have considerable impact. You will also start noticing that you are held to a different standard. Excuses that may be tolerated for employees will no longer be acceptable for you. You will realize soon enough that leadership isn't about excuses—it's all about accountability for results.

The first time you decide to become a supervisor or manager of people is one of the most important leadership decisions you will ever make. We work with front-line leaders in *The Accountable Manager* development program. One of the first important insights we share with these leaders is that they must stop thinking of themselves as individual contributors.

It's no longer about you. You have made the decision to stand apart from the pack and be the leader, someone committed to adding more value to your organization. You have suddenly entered a different zone, and it will affect you in ways that you never would have suspected.

Take Thomas, for example. He became the supervisor of a team that he was a member of. It changed the relationships that he had with his peers. He knew that. What he didn't realize is how much those relationships would change. This became clear to him when the team organized a summer outing and didn't invite him. At first, he was hurt. But when he put his leadership hat on, he understood that it was good for his team to do social things without the boss. He realized that's the price one pays as a leader.

One of the things I realized when I was a front-line leader is that your team also makes a leadership decision: They decide whether they will follow you. If they do, your job will be a lot easier. If they don't, you will have some hard work ahead. So pay attention to your team. Be deliberate when making small d leadership decisions during team meetings. You'll be amazed how far deliberateness and consistency on your part will go in helping your team drive high performance.

What you will also find as a front-line leader is that you start really thinking about the responsibility and obligations you have to your organization (or at least you should). Your core obligations are twofold: to drive the performance of your team and to learn the essentials of your new role.

You'll quickly realize that you are now accountable for the performance of your team. Depending on your role, your span of control can be considerable. You may be responsible for 10, 20, or more direct reports—no easy task. In fact, the larger your group is, the more you may start feeling a bit of the heat as a leader because you are truly accountable for their performance.

You will also need to master the leadership essentials that you will count on for the rest of your career—key skills such as coaching, listening, delegating, setting clear expectations and managing performance, holding people accountable, and confronting conflict. Again, it is best that you learn to master these skills now, because if you don't, your effectiveness will suffer if and when you take on a more senior leadership role later. You will find your day will become consumed by people issues. In fact, you'll be surprised how much time they will take and how much personal energy they will sap from you.

Although you may not find your obligation to your communities as obvious, I encourage you to find ways to give back to society. It's important that you develop the ability to pay attention to this broader obligation now, because it will increasingly be expected of you as you move into more senior-level roles.

Some of the hardest work you will face as a leader centers on the shift from being a doer to becoming a delegator. Many front-line leaders struggle with it. You may have a role that still demands that you do the work in addition to managing others. You will most likely also have the greatest technical expertise on the team. Your team will look to you as the expert, which can be a difficult transition for some people.

The other hard work that you will need to do is to shift where you get your personal sense of gratification. As an individual contributor, it primarily would have come from your own accomplishments. Now you need to shift so that you gain personal gratification from building your team and watching everyone grow. You will need to let go of the desire for personal glory and replace it with the desire for glory for the team. You will have to let go of rating your performance based on your own contribution and instead be judged by your team's contribution.

Your final challenge at this level is to not isolate yourself. Reach out to leaders at your level in your own organization. Find ways to connect with them at work or after work outside the office. Day to day, it's also important to build the habit of connecting with your fellow leaders in real ways. Instead of always sending e-mails, pick up the phone. Better yet, walk down the hall and sit with a colleague to discuss an issue. These small but important practices to connect with other leaders will be invaluable to you over your leadership career.

A few final thoughts for front-line leaders: There will be times when you feel ignored by your organization. It's nothing personal; it's just the way some organizations run. Don't let this get to you. The good news is that more and more organizations are recognizing that front-line leaders are critical to their overall success. In fact, I believe there has never been a better time to be a front-line leader than today.

Turning Point 3: Mid-Level Leaders

Mid-level and senior leadership roles are the glue within any organization. At this level, it's all about your ability to have organizational impact; this skill is what you will be judged on as a leader.

As you make the leadership decision at this level, you will come face-to-face with the challenge of letting go. What drove your success up to this point—your strong technical expertise—is now being replaced with that murky world of organization-wide leadership. In this world, your success is defined and measured largely by your ability to influence, collaborate, and drive innovation. You will need to break down silos to get the work done and meet customer needs.

What I realized when I had a role at this level is that the leadership decision is not a onetime single event. Every day you'll show up to work and face significant challenges and demands, and they'll force you to regularly ask yourself: *Am I up for this? Am I prepared to do what is necessary? Do I have the stomach to take this on?* Depending on your day, you may be asking these questions a lot.

These questions are critical because this is the level where you may find yourself checking out or starting to settle. When this happens, you run the risk of merely going through the motions as a leader. If you find yourself doing this, stop and question your leadership decision altogether.

Your core obligation at this level is to have organizational impact. This means not looking to your executives for permission or approval to do things. You must be able to effectively work across your organization with other leaders to drive change and create high performance. It will no longer be about your own team or department. For probably the first time, you'll start realizing that your obligation is to be an ambassador of your organization now. *You are the company!* You are expected to lead inside and outside. You will start thinking much more about your obligation to the communities in which you do business. Depending on your role, you may be the face of your company to your local community.

There is a lot of hard work at this level. The people issues continue, but they will feel harder to handle because now you are also dealing with other senior leaders. You will face your fair share of big egos and petty politics.

The drama can be intense at times, and you will need to learn how to deal with it. You will be challenged to be strategic at the same time that you're dealing with tactical priorities. You'll be in the middle—caught between pressures from the front-line and from the executive level. You'll feel like you are always reacting, or in firefighting mode.

This is the world of big project implementation. You may not be a sponsor of these big projects, but you will own their successful execution. And although you will live in one department or line of business, you will also need to start having an enterprise-wide perspective.

It is at this level where your resilience and personal resolve will truly be tested. You will learn whether you are up for it. You will also start getting a glimpse of whether you have what it takes to succeed in a more senior-level role. But to move forward, you will need to overcome some of the traps that weaken mid-level leaders.

One leader whom I worked with was a brilliant individual. Tazeen's personal performance was outstanding. She had also developed strong personal relationships with her team members. Unfortunately, she blurred the line between being a leader and being a friend to them, and team members behaved very causally with her. She wanted to be seen as one of the team and, as a result, she didn't tackle performance issues.

Some members of the team took advantage of her good nature. Although she was liked, she was seen as being a weak leader. Ultimately, this stalled her career. Executives saw her as a capable middle manager, but they didn't have the confidence that she would succeed at more senior levels of the organization. Tazeen was struggling with her role and the power that came with it.

As a senior leader, you will have more power than you did at lower levels. It's important to understand how to handle it, how to share it with others, and how not to abuse it.

All the hard work at this level is critical and necessary because it will prepare you for what's to come in a more senior leadership role. One of the changes you will experience is that you will now manage other managers, many of whom have greater expertise than you do in their own specialty areas. The hard work before you is to forge a strong team, even without that technical expertise. You will need to rely on the advice and judgment of others and make decisions based on their suggestions. This level of trust may be unsettling for you.

All this pressure can get to you, and, at times, you may feel disconnected and isolated. Yet the irony is that it is at this level precisely when a true community of leaders can be created. The challenge you will face is that you will be living in a stable of thoroughbreds. Your day-to-day climate may be one of internal competition—silos fighting silos.

You must change that climate. You must reach out to your fellow senior leaders. Because you will be collaborating on many company-wide projects, there will be natural opportunities to connect. Take the time to build truly positive and healthy relationships with your peers, relationships that will have a positive impact on the work you are doing. Form your own support group within your organization, made up of a small number of trusted colleagues. Leverage social media tools to connect across geographies. There are more ways to connect with fellow leaders today than ever before.

It's also important that you not insulate yourself or stay too internally focused. Stay connected with leaders in your industry outside your organization. At this level, you have a huge opportunity to transform your relationships with peers and colleagues to ones based on trust, respect, and mutual support.

I find many mid-level and senior-level leaders underestimate the impact that they can actually have on their organizations. The reality is that as organizations continue to become more lean and streamlined, leadership roles at the middle are critical. Don't lose sight of this. Your company's success is in your hands. As always, the decision is yours. I encourage you to make it and lead your company to greatness.

Turning Point 4: Executive Leaders

Welcome to the big leagues. You've finally made it to an executive or C-suite leadership role. Everything will feel more intense: the accountability, the scrutiny, the need for professional maturity. At the same time, becoming an executive leader is an amazing opportunity to shape the future of your organization.

The way you decide to take on one of these roles is also critical because your impact is very significant. Although these roles have big titles, big compensation, big perks, and so on, you need to decide why you really want the role. Are you genuinely motivated to have a positive and enduring impact on your organization? Or is it all about you—your ego and your personal needs? Are you prepared to take your leadership to a very different level by becoming a great leader, one whom your employees and stakeholders will look up to?

An important factor in making a leadership decision at this level will be your relationship with your boss: the CEO or chair of the board. This relationship will need to be strong for you to have any chance of succeeding. Make sure you take the time to truly gauge what this relationship will be like. If your sense is that it won't be strong, then you need to address this before you decide to take on the role.

Your Big D leadership decisions will demand that you be honest with yourself. Many leaders aspire to the executive ranks, but few make it—and even fewer succeed. You need to have the self-awareness to know whether you are cut out for these demanding roles. You may find you are better suited to remain in a mid-level or senior leadership role. This is perfectly fine. Our organizations need strong leaders at all levels.

Your obligation as an executive leader is fairly straightforward—you must lead the future. You need to shape your environment, create a strategy that will drive sustainable growth, and establish a strong culture that will attract and keep the best talent. You should feel the weight of your obligation to your customers, employees, fellow executives, board, and shareholders. The game changes once again—now you really start to understand the many obligations you must live up to.

You should also start recognizing that as an executive, you have moral and fiduciary obligations. *You must leave the organization better than you found it.* You must scale the organization beyond yourself and create a business model that will drive sustainable growth. You must be externally focused and build strong stakeholder relationships.

Your time is no longer spent reacting—anticipating, shaping, and executing are your new priorities. You should also realize that your role is no longer just about your function or line of business. You must wear the proverbial corporate hat, thinking about the success of the entire enterprise.

Another key obligation is to build a strong management team and ensure you have succession in place. In fact, many CEOs I've worked with believe building a strong team is one of their most critical obligations to their company. Boards judge CEOs on their ability to build strong teams. Teams at the top are vital to the success of your company—not only because they are necessary to drive company performance, but also because you have an obligation to build leadership continuity and ensure succession issues are being addressed.

There is considerable hard work at this level, much of which is made more difficult because of the constant scrutiny you will face. As we've explored earlier in this book, when you are under this kind of scrutiny, fear may creep into the back of your mind. You don't want to be the leader who screws it all up or brings your organization down. Your mistakes could make it to the front pages of newspapers and business magazines or go viral on Twitter. Those are the risks and the challenges. You are the face of your organization, and its reputation often hinges on yours. Your resilience and resolve will be tested in a completely different way.

I worked with a small group of CEOs who were in transition and were clients of our Executive Outplacement Program. We were talking about the ideas of the leadership contract and spent considerable time talking about the hard work at the executive level. They commented that some of the hardest work is making difficult business decisions such as terminating an employee or closing a failing business unit. Even if these decisions are the right ones for the company, they still carry a personal toll for leaders.

Of the four leadership turning points, it is at the executive level where you can make the greatest impact in your organization by creating a true community of leaders in a way that will become the ultimate differentiator for your company. At a personal level, you can set the pace for others and model great leadership and ensure your senior team does as well.

As we discussed earlier in the book, executive roles can be isolating, and even lonely. You need to break this sense of isolation. Build a network of close relationships inside and outside your organization. I find many CEOs, for example, will have a small team of external advisors and colleagues they can go to for advice, support, and a sense of community. You don't have to be a CEO to establish this. Reach out and find leaders who are in a similar role as yours (inside or outside your organization) and connect on a regular basis. In the end, leadership is all about the connections you make.

I believe there is no better time than today to be an executive-level leader. If you can figure out how to leverage social media, you now have a platform to share your organization's story in ways that you couldn't a decade ago. If you are able to create a truly inspiring place to work, you will attract the best and the brightest in your industry. You also have the opportunity to have an impact on global and social levels. These opportunities are what the executive level puts before you.

Final Thoughts—The Turning Points of Leadership

As I described earlier in this book, as organizations have become leaner over the years, many critical roles no longer exist. In the past, these roles acted as stepping-stones to help you grow and mature as a leader. Today, the stepping-stones are gone, and the transition between each of the turning points can feel like a considerable leap. I believe this is why so many leaders derail within the first one or two years in their roles. They have made the leap without truly understanding the fine print and the expectations of the leadership role. The good news is that the four terms of the leadership contract provide a practical and useful way to help you gain a clear understanding of what you are signing up for, what you have to pay attention to, and what you must do to become a great leader at each turning point.

The Gut Check for Leaders—The Turning Points of Leadership

As you think about the ideas in this chapter, reflect on your answers to the following gut check questions:

1. What does the leadership contract mean to you? What new insights did you gain about your leadership role?
2. What specific areas must you pay attention to now as a leader?
3. What clarity did you gain about how to apply the four terms of the leadership contract to your role?
4. In what ways has this clarity affected your commitment to be a truly accountable leader?

CHAPTER 11

Living the Four Terms of the Leadership Contract

I magine for a moment you are about to take on a new leadership role. You are full of energy, ready to take on the challenge. You are brimming with confidence, and excited about the new title, increased compensation, and extra perks you will receive.

Now just before you start your new role, you and I have a conversation. In that discussion, I tell you that within the first year of your new job you will experience a significant crisis. News will break revealing that one of your company's products is faulty and responsible for the death of more than 100 people and the serious injuries of even more.

As a result, you and your company will experience a firestorm of harsh criticism from the media and the public. Your every word and move will be scrutinized on the nightly news. Within months, you will be testifying in front of the Senate as your company is eviscerated in a hearing on Capitol Hill.

If I told you that all those things would happen, would you still take on your new leadership role? Would you be as excited and as confident?

This is exactly what happened to Mary Barra, the CEO of General Motors (GM). Barra was appointed to her new role in December of 2013. When news of her appointment first broke, most of the media focused on the fact of her gender. Choosing a female CEO was undeniably a great step forward for GM and for corporations around the world. It was great for Barra, who over a 33-year career at GM, held a number of executive posts including vice president of global human resources and, most recently, vice president of product development.

But no one could have predicted the leadership challenges she was about to face. It all started when we learned that the company's faulty ignition switches had resulted in all those deaths and injuries. Barra initiated a 30-million-car recall. She was under intense scrutiny. The pressure must have been enormous for her and her leaders and employees.

Through it all, Barra was praised for how she handled the crisis. As described in *Fortune* magazine, Barra had a unique combination of honesty, humbleness, and a sincere desire to fundamentally change the errors that led to the company's problems. Barra wasn't interested in denying or diminishing what happened. She wanted the scandal to remain a constant reminder of what happens when a company fails to do the right thing for customers and society as a whole. She took full accountability and never passed the buck.

But there's more to Barra's leadership. She also appears to be a community builder who is positively regarded for her approachability and strong listening skills. Colleagues and GM insiders describe her as an inclusive leader who engages employees and leaders. For example, she holds frequent town hall meetings that help her get input on the status of projects and fuel decision-making. She relies on those skills to drive the culture change she's leading at GM.

I believe Barra's story is a perfect example of the kind of complex challenges that leaders face today and will continue to face in the future. Your challenges and pressures will undoubtedly be different from hers, but they may be just as difficult to manage.

What has also changed for leaders is the high level of scrutiny they're under from multiple perspectives—customers, employees, shareholders, stakeholders, and market analysts are all watching closely. The world for leaders is a very different place than it was just a generation ago.

This is why we need a leadership contract. I believe you can't lead without making the conscious and deliberate decision to be a leader. The pressures will tear you apart if you don't have true clarity and commitment. Barra's story illustrates that you can't lead without clarity about your obligations and a clear sense of commitment to yourself, your customers, your organization, your employees, and the communities in which you operate. You need to have the resilience and resolve to tackle the hard work. Finally, you need to be a community builder and take an inclusive approach to leadership.

In this chapter, we will explore how to put the leadership contract into action and become a truly accountable leader by implementing:

- Four foundational practices tied to each of the four terms.
- A series of daily, quarterly, and annual practices to ensure you keep living up to the four terms of the leadership contract.

The Four Foundational Practices for Living the Leadership Contract

There are four foundational practices, each tied to one of the four terms of the leadership contract (see Figure 11.1). I have found these practices to be the basis from which to start your own journey to become a truly accountable leader. To help you implement these practices, you may want to pick up a copy of *The Leadership Contract Field Guide* (Wiley, 2018). It is filled with practice activities to help you become a truly accountable leader.

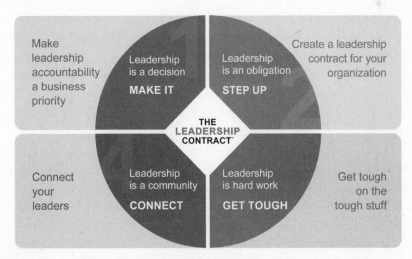

Figure 11.1   Living the Leadership Contract—The Four Foundational Practices

1. *Understand and Share Your Personal Leadership Story*

When my team and I work with leaders in our development programs, we ask them what has most influenced their leadership. They all say that experience was the best teacher. But you learn from your experiences only if you take time to reflect on them and consider how they have shaped you. When you don't know what your experiences have meant to you, you don't have the necessary foundation to put the leadership contract into action.

Start building this foundation by thinking about your own personal leadership story. I've outlined the steps for you here.

Determine Your Critical Leadership Experiences   Pause for a moment and think about the critical experiences that you believe have made you the leader you are today. I bet stories are already coming to mind. Some may be of peak experiences when you had a significant impact as a leader—when you were at your best. Other stories may be more negative, moments in which you struggled, worked for the worst boss on the planet, faced adversity, or had your personal resolve tested.

Identify Common Themes and Patterns   Once you've determined your critical leadership experiences, look at them as a whole and identify any common patterns and themes. What are you most proud of? How did you handle adversity? What insights can you glean about your personal resilience and resolve? What we generally find with this activity is it immediately gives leaders a sense of clarity regarding who they are as leaders and why they lead in the way they do. This level of clarity will enable you to be much more effective in making good leadership decisions.

Let's return to the example of Mary Barra that I shared at the start of this chapter. The more I learned about Barra's experience as a leader, the more I was struck by her personal leadership story. Simply put, Barra is a living, breathing example of the American dream. She comes from humble beginnings. Her father was a Finnish immigrant who worked at GM in Detroit for 39 years as a die maker. She started working for the automaker when she was 18 years old, eventually enrolling in General Motors Institute (now known as Kettering University) to study science.

She also earned a GM fellowship at the Stanford School of Business, where she obtained her master of business administration (MBA).

Why should this matter? Let's face it; the appointment of a new CEO can be an unnerving experience for any large organization. At GM, when Barra stepped up into her new role, employees at the very least had the comfort of knowing the new CEO had been with the company through good times and bad. She was a GM lifer. Barra's connection to the company is baked into her family history. I believe it's one of the key reasons she succeeded in managing the crisis she experienced in the first year of her job. For Barra, being the CEO of GM wasn't just a job; it was part of her leadership and life story.

This is why it's important to know your leadership story. Understanding what has shaped you makes you a more effective leader. You understand the leadership decisions you have made in the past, you appreciate how you've handled success and failure, and all of these lessons help you take on future leadership roles.

Share Your Leadership Story   Once you understand your personal leadership story, it's important that you share it with those you lead. In fact, I believe it's one of the most powerful things any leader can do. After I published the first edition of this book, I was surprised by the impact it had on my colleagues because they read about my own personal leadership story. My team members felt they understood me in ways that they hadn't before.

A client of mine, an accomplished CEO, once shared with me stories of his childhood growing up in rural England. He was from a poor family, and when he attended private school, his classmates tormented him. As a result of those experiences, he firmly decided at the age of eight that he was not going to be poor when he grew up. Everything he accomplished later in life was a result of his experiences as a young boy. Those experiences drove his desire to escape the poverty of his childhood.

It was a great story. But when I asked him whether he had ever shared that story with the people he led, he shook his head. His answer was no— only his closest colleagues knew of his history.

Isn't that a waste? He missed an opportunity to better connect and relate to the people he led. He missed the opportunity to inspire others in a very personal way.

Every time I work with leaders at an event where their employees have gathered, I encourage them to share a little bit about their personal history. Some are excited to do so. Others hesitate, uncertain how it will affect the way their employees perceive them. For those who have the courage to share their stories, I find it makes them more human to their employees, which leads to a deeper and more meaningful employer–employee relationship. This is the connection that great leaders have with their employees—the bond that produces greater commitment and effort. It also shows you are strong enough to be vulnerable in front of others.

Now I know some of you may struggle with this idea; you may be a private person. I can completely relate to this. However, it's important to recognize that employees today want to connect with their leaders at a more personal level. They want to know you not just as their boss or manager but also as a person.

The power of sharing one's leadership story was really made apparent to me soon after the announcement of Adecco/Lee Hecht Harrison's acquisition of Knightsbridge. A few of us on the executive team were invited to take part in the company's Global Conference.

Peter Alcide, the president and COO of Lee Hecht Harrison, opened the conference. He welcomed everyone and shared his reflections on the company's performance. I was impressed by the company's scale and global success.

Then Peter mentioned that the company's most recent employee engagement survey had revealed that many employees didn't really know him at a personal level. So like a strong, accountable leader, Peter began to remedy this situation and started to share his personal leadership story.

He talked about his humble upbringing. He shared how most of what he learned in life came from his parents and family life. Peter is one of four boys in his family. He told us how his parents never went to college. His father was a bus driver in New York City. Peter said his dad would leave their house at 3:00 AM and return home by 4:00 PM. The family would have dinner together at 4:30 PM on the dot every day. Then Peter's mother would go to work at the catalogue store of a large retailer. His parents always made sure that one of them was at home to watch over the four boys. Peter talked about how this shaped his own parenting style.

Peter said it was important to him to drive a successful company. He was a competitive person by nature and liked to win. But above all of that, he wanted to make a difference in everything he did. In fact, the culture of

Lee Hecht Harrison is rooted in this idea of making a difference in the lives of our customers, whether it is an individual going through career transition, a group of leaders working together to make their company successful, or a company trying to navigate change in a complex world.

All of us as leaders have a personal leadership story—one that defines who we are as leaders. I find few leaders are clear on what that story is about and even fewer ever share their leadership stories with the people they lead. When you do, you will find people will connect with you in a very powerful and visceral way. Don't miss the opportunity before you.

2. Define Your Value and Desired Impact as a Leader

I worked once with a leader who was the founder and CEO of his company. He was known to be a patriarchal leader. He also could be really rough with his people. I was lucky to have an hour of his time, because he didn't like consultants. He thought all the leadership development stuff we talked about was just fairy dust.

Yet now that he was in his early seventies and his career was coming to a close, he felt he wanted to leave a legacy for his company—one centered on building strong leadership for the future.

At one level, I respected him for this idea. Yet, at another level, I recognized that his thinking was faulty. This leader didn't realize that he didn't have to wait until the end of his career to start thinking about his personal leadership legacy. He had an opportunity to leave a leadership legacy every day of his career while he was running his company.

I have discovered that a lot of leaders tend to think about the idea of a leadership legacy only late in their careers. This is an outdated concept. The reality is that each of us leaves a legacy every single day. The question is: _Are you leaving a legacy you are going to be proud of?_ What is the value you need to create? What is your desired impact on the people you lead?

You have to remember that once you decide to lead, you are going to be held to a higher standard. You have obligations that go beyond yourself. You have obligations to your customers, employees, shareholders, and communities.

To fulfill those obligations, you need to be clear on the value you must deliver as a leader—the desired impact you will have. It's about being clear on the legacy you need to leave. Take a moment to think about the people you're accountable to and ask yourself: How would they define the value I have to bring as a leader? What's the impact I need to have?

Better yet, go ask them. Talk to your customers, employees, peers across your organization, and stakeholders in your community who depend on you and your organization. They will have an answer. You will learn whether they see you as a leader with credibility. You just need to ask.

I've developed a set of six questions that I use in my own leadership role. These questions help me determine my value as a leader through the perspective of my customers, employees, and internal and external stakeholders:

1. What is the primary value that I provide as a leader?
2. What are my personal strengths as a leader?
3. Where do I need to be stronger as a leader to have greater impact on the organization?
4. What blind spots must I pay attention to?
5. How am I living up to the four terms of the leadership contract?
6. What is one action that I must implement to increase my value and impact as a leader?

I find this set of six straightforward questions is one of the best ways to get feedback on yourself as a leader. The feedback is always candid, direct, and extremely insightful. Instead of guessing what your key stakeholders value, go find out directly. The mere act of asking already demonstrates that you are an accountable leader who is committed to living up to your core leadership obligations. Once you have everyone's perspective, create a clear leadership obligation statement for yourself—one that clearly outlines the desired impact you must have as an accountable leader.

I find the truly great leaders with whom I've worked always have this obligation statement very clear in their minds. It becomes a central point of focus for their leadership.

3. Have the Tough Conversations

My colleague and I were conducting the final activity at a leadership forum event we were facilitating for the top 60 leaders of a global company. It was a three-day session with the first part dedicated to understanding the ideas of the leadership contract, and the rest of the meeting focused on the new business strategy for the company.

Throughout the three days, it became clear that although the company was successful, there were things that were still getting in the way. The leaders lacked the courage to have tough conversations with their direct reports and with one another.

Since launching this book, I have found this to be a recurring theme with many organizations. As we explored in Chapter 7, "Leadership Is Hard Work," many leaders struggle with the hard work of their roles, such as giving candid feedback, managing poor performers, or calling out bad leadership behavior on the part of a peer or colleague. As we discussed, when we avoid this hard work (and it is hard work), we become weak and we make our organizations weaker.

Steve Jobs's reputation for candor—even mercilessness—is well-known. He clearly wasn't afraid of having tough conversations. According to *New York* magazine, when Sir Jonathan Ive, the chief design officer at Apple, saw his colleagues devastated by a conversation with Jobs, he challenged his boss. Jobs's response was, *Why be vague?* Jobs believed that ambiguity was a form of selfishness because it was rooted in a desire to be liked. This desire gets in the way of doing the right thing for the company and, ultimately, the individual. Remember what I also said in Chapter 7: *Being liked as a leader is often overrated.* It can lead you not to do the hard work of leadership for fear that others won't like you.

It's important to note that many people saw Jobs as a real jerk. And it's true he could be harsh. I suspect that had to do more with his style—in how he had a tough conversation. He probably confused being rough with tough. Despite this, it seems he was clear on his leadership accountability to have tough conversations when required.

How about you? As leaders, we all need to commit to have tough conversations—it is part and parcel of being a truly accountable leader. You do need to call out poor performance. You do need to speak truth to power and raise concerns that senior management may not want to hear. You do need to give feedback, even when it will be difficult for someone to hear it. You do need to engage in dialogue, even when there are dissenting views.

I find that the biggest barrier for most leaders isn't that they lack the skills to have these tough conversations but rather that they need the right mindset.

Here's what I've learned through my own leadership roles and through working with accountable leaders at all levels: Ultimately, having a tough conversation is rooted in *caring*.

How can that be? Take a second to think about the people in your own life whom you would label as being tough. They were the ones who called you out when you needed calling out. They were the ones who sat you down and gave you the feedback no one else had the courage to give. These people may have seemed uncaring. But it's the complete opposite. They had the courage to have tough conversations with you because they cared deeply about you. Those individuals cared so deeply for you that they had the courage to sit you down and set you straight when you needed it.

By having the tough conversation with you, they were essentially saying: I care so much about you that I will give you the candid feedback you need to be successful.

I've seen this play out many times. The courage to have a tough conversation comes from the degree to which you care about a person, about the success of your company, and about positive outcomes for your stakeholders. If you didn't care, everything would be so easy. If you didn't care, you wouldn't bother having the tough conversations; you would just go on managing your own affairs and minding your own business.

However, when we do this we are doing a huge disservice to our people and our organizations. I've seen too many people not being given the feedback they need. Something they are doing is getting in their way and they are unaware of it. No one has the courage to speak up, and the person keeps going on, naïve and unaware. There is snickering behind his or her back. Eventually, the person might start to get an uneasy feeling that something is going on. But until someone has the courage to have the conversation, nothing will change.

Now one could argue that people need self-awareness so this doesn't happen. I agree with this, to a point. But in reality, some people just don't have that self-awareness. And holding back on constructive feedback does them a disservice. They keep on behaving the way they've always behaved until the day comes when something happens, and they are shocked that everyone knew but them.

I experienced this recently with a colleague. We were facing a challenging business situation, and he was struggling coming to a tough decision. He was taking forever to make up his mind. He didn't realize how the situation was eroding his credibility with his peers. It was clear to all of us what he needed to do, but he was struggling.

I reached out many times to have the discussion with him but he resisted. When we finally were able to have a discussion, he actually questioned whether my intentions were truly positive. I said, "If I didn't care, I wouldn't be putting myself through all this stress. I would just focus on my own business and let you manage your own. But because I care about you, your team, and our company, I believe it's important for us to have this discussion. I hope you can see that." He did and quickly made his decision.

Does this resonate with you? Have you been in this situation before?

I find sometimes leaders struggle with having the tough conversation because they worry about the technique or how to structure the discussion. This certainly can be a barrier, but I find it can also be an excuse. The *how* is important. You certainly shouldn't have a tough conversation when you are angry or in a vengeful state.

In my experience, the first step is actually to focus on how much you care about the person, your company, and your collective success. When you begin from this starting point, having the conversation is easier because at the end of the day the person will know you have his or her back. The person may still not like what he or she hears but will appreciate your courage and the fact that you're looking out for his or her best interest. You will actually strengthen the level of trust between you and that person.

It's time we create organizations where we can have candid, frank, and adult conversations about our business, each other, and our collective performance. Our inability to do so wastes time, creates roadblocks that slow down our progress, and interferes with our success. Here's your challenge: *to be the leader who commits to doing the hard work and having the tough conversations in your organization.* Be that leader!

4. Be a Community Builder

The accountable leaders of the future will be community builders. Like Mary Barra of GM, they will take an inclusive approach to working with others. They will find ways to connect on a personal level with peers and colleagues. As we discussed in Chapter 7, too many leaders feel disconnected and isolated. We need more community builders to create that sense of connection we so desperately need and want. We need to create a new way of working across our organizations. It's a bold vision which I've summarized for you in *The Community of Leaders Manifesto*. Read it now.

THE **COMMUNITY** OF **LEADERS** Manifesto

WE ARE **DONE WITH THE OLD MODEL** OF LEADERSHIP THAT HAS GLORIFIED HEROES.

WE ARE DONE SETTLING FOR **MEDIOCRITY**. WE WILL NOT BE **LAME LEADERS**. WE WILL STOP GOING THROUGH **THE MOTIONS**. WE WILL PUT AN END TO THE **ISOLATION** THAT WE FEEL EVERY DAY.

WE WILL **NOT BE DISCONNECTED FROM** ONE ANOTHER. WE WILL **NOT PUT UP WITH A CLIMATE OF APATHY** AND LOW TRUST. WE WILL **PUT AN END TO ALL THE INFIGHTING** AND COMPETITION. WE WILL STOP BUILDING SILOS. WE WILL **STOP WORKING AT CROSS-PURPOSES**. INSTEAD,

WE RESOLVE TO **CREATE A STRONG** COMMUNITY OF LEADERS—ONE WHERE THERE IS **HIGH CLARITY** ON WHAT WE ARE TRYING TO ACCOMPLISH AS LEADERS TO **MAKE OUR** **ORGANIZATION GREAT**.

WE WILL **SHARE A COLLECTIVE ASPIRATION** AND PASSION FOR **GREAT LEADERSHIP**. WE WILL **SET AN EXAMPLE** TO OTHER ORGANIZATIONS.

WE WILL BUILD THE **BEST** **LEADERS** IN OUR INDUSTRY.

WE WILL OPERATE AS **ONE** **COMPANY**.

WE WILL BE ALIGNED TO **OUR** **STRATEGY**.

WE WILL **DRIVE COLLABORATION AND INNOVATION** ACROSS OUR ORGANIZATION. WE WILL **BUILD STRONG RELATIONSHIPS** WITH ONE ANOTHER. WE WILL **MAKE EACH OTHER STRONGER**. ONCE WE BUILD A STRONG COMMUNITY OF LEADERS, IT WILL BECOME OUR **ULTIMATE DIFFERENTIATOR**. IT WILL BE OUR **TRUE AND EVERLASTING SOURCE OF COMPETITIVE ADVANTAGE**. IT ALL STARTS WITH EACH ONE OF US. IT ALL STARTS WITH A DECISION TO LEAD MORE DELIBERATELY—WITH GREATER PERSONAL **CLARITY AND COMMITMENT**.

As you can see, *The Community of Leaders Manifesto* outlines the commitment that you must make to create a strong community of leaders in your organization. It clarifies what you and your fellow leaders need to aspire to create. Use it as an on going source of inspiration for yourself and your fellow leaders. Imagine if your employees went to work each day knowing their leaders were truly committed to putting the ideas in this manifesto into practice. It would be a game changer—it would truly transform your culture!

Take *The Community of Leaders Manifesto* and share it with your colleagues. Discuss whether you are living up to the vision it presents. You can start with a small team of fellow leaders and make a commitment to one another. You can also work to implement it more broadly across a level of leaders or your entire leadership cadre. Don't worry that other leaders won't find this change worthwhile. In my experience, people are hungry for an open and honest conversation about leadership. This manifesto gives you the language to start having those conversations in your own organization.

The good news about building a strong community of leaders is that it rests on a few simple actions you can implement every single day. My team and I often ask participants in our leadership programs to identify the actions that build a strong leadership community within an organization. We hear the same ideas no matter what organization or industry we work in. These ideas are all based on connecting with others and are staggeringly simple. Here are the top five actions we hear all the time from leaders like you:

1. *Connect Informally.* Spend time over coffee breaks to get to know colleagues personally. It's hard to build community with strangers. Get to know your fellow leaders better.
2. *Connect Over a Meal.* It's surprising how often this idea emerges. It seems there's something really important about having a meal together with colleagues. It builds stronger connections. Now these should not be stuffy business meetings, but rather casual forms of conversation over some good food. Current research supports the value of connecting over meals. For example, an interdisciplinary group of researchers led by Kevin M. Kniffin, an economist at Cornell University, explored the interaction between eating together and group performance among firefighters across 50 firehouses. The researchers found that when firefighters ate meals together they tended to demonstrate stronger group performance compared to those who preferred solo dining.

3. *Connect across Departments.* Invite colleagues from different business units to your own meetings to learn about what they do and how you can work more effectively together. It's surprising to me how many leaders don't think to do this, and yet it's so simple to do. You don't need senior management's permission. Just do it.

4. *Connect via Technology.* There are so many more options available today to connect using technology. More and more of us work virtually across time zones and geographies. In a world of text messaging, e-mails, and collaboration tools, people still feel disconnected from each other. Despite all the tools, real relationships are lacking. In practice, I've heard over and over again the need for leaders to commit to simple ways of connecting via technology. What is the single most frequent strategy I hear all the time? Get ready for it: Pick up the phone. That's right. While we have more technologies to keep us connected, few feel a real sense of connection with the people we work with. The technologies can be great, but we need to infuse the human element—a voice or an image. So when you have a few minutes to spare in your day, pick up the phone or have a Skype call and make a real personal connection.

5. *Connect People to One Another.* Be the person who helps others build a network of relationships. Make introductions. Bring colleagues together. Many leaders excel at this externally. I've known some to be really well connected within their industry, yet they rarely think to apply those same skills within their organization. Be the person who helps others connect to others within your company. Be the connector.

Regular Practices for Living the Leadership Contract

By this stage, I'm sure it's becoming clear to you that the four terms of the leadership contract don't exist in isolation from one another. They are interdependent and represent an integrated way to help you become a more accountable leader. They evolve every single day as you lead. In other words, you don't put them into effect only once; you must put them into action daily, quarterly, and annually.

Daily Actions

After the senior vice president of human resources for a large financial services organization read about the leadership contract, she sent me an e-mail telling me how much she loved it. She also said she would put the four terms into action daily by asking herself the following four questions every single morning before she started work:

1. What leadership decision do I have to make today? Is there a Big D or small d leadership decision that I will face?
2. What leadership obligation do I have to live up to today?
3. What hard work do I have to tackle today as a leader?
4. Which relationship with a colleague do I need to make stronger today to continue to build a community of leaders?

Imagine the focus that answering these questions brings to her leadership role. When I do my keynote presentations with audiences, I typically give out a small card that has these four questions on it. The participants in these sessions love taking the cards. They often ask for extras for their colleagues. It seems having a simple set of questions to focus one's leadership mindset every single day is valuable to many leaders.

Other leaders have shared with me that they also use these four questions when they are dealing with a business or leadership dilemma and no clear answer is apparent. Imagine that something comes up during the day, something that's a real challenge for you: an issue with an employee, a serious conflict with a customer or supplier, or something that's gone awry with a stakeholder.

All eyes are on you. You have to resolve the issue. How do you make sure you respond in the best possible way? Ask yourself the four questions presented in this chapter, and the way forward will be perfectly clear. You'll immediately know what you have to do as a leader. I know this because I've done it many times in my own role, and it works. These questions force you to think about your dilemmas more objectively. You'll keep your leadership obligations in sight. You'll end up doing the right thing as a leader.

Quarterly and Annual Actions

Each quarter, set aside two to three hours to reflect on your leadership. How did you do over the past three months? What were some of the critical leadership decisions (Big D and small d) that you made? What value did you bring to those you are obligated to? What hard work did you tackle? What hard work did you avoid? Over these months, did you become stronger as a leader or weaker? How did you strengthen the sense of community among the leaders in your organization? Looking ahead to the next quarter, how will you continue to put the four terms of the leadership contract into action? If you are working with a leadership coach, discuss these questions with her or him. You may also find it helpful to work with a trusted colleague who is part of your community of leaders.

I believe it is also important to invest some time annually to reflect more formally on your personal level of leadership accountability. Here are some questions (categorized under each of the four terms) that you can use to assess your own level of accountability as a leader.

1. Leadership Is a Decision—Make It
   - In what specific ways did you demonstrate your decisiveness as a leader?
   - Describe how you fully embraced the challenges and difficulties that come with being a leader?
   - Are you still excited about your leadership role, and do the people you lead know it?
   - How did you pay attention to how you showed up as a leader each and every day?
2. Leadership Is an Obligation—Step Up
   - Do the people you lead know you are fully committed to being the best leader you can be?
   - In what ways did you put what is best for your organization ahead of what is best for you personally?
   - How did you actively work to leave your organization in better shape than you found it?
   - Do you remain clear on what your personal obligations are as a leader?
3. Leadership Is Hard Work—Get Tough
   - In what ways did you effectively handle the pressures and scrutiny of your leadership role?
   - Did you consistently tackle the tough conversations with the people you work with?

- What difficult decisions did you make, even if they were unpopular with those you lead?
- How did you demonstrate resilience and resolve in the face of adversity?
4. Leadership Is a Community—Connect
   - How did you lead with a one-company mindset?
   - What relationships with direct reports, peers, and colleagues did you make stronger?
   - How did you look for ways to collaborate with your peers and colleagues?
   - Who did you support so that they could become better and more accountable leaders?

Solicit Feedback from Others   It's always important for leaders to know how others see them. One approach my team and I have used over the years is to send out an anonymous survey to members of our team, colleagues across our company, and select customers and other stakeholders. The survey includes the six questions I shared earlier that help determine your leadership value.

Once all the responses are back, I go through them to identify key themes and summarize the data. My team members do the same. Then we meet to review our results, clarify the themes, gain more insight, and personally commit to improve how we are leading and how we are supporting one another. I've worked on many multi-rater and 360-degree projects with clients, and I find this set of six straightforward questions to be one of the best ways to get feedback on yourself as a leader. The feedback is always candid, direct, and meaningful.

Determine the timing that works best for you. We've always done ours to align with the midpoint of our fiscal year. This way we can get feedback on how we have done in the first half of the year and figure out what we need to focus on for the rest of the year. You may find it helpful to apply a similar strategy, or you may want to align your annual leadership checkup with your organization's performance review process. In the end, the important thing is to make a yearly commitment to review the four terms of the leadership contract and evaluate how you are putting them into action to become a more accountable leader.

Sign the Leadership Contract at Each Turning Point   As I noted in Chapter 10, the four leadership turning points are critical moments in your career as a leader, and at each one you must pause and reflect on what you are signing up for. When you face one of these turning points, you need to understand that your world will change as a leader. Each one of these moments represents a Big D leadership opportunity. You need to pause and get clarity by asking yourself:

- What's the role really about?
- What are the expectations?
- What will success look like?
- What value must I bring as a leader?
- What impact must I have?
- What temptations might I need to manage?

You must also pause and reflect on your degree of commitment by asking yourself:

- Am I up for this?
- Am I fully committed to doing what I need to do to make my team and company succeed?
- Am I prepared for the hardships that will come my way?
- Am I committing for the right reasons, or am I doing this only to feed my ego?

Once you are satisfied with your answers to these questions, re-sign the leadership contract to solidify your commitment with yourself to be a truly accountable leader.

Create Your Own Personal Leadership Contract   Some leaders I know are so passionate about becoming great leaders that they are motivated to create their own personal leadership contracts. If you are one of these leaders, then I applaud you. Take the leadership contract we reviewed in Chapter 9, and modify it for your own needs.

If you go through the effort to create your own leadership contract, I strongly encourage you to share it with your team. You'll be amazed at the impact it will have on them and the way they will see you. But it's important not to share it with a sense of arrogance. You'll come off as pompous and pretentious. Instead, let your genuine commitment come through, coupled with a sense of humility. This is a powerful combination. Don't stop there—share your personal leadership contract with me at www.theleadershipcontract.com.

Final Thoughts—Becoming a Truly Accountable Leader

Now, the good news is that if you commit to living the four terms of the leadership contract, then you will create the necessary foundation to become the accountable leader that your organization and employees need you to be. Commit today to living the leadership contract.

The Gut Check for Leaders—Living the Leadership Contract

As you think about the ideas in this chapter, reflect on your answers to the following gut check questions:

1. How does understanding your personal leadership story help you become a more accountable leader?
2. How does having clarity regarding your value and desired impact help you become a more accountable leader?
3. How will having tough conversations make you a more accountable leader?
4. In what ways will you be a community builder within your organization?

CHAPTER 12

Embed the Leadership Contract in Your Organization

S everal years ago, my team and I worked with a financial services organization. It was in trouble. Its performance was in decline and its leadership culture had become complacent. We were brought in to work with the new CEO, who was trying to turn this company around. He was particularly struggling with his top 50 leaders. "I can't seem to light a fire under them," he said in our first meeting.

Nothing he tried seemed to work. He tried to be inspirational and paint a great vision of the future. No response. He tried to scare them by giving what I call the "You're either on the bus or off the bus" speech. He tried to be their friend, appealing to their sensibilities. Nothing worked. I could tell he was at his wit's end and losing patience when, near the end of that meeting, he said, "I should just fire them all!"

As we started to get to know this organization and its leaders, it became evident that they had become a rotting of zombies, which I described earlier in Chapter 8. They were all nice people who showed up every day just going through the motions but with no excitement for their roles. It seemed the complacency had taken over all the senior leaders. Apparently, the previous CEO had tolerated this mediocrity for a long time.

After our preliminary analysis, we came up with a strategy to drive strong leadership accountability. First, we would work with these senior leaders through a series of leader forum meetings. At the same time, we worked in parallel with the HR department to help it start articulating a set of clear leadership expectations—something that had never been done before.

The first session with those leaders was exactly what you would expect with a room full of zombies—the apathy and mediocrity were high. It was like an episode of the TV series *The Walking Dead*, without all the blood and gore. We did a baseline measure of their leadership culture, and to no one's surprise they rated themselves quite low, both in terms of their clarity on strategy and leadership expectations as well as their collective commitment to the company. In our discussions, they cited multiple examples of working at cross-purposes with one another and few examples of collaboration across their company. Many also admitted that they had checked out as leaders.

The good news, amid the stench of lame and mediocre leadership, was the fact that they acknowledged their problems. Now the question was: Were they prepared to do something about it? I've learned over the course of my career that it's easy for zombie leaders to be in a meeting and nod their heads in agreement on any issue. It's something else to move them to real action.

In each of the remaining sessions, we tackled the problems they identified in the baseline survey. We also started to increase the expectations of their personal and collective leadership accountability. We asked the leaders to make public commitments on actions they were going to bring back to their business units and then to report back in the next session. At first, adoption of this practice was weak. Given their history, it took a while for them to even understand what it really meant to be accountable. But we called out their behavior and lack of leadership. They didn't like it, but we kept pushing. It's hard to bring zombies back to life. Slowly but surely, we began to see small signs of change starting to take hold.

In one session, we had a breakthrough. Both my colleague and I saw this group of leaders shift right before our eyes. It was the kind of moment that every facilitator, trainer, or consultant lives for—that instant when the leaders go from being lame to being accountable. All the hard work we had been doing seemed to click in an instant.

Even the leaders noticed the change. They were no longer the same leaders they had been—they were on their path to becoming accountable leaders. The energy in the room completely changed. They stepped up and took ownership for their problems and, more important, the solutions. As the day unfolded, my colleague and I drifted into the background as these leaders took over the meeting. They started to self-organize. They started to come up with their own solutions. They got clear on who would do what and by when. They finally made decisions on chronic issues that had remained unresolved for months. You could feel the momentum starting to take hold. They went from being lame and mediocre to inspiring and accountable. The energy at the end of the day was so high that no one wanted to leave the meeting room. Everyone lingered, talking to one another. They were feeling the connection, the commitment, and the clarity they all shared.

At the next session, we repeated the survey on their leadership culture, and sure enough, it had improved considerably. The changes were taking hold. The leaders reported having greater clarity on the company's strategy. They knew what was expected of them. They reported much stronger personal and collective commitment to drive the company's success.

It turns out the CEO didn't have to fire them after all. He did, however, have to make leadership accountability a priority and be deliberate about setting clear leadership expectations. In the end, these leaders had to learn how to work together as a real community. The timing couldn't be better for them. Why? What those leaders didn't realize at the time was that within just a few weeks they would be dealing with one of the biggest business challenges of our generation—the global financial crisis.

When it hit, this company (like so many others in the financial services sector) was left reeling. However, the leaders of this particular company were able to weather the storm because they had become individually and collectively stronger.

Imagine for a moment if all this work hadn't happened. Imagine if they had still been a rotting of lame and mediocre zombies trying to deal with one of the worst financial crises of all time. I can guarantee you that they would have failed miserably. It certainly wasn't an easy time for them. It was hard on everybody in the company, but the leaders managed through it all and kept the company going while others in that industry had a much different fate.

This is the kind of dramatic impact that can happen when an organization takes responsibility for driving strong leadership accountability.

We already know that it is important for leaders to step up and be accountable at an individual level. That's been the primary focus of this book. But organizations have to step up, too. And when I say organizations, I mean senior management, HR, and even the board. They must all work together to go from individual leadership accountability to building collective leadership accountability across an entire organization.

In this chapter, we'll focus on how to make this happen. More specifically, we'll examine four strategies to embed the leadership contract into your organization.

The Four Strategies to Drive Strong Leadership Accountability

There are four strategies that can help drive strong leadership accountability in your organization (see Figure 12.1). As you will see, each ties to one of the four terms of the leadership contract.

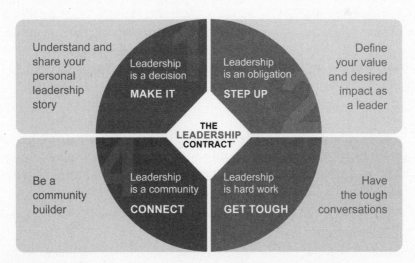

Figure 12.1   The Four Strategies to Drive Strong Leadership Accountability

1. *Make Leadership Accountability a Business Priority*

The first term of the leadership contract says that leadership is a decision. Chapter 5 described in detail what this means for individual leaders.

Organizations also need to make a decision which centers around making leadership accountability a business priority. As we explored in Chapter 3, 72 percent of organizations believe leadership accountability is a critical issue, but that doesn't necessarily mean they've taken action to make it a real business priority. What would this kind of action look like in practice? It would mean a shared sense of clarity among the board, the CEO and executive team, and HR on the organization's responsibility to support leaders to drive strong leadership accountability across the enterprise.

What I've seen many times is uneven commitment and lack of clarity as to who must own leadership accountability as a business priority. For example, I've seen many cases where the CEO assumes complete and sole accountability. He or she is the only one in the entire organization who is passionate and paying attention to leadership accountability. The problem is that if the CEO leaves the organization, things begin to crumble and leadership accountability is no longer an area of focus. Whatever progress was made evaporates.

I've also seen companies in which a very progressive senior HR leader single-handedly takes on the responsibility for driving leadership accountability. This creates problems similar to the first scenario. Other executives don't step up or take it seriously. The HR leader feels like he or she is pushing a boulder uphill and eventually gives up.

The ideal scenario is when the CEO, HR, senior management, and the board all have clarity and commitment around driving strong leadership accountability. When this total accountability is in place, terrific things can happen.

Conduct a Leadership Accountability Audit   You can start making leadership accountability a business priority today by conducting an audit of leadership accountability in your own organization. You can use the questions below:

- To what extent is leadership accountability a business priority in our organization?
- In what ways can we make leadership accountability a topic of conversation for the senior management team or the board?

- How satisfied are we with the degree of leadership accountability demonstrated by our leaders?
- Do we see leadership accountability gaps by level (front-line, mid-level, executive ranks)?
- To what extent has our organization set clear leadership expectations for our leaders?
- Are we confident that we have a strong leadership culture, and one that will ensure our future success?
- To what extent do we believe our leaders are fully committed to their roles as leaders?
- Does our organization have the courage to identify and address mediocre and unaccountable leaders?

Answering the questions above as an executive team (or even with your board) will certainly foster robust and meaningful dialogue, possibly even a much-needed healthy debate.

Once you've made the decision to make leadership accountability a priority in your organization, you need to reinforce this decision in visible and tangible ways.

Senior Management Must Be the Example of Accountability   Our global research also revealed that only 31 percent of organizations are currently satisfied with the level of accountability among their leaders. In order to build a culture of accountability, you first need to ensure that senior management and executives set the example of strong leadership accountability. As you know through your own experience, if senior leaders are not setting the tone for other leaders in the organization, you won't succeed. So it's important that your senior leaders personally understand that leadership accountability starts with them.

A great example of this comes from Harry S. Truman, the thirty-third president of the United States. He kept a sign on his desk in the Oval Office that read, "The buck stops here." It's a phrase he made popular, and it signified that, as the ultimate leader of his country, he had to make decisions and accept the full accountability for them. What makes this story interesting to me is that the sign on his desk was Truman's own personal reminder to be an accountable leader. If he needed a reminder, then most of us do as well. But I find too many leaders just assume that because they are at the executive ranks, they automatically have strong leadership accountability. That's a dangerous assumption.

Human Resources Needs to Set the Leadership Bar High for Itself   Often, the HR function is at the center of this work of creating a leadership contract for the organization. And just like senior management, if the HR leaders of the organization do not internalize the terms of the leadership contract, the ideas get watered down. I've seen far too many lame HR departments trying to drive culture change without recognizing the need to change themselves first. I've also seen some amazing HR departments, led by truly accountable and inspirational leaders, set the tone for an entire company. If you are leading the HR function for your company, I encourage you to step up to your leadership accountability. Be the leaders everyone else in your company wants to emulate. I believe this is the biggest missed opportunity for HR leaders today.

I spoke recently to a CHRO of a large telecommunications and media company about how his company successfully transformed itself. During our discussion, he shared that before the company started to work on its transformation, he actually began to transform his HR team. "I knew if I didn't have a strong team in place, the transformation would not be successful," he told me. "My team were going to be critical in supporting leaders to lead very difficult and complex change."

This was a senior HR executive who set the bar high for himself and his team. His story showed how critical HR leaders and professionals are to helping a company when it's transforming itself. It's these leaders who have the expertise in leading change and helping leaders acquire new mindsets and capabilities; but if they are weak, then it creates executional risk.

If you are a senior HR leader, ask yourself: Do you have the team your company needs to help drive its success? Are your HR leaders models of strong leadership accountability? If you answered no to either of these questions, you have some work to do.

2. Create a Leadership Contract for Your Organization

Once your organization makes the decision to ensure that leadership accountability is a critical business priority, then you must be clear on your obligation: to create and communicate clear leadership expectations to your leaders. According to our survey, just under half of organizations have done this well. The best way to set clear expectations for your leaders is by creating a leadership contract for your organization.

Since we launched the first edition of *The Leadership Contract*, we've seen many organizations begin to step up to their obligation and be deliberate about setting clear leadership expectations. They've done this by creating their own company-specific leadership contracts. In every case, their leaders responded favorably because they knew what was expected of them.

For example, we worked with the CEO and senior vice president of strategy and talent of a health care organization that was transforming itself to become a biologics manufacturer. This team was so excited about the idea of the leadership contract that they wanted to create their own. They felt the timing was right because the organization was at an inflection point and going through a fundamental change in its strategy. As a result of this change, what it meant to be a leader also needed to evolve. They were about to introduce a new strategic plan to the top 120 leaders, and they wanted to make sure the leaders not only understood the strategy but also were clear on their role in executing it.

The organization hadn't done a great job previously of developing and supporting its leaders. It was time to change that. My team and I helped it create a custom leadership contract. We conducted interviews and focus groups to understand all the issues and then began to draft a set of terms. We validated these terms with other leaders and then designed a two-day leadership forum.

On day one, the CEO revealed the new strategic plan. On day two, we introduced the leadership contract and began the process of helping the leaders understand the terms so that they could sign it (see box).

The Leadership Contract for a Biologics Manufacturer

I, as a leader, commit to the following terms of our leadership contract:

- I will lead with courage. I will make tough decisions and have difficult conversations that are in the best interests of our organization.

- I will lead by developing myself. It will also be essential that I create engaging environments in which people have meaningful opportunities to grow.
- I will lead through relationships. Successful strategy execution is ultimately a function of having these strong relationships with employees, patients, funders, and other key stakeholders.
- I will lead with the big picture in mind. I will align both business and team priorities. This enterprise-wide perspective is necessary to effectively operate across the organization to achieve shared strategic goals.
- I will lead with accountability. I will step up, tackle challenges, and bring solutions rather than problems to the table.

We will work together to lead as one community of leaders.

The leaders had a very strong positive reaction to their own leadership contract. Many said they were both exhilarated and scared by the terms. Their organization was drawing a line in the sand about great leadership—something that leaders desperately had wanted to do but didn't know how to until now. The leadership contract gave them a way. But they also understood the contract meant increased accountability—no more excuses. They were now going to lead as one community of leaders with clarity and commitment.

Six months after the leaders signed their leadership contract, I was chatting with Andy, the senior vice president of strategy and talent. He said to me, "You won't believe what this leadership contract has done for our organization. It's gone viral. Managers have taken it to their teams. Employees have embraced it. Our manufacturing facility created a huge poster that all the employees signed. Everyone is taking it seriously. It's clear that there was a hunger for accountability, real clarity, and real commitment on the part of leaders and employees. The amazing thing is that it just happened—the executive team didn't force it. It came from the organization."

I was surprised by what Andy said. I knew the potential power of the ideas of the leadership contract and its four terms, but I didn't realize it could have such widespread impact.

I really admire this organization's determination to put the leadership contract into action for all leaders. They are starting to realize what I've believed throughout my 25 years in the leadership industry: When all your leaders share the same aspirations, the same clarity about what they are trying to do as leaders, and the same deep commitment to executing your business strategy and creating a community of leaders, something powerful will happen—something that will become the ultimate competitive advantage!

This organization isn't alone. Over the last couple of years, we've seen many organizations create company-specific contracts to help them set clear leadership expectations. These organizations represented a cross-section of industries, from financial services to technology, health care, education, the public sector, and more. This widespread implementation of company-specific leadership contracts really points to the need that organizations have to set clear leadership expectations and to do it directly and practically. What we've also observed is that these leadership contracts are either replacing traditional leadership competency models or integrated with existing leadership frameworks. The difference is that leadership contracts are written in simple, clear, and compelling language. They aren't full of the kind of jargon or corporate-speak that doesn't resonate with actual leaders. Instead, they are personal, visceral, and aspirational.

Creating a leadership contract for your company is just the start. You must then ensure it is truly embedded in your organization. Below, I outline a number of strategies for you to consider.

Have Leaders Sign the Leadership Contract at Each Turning Point   As we explored earlier in this book, there are four key leadership turning points that leaders face throughout their careers. At each, they assume more senior roles, and each step places greater expectations and demands on the individual. Organizations must be aware of this and support leaders during these times to ensure they succeed in their transitions to bigger leadership roles.

One of the ways to do this is to use your own leadership contract to have discussions with leaders as they transition into new roles. It's important for leaders to appreciate the transition, how their roles will change, and how they must step up to their increased leadership expectations.

We worked with a large energy company that created a half-day Leadership Contract workshop for employees in professional roles. These roles were essentially feeders into front-line management positions. The workshop helped the employees gain a better understanding of what it means to take on a leadership role. The company found that those leaders who continued to express interest in becoming managers after going through this program were more focused and committed than others. They had a better sense of what was expected and how they needed to focus their development to tackle the hard work ahead.

Another client, a large financial institution, used its leadership contract to provide coaching to new vice presidents in the bank. It found that this process helped its leaders integrate into their roles more quickly and confidently.

These are just a few examples of what happens when an organization creates a company-specific leadership contract and then uses it to help leaders at all levels understand what it means to be an accountable leader.

Anchor Your Leadership Contract in Your Development Programs   Your company-specific leadership contract becomes the foundation that defines what it really means to be a leader in your company. In our experience, we find it important to remind leaders of these expectations regularly. One way to do this is to include your leadership contract in all your development programs. One client of ours set aside time in every leadership development workshop and seminar to review the leadership contract and expectations.

In response to client demand, we have also included many of the ideas of this book in our own coaching process. This way our clients worldwide know that our coaches are driving strong leadership accountability in every coaching session.

Leverage Your Leadership Contract at Key Inflection Points   My colleagues and I recently launched another Leadership Contract initiative with a European client that is one of the world's leading suppliers to the industrial and automotive sectors. The company is more than 100 years old.

The managing director of Italian Operations began our session by talking to his top 30 leaders. He had just come back from a corporate leadership meeting where the discussion was all about change and transformation. He said the company was at an inflection point, and they needed to transform their leadership culture to drive success in the future.

Although the company has been a dominant industry player for many years, it is at a point where it must now evolve. New competitors are fierce. Increased customer expectations are challenging pricing; raw materials are no longer cheap.

This is becoming a common and recurring story with companies everywhere. Andrew Grove, former chair of Intel, wrote and spoke a lot about inflection points as far back as the late 1990s. Unfortunately, Grove died in 2016, but his ideas have had an enduring quality that is rare in business.

For Grove, a strategic inflection point occurs when a company experiences a major change in its competitive environment. This major change can be the result of a number of factors, including the introduction of new technologies, a shift in the regulatory environment, or evolving customer values. My client is experiencing all three.

Common to all organizations facing an inflection point is the need to make fundamental changes in business strategy. This will put tremendous stress and strain on leaders who will be responsible for affecting those changes. If they fail, it could be the beginning of the end.

In a recent article by McKinsey & Company, the authors argue that strong, dominant, incumbent players in certain industries "needn't be victims of disruption if they recognize the crucial thresholds in their life cycle and act in time."

The article repeats a quote from Reed Hastings, the CEO of Netflix, who noted that many organizations fail to try new things out of a fear of hurting long-standing, core activities. "Companies rarely die from moving too fast," Hastings has said, "and they frequently die from moving too slowly."

We all know of companies that have failed to react to inflections in their industries. Leaders at those companies may have seen what was happening but didn't respond, resulting in a downward spiral. At least our client is responding early and has identified the need to transform.

The big lesson here is that just saying your company has to transform is very different from successfully transforming.

Back to our European session. When it was time for the head of HR to speak, he continued to challenge his leaders. He used the analogy of an iceberg—everything above the water surface represents the behavior and actions of leaders; everything below represents their fundamental assumptions, values, and mindsets. In order to transform the company, leaders need to first transform themselves. This will require them to act and behave differently, but only after they change their mindsets and core assumptions.

As we began to share our work in the area of leadership account-ability, we focused the discussion on what exactly they must do individually and collectively to successfully lead the company through their own inflection point. These leaders will need to pause from their day-to-day grind to reflect on their roles, challenge the assumptions they have made about the company, and begin to learn new ways to be accountable as their company heads into the next 100 years.

Does this sound familiar? Are you going through a period of significant transformation? How are you and your fellow leaders responding? Are you challenging old assumptions and mindsets? These are questions we all need to grapple with as leaders.

Organizations today are always facing change—sometimes transfor-mational change. At these inflection points, everything is reexamined: the markets in which you operate, the business strategy of your company, and ultimately the kind of leadership you will need to be successful in the new future. Navigating through an inflection point represents a signifi-cant challenge. Not every organization is successful. We have found that a company-specific leadership contract becomes a powerful way for leaders to understand new leadership expectations quickly. In fact, some of the most important and rewarding work that my team and I have done is in helping leaders and their organizations successfully transition through a critical inflection point.

Use Your Leadership Contract to Build Accountable Teams Since writing the first edition of this book, my team and I have had many conversations with our clients about how to apply the ideas in their organizations. One of the areas that I always believed was ripe for application was in using the four terms to help build truly accountable teams.

In my own experience working with senior teams across many industries, I find that ultimately their long-term success is a function of how each individual shows up as a leader. Do they bring a real sense of clarity and commitment to make the team successful?

So it wasn't a surprise to me when one of our clients approached us with an interesting request. She was a big fan of *The Leadership Contract*, and she asked us how she could use the four terms with her newly formed senior leadership team. Our client shared that she had an upcoming one-day offsite and she wanted to make sure she was able to set up her team for success. So we went away and reflected on her needs. We came back to her with an agenda for a one-day session that was based on a series of questions for her to use with her team. Here's what we shared with her. You may find these questions valuable with your own team.

1. Leadership Is a Decision—Make It
   - What is our vision of a truly accountable team?
   - Are we "all in" as individual team members and fully committed to create and sustain a truly accountable team?
   - Do we have clarity regarding our mutual expectations of one another?
   - What are the Big D and small d leadership decisions that we will need to make as a team?
2. Leadership Is an Obligation—Step Up
   - What is our core obligation as a team?
   - In what ways will we individually and collectively step up to our core obligation?
   - How do we intend to leave our organization in better shape than we found it?
   - How will we set the tone and be an example of a truly accountable team to others in our organization?
3. Leadership Is Hard Work—Get Tough
   - What is the hard work that this team must tackle in order for us to be successful?
   - What is the hard work within our own organization that we must address head-on?
   - What are the tough conversations we must have as a team? And with other teams we will work with?
   - How must we demonstrate resilience and resolve as a team?
4. Leadership Is a Community—Connect
   - How will we establish a real sense of community within our team?
   - In what ways will we have each other's backs?

- How will we celebrate our key milestones and successes?
- How will we support the success of other teams that we will work with across our organization?

Since that request, we had more, and so we responded by building *The Leadership Contract for Teams* solution. It's been extremely gratifying to see how the ideas of the book have translated so effectively to help teams become more accountable. Many teams within my own company have been early adopters and have become stronger and able to drive greater success for our company. You can also review *The Leadership Contract Field Guide* book for ideas and strategies you can use to build your own accountable team.

3. Get Tough on the Tough Stuff

This next strategy is anchored on the third term of the leadership contract which says that leadership is hard work and leaders need to get tough. As we explored, many leaders struggle with the hard work they face in their roles, such as giving candid feedback, managing poor performers, and having tough conversations. Getting tough as a leader isn't easy, and it requires concerted effort at the individual level. But if all that happened was that we set the expectation for leaders to get tough without supporting them, then progress will be limited.

Organizations, meaning senior management and HR, need to do some of their own hard work at an organizational level. They have to get tough on the tough stuff as well. Below are some ideas.

Promote Leaders for Being Accountable, Not Solely for Being Strong Technical Experts   As I shared earlier in the book, one of the challenges organizations have typically faced is their reliance on promoting technical superstars into leadership roles. The tough work for an organization is to resist this temptation. Sometimes it's done because it's expedient and easy to do. Other times, it's done because we don't have a clear idea of what accountable leadership actually looks like.

Let's go back for a moment to the global research I referenced earlier in this book. We asked respondents to identify the behaviors they most associate with truly accountable leaders. It's a great list and brings much-needed clarity in terms of what accountable leaders do differently than unaccountable ones do.

Accountable leaders:

- Hold others, including their team (or direct reports), accountable for high standards of performance;
- Tackle tough issues and make difficult decisions;
- Effectively communicate the business strategy throughout the organization;
- Express optimism about the company and its future; and
- Express clarity about external trends in the business environment.

Review this list and see whether it aligns with your own definition of the critical behaviors of accountable leaders. Use this or your own list, as the basis for making promotions. Don't simply take the easy way out and promote based solely on technical expertise.

Make It Safe to Speak Truth to Power   Often, one of the hardest things for leaders to do is to *speak truth to power*. This means having the courage to raise and bring forward issues to senior management, even when they might be contentious. For many leaders, speaking truth to power isn't easy. Many agonize about sharing their opinions. Others simply keep quiet—seeing playing it safe as a better option. These leaders fear the potentially negative reaction from senior management.

The reason this is so difficult is that, traditionally, many companies have had a shoot-the-messenger mentality. Perhaps it's rooted in senior management's desire to hear good news only. Perhaps it's their insecurity. But when someone speaks up and is then attacked, demeaned, or fired, it creates an unsafe environment. Other leaders immediately learn that if they stick their necks out and raise an important or controversial issue, their heads will be chopped off. So everyone keeps quiet, and nothing changes. The hard work becomes even harder.

It's also hard for senior executives. It isn't easy listening to someone speak the truth or call you out on something that isn't working. You have to learn to manage your own reaction in these situations. I worked with one leader who had a tendency to lose his temper completely when his leaders spoke truth to power and raised important issues. He couldn't control himself. He would go on a rant and even be verbally abusive. His leaders quickly learned that despite all the talk about creating an open culture, the reality was much different. If this is you, you really need to work on yourself. Jim Collins in *Good to Great* talked about the need for leaders to accept the brutal truth. But it isn't always easy. I know from my own experience. It's really tough to hear about things that aren't working in your company when you are giving your job everything you've got.

It's important for all leaders to appreciate that when you do speak truth to power, you should do it in a way that demonstrates accountability. You can't simply come off as a complainer. You need to present your concerns in a constructive manner. I know many CEOs who react strongly when leaders share information in a blaming tone or do it in a way that shows they aren't stepping up to fix the situation. They are perceived as whiners and erode their credibility.

So get tough on the tough stuff and start making it safe for your leaders to speak truth to power. When you do, you'll tackle the real issues that may be holding your company back.

Stop Tolerating Mediocrity   My colleague and I were speaking at a conference on the ideas in this book. The question-and-answer segment with the audience became quite lively as everyone was grappling with the issue of leadership accountability.

One delegate asked us a final question: "If there were one or two things my organization could do to drive strong leadership accountability, what would they be?" I said there were two things: first, to set clear leadership expectations and, second, to stop tolerating mediocrity from your leaders.

After our session, we had many delegates thanking us for our comments. Many said that upon reflection, their organizations did indeed tolerate mediocrity and it had to stop.

I've come to learn through my own leadership role and through my work with clients that there is a price every organization pays for mediocrity, and it's significant. Consider, for example, some great research that recently came out of the Gallup organization. In 2015, it conducted a major survey of 2,564 managers, called *The State of the American Manager: Analytics and Advice for Leaders*.

Gallup found that a whopping 51 percent of American managers are not engaged and another 14 percent are actively disengaged. When you combine the impact of these numbers, Gallup estimates the costs to be anywhere from $319 billion to $398 billon to U.S. companies. This is staggering.

According to Gallup, these findings suggest that two-thirds of leaders in our organizations have essentially checked out, meaning they care little about their jobs, their people, and their company. How can we ever hope to be successful if we tolerate this?

But there's more. Gallup also found what it calls *the cascade effect*, which essentially means that an employee's sense of engagement ties directly to his or her manager's sense of engagement. In fact, employees who are led by highly engaged managers and leaders are 59 percent more likely to be highly engaged themselves.

In many ways, these insights should be obvious. Think about your own experience. I suspect it would align with these survey findings. I certainly know that when I was at my best over my career, it was always because I was working for a great leader I admired, and I showed up every day being accountable and fully engaged. What's been your experience?

It's time to start doing the tough stuff and stop tolerating mediocrity in our organizations. The price we are paying is too high.

The good news is that a company-specific leadership contract goes a long way toward achieving that goal because at least it makes your leadership expectations clear. Those leaders who don't want to be—or shouldn't be—leading know what's expected of them. They then need to make their own decisions. Or you can help them with their decisions. That's where we are going next.

Identify and Address Unaccountable Leaders   Too often, attempts to build strong leadership accountability are undermined because we fail to take action on leaders who simply are not prepared to be accountable. Keeping these leaders in their roles has consequences. It sends the message to other leaders and employees that you are prepared to tolerate mediocrity in your organization. It also disengages your high performers, who are truly accountable, as their contributions are minimized.

Our research revealed that only 20 percent of companies believe they have a culture that actually addresses unaccountable and mediocre leaders. When I traveled to cities around the world and spoke to leaders, they confirmed this. Many said, "We know who our unaccountable leaders are, but we choose to do nothing about them." How is this possible?

It's time you get tough as an organization and identify the leaders who are struggling in their roles. Maybe they need support. Maybe they shouldn't be in leadership roles. Maybe they don't really want their roles and are looking for a way out. Maybe they are better suited for an individual contributor role. Maybe you should have left them as technical experts and not promoted them into leadership roles. Maybe they need to leave your organization. Whatever the outcome, as an organization you need to do your part and act on unaccountable leaders. I know this will be a hard message for many of you, but I think you know this is something you must do.

A client of mine in the insurance industry was going through transformational change. The way the company had operated for decades needed to change. A new CEO arrived and soon brought on a new head of HR. These two began to set a new course for the future. A critical part of their approach was to set clear leadership expectations for all leaders. The board was completely supportive of this work.

They ended up creating a set of leadership expectations that they called their "price of entry" conversation. They made things very transparent to their leaders. Their price of entry included a list of criteria and expectations that would be required of leaders of the future. Those criteria were also used to evaluate their cadre of leaders—to identify those who were not living up to these new expectations.

There were some very tough and frank discussions. Many leaders ended up leaving the organization. Some left voluntarily, and others were pushed out. It was a tough period, but in the end the organization became stronger because the leaders who remained were totally clear and committed to leading in a new way. They were the accountable ones.

Is this too drastic an approach? Some of you reading this might feel like it is. But at the end of the day, this is what it means to be serious about driving real leadership accountability. We need to wake up and stop being naïve, assuming that lame, mediocre, and unaccountable leaders will help us become successful. They never have. It's time to get tough and do the tough stuff.

4. *Connect Your Leaders*

The fourth term in the leadership contract asks leaders to connect with one another to build community and a strong leadership culture. Only

27 percent of organizations feel they have a strong leadership culture today according to our survey. Connecting with other leaders is a crucial step for individuals to take, and it's crucial for any organization that wants to build an accountable leadership culture to support these kinds of connections. Why?

More and more organizations are starting to recognize that collaboration is the key to driving real innovation and sustained success today and in the future. Entrenched silos, infighting, and competition are not the way to achieve this success. Instead, organizations need leaders who understand the whole, appreciate what they need to do in their own divisions and business units, and work across organizational boundaries. We need leaders who have a one-company mindset and are able to act as an aligned community of leaders.

In Chapter 7, I presented several strategies that individual leaders can implement to build a community of leaders. Here, I'll focus on how organizations can help their leaders connect with one another.

Assess Your Current Leadership Culture   Before you start having your leaders connect, it's important to understand what you currently have in place by creating a baseline measure of your leadership culture. We often use our *Community of Leaders Survey* with our clients, and Figure 12.2 shows several statements from that survey that you can use to assess your organization.

As you review your responses, what patterns do you see? What are some areas of strength? What are some areas of weakness that you may need to address? See the remaining strategies below for ideas on how to build a strong community of leaders.

Hold Regular Leadership Forums to Help Leaders Build Relationships   As I said earlier in this chapter, one of the important organizational practices that industry-leading companies put in place is having regular leadership forums that bring leaders together. Our own client experience validates this practice. Regular forums give leaders the opportunity to come together to network with one another and build relationships. These forums help counter the isolation that many leaders experience day to day.

When done right, leader forums can help clarify your business strategy and reinforce your leadership expectations. They provide a

Instructions:

Rate your organization's leadership culture on each of the statements below.

Your Organization's Leadership Culture	Not At All True		Somewhat True		Completely True
1. Our leaders are clear on the strategic direction of our organization.	①	②	③	④	⑤
2. Our leaders create excitement about the future of our company.	①	②	③	④	⑤
3. Our leaders share a common aspiration to be great leaders.	①	②	③	④	⑤
4. Our leaders lead as a united front with a one-company mind-set.	①	②	③	④	⑤
5. Our leaders hold one another accountable and call out unproductive leadership behavior.	①	②	③	④	⑤
6. Our leaders celebrate success and key milestones.	①	②	③	④	⑤
7. Our leaders break down silos and collaborate effectively.	①	②	③	④	⑤
8. Our leaders make sure that internal politics and personal agendas take a back seat.	①	②	③	④	⑤
9. Our leaders demonstrate resilience and resolve in the face of adversity.	①	②	③	④	⑤
10. Our leaders support one another—they have one another's backs.	①	②	③	④	⑤

Figure 12.2   The Community of Leaders Survey

venue for leaders to network and build relationships with one another. We have learned that it's really hard to build a community of leaders among a group of strangers. When you get it right, you will find leaders better able to collaborate, innovate, and hold themselves and one another accountable for performance.

What makes for a great leader forum?

First, it's important to be clear on who should be in the room. Often, it is the top two or three layers of leaders and high potentials.

Second, the event should begin with opening remarks from the CEO to provide an update on the state of the business, a review of the corporate strategy, and a reminder of the leadership expectations.

Third, the agenda should tackle meaty business issues that are all about leading more strongly as a collective group of leaders. Usually, these are not divisional or operational priorities but key challenges facing leaders across the enterprise. Ensure that leaders are able to drive to recommended actions that will form the basis of personal commitments.

Finally, I find the best leader forums close off with a strong *call to action* by the CEO. Set the bar high for your leaders. Reinforce the importance of individual and collective leadership accountability.

Set Up Leadership Accountability Peer Groups   We worked with one client recently to help design and deliver a leader forum. One of the themes we heard from leaders during the planning process was their sense of isolation from one another. We recommended that after the leadership forum, small groups of six to eight leaders hold a monthly conference call solely focused on discussing their leadership challenges and ensuring they hold one another accountable in their leadership roles.

When we proposed the idea, the CEO said her leaders were so busy that they wouldn't find 12 hours over a year to commit to this. We knew there was a hunger for connection so we pushed the CEO a little. Eventually she agreed to let us propose the idea at the forum, and based on the leader response we would either move ahead or kill the idea.

Guess what happened?

When my colleague presented the idea, the leaders overwhelmingly jumped at the opportunity. We set up some simple guidelines for them, but mostly left them to plan the calls themselves. Remember, this was to be self-managed. It was the ultimate test of their personal and collective accountability as leaders.

One year after launching this practice, the leaders were still meeting in their leadership accountability groups. To me, this is a testament to the need for leaders to connect, learn from one another, and support one another to drive real leadership accountability.

What happens in a leadership accountability peer group? Leaders begin the session by providing an update on how they are doing in their own leadership roles. They then review the commitments they made in their previous session and discuss what worked and what didn't work. Leaders then support one another by providing insights to help one another be more effective. Sometimes leaders can tackle a topic that's acting as a roadblock organizationally, such as how to drive collaboration across business units and departments. The leaders would explore this topic and identify strategies to put in place, and everyone would make a personal commitment to moving things forward in his or her own area to drive greater collaboration.

Final Thoughts—Building Strong Leadership Accountability In Your Organization

As we've discussed, the leadership accountability gap is a real challenge facing many organizations. Based on our research, about three out of every four organizations we surveyed state that leadership accountability is a critical business issue. There's a good chance that your own organization is also struggling with this issue. The ideas in this chapter present a road map to embed real leadership accountability in your organization.

It begins with deciding to make this a priority for your organization. You must then set clear expectations of your leaders through a company-specific leadership contract. You must have the courage to do some hard work necessary to establish the foundations of enterprise-wide accountability. Finally, you must find ways to build a strong community of leaders, by fostering relationship-building among your leaders at all levels.

The Gut Check for Leaders—Embed the Leadership Contract in Your Organization

As you think about the ideas in this chapter, reflect on your answers to the following gut check questions:

1. To what extent has your organization made leadership accountability a business priority?
2. How can you do a better job of setting clear leadership expectations for your leaders?
3. In what ways do you need to get tough on the tough stuff?
4. Are you tolerating mediocre and unaccountable leaders in your organization?
5. How can your organization foster the ability of leaders to connect with one another?

AFTERWORD

The Future of Leadership Is You

I began this book with a simple question: What does it mean to be a leader?

As I explained, it's a question I believe every single one of us in a leadership role needs to answer. The reason is that the world in which we lead is more dynamic and complex. Organizations are facing unprecedented disruption, change, and transformation. Our world also faces complex societal problems. This is placing intense pressure and scrutiny on you and others in leadership roles.

What we know is that the models of leadership of a generation ago are insufficient for today's world.

In essence, we need leaders to be stronger than they ever have been. Yet, every day we see signs that suggest this is not the case. Many leaders have become outright disappointing—and at times even disgraceful. This erodes the trust that people have in leaders throughout society and in the business world. It erodes the engagement of employees.

My work and research have revealed that the root of the problem is a leadership accountability gap. We need leaders in every facet of society to step up and be truly accountable. We need leaders who can lead transformational change and make their companies successful and our world a better place.

Truly accountable leadership is the only way to build an organization that can not only survive in our increasingly complicated world, but also succeed and grow. Truly accountable leadership is the only way we can create vibrant countries and a secure society for all people to lead meaningful lives.

The solution begins by understanding that when you take on a leadership role you are being held to a higher standard of behavior. Many leaders seem to not be fully aware of this. This is why the idea of a leadership contract is so important today. You need to understand that when you take on a leadership role, you are signing up for something important. You just can't take on a role for the title, the perks, or the increased compensation. You need to pause and reflect on the four terms of the leadership contract:

- Leadership Is a Decision—Make It
- Leadership Is an Obligation—Step Up
- Leadership Is Hard Work—Get Tough
- Leadership Is a Community—Connect

When you internalize these four terms and commit to living them on a daily basis, you will reap many rewards:

- You will stand out as a role model to others because your decision to lead means you are setting the pace for other leaders. You will be the leader others want to emulate.
- You will bring greater value to your organization because you'll never lose sight of your leadership obligations. You'll be clear on the value you must create for your customers, employees, stakeholders, and the communities in which you do business.
- You will continually move your organization forward because you won't shy away from the hard work of leadership. You will have the courage, resilience, and resolve to take on the hard work because you'll know that if you don't, no one else will. You will have the courage to have tough conversations.
- Finally, you'll be seen as a community builder. You'll commit to connecting with your colleagues across your organization. You'll help create a climate of high trust and mutual support. You will create a strong leadership culture that will become the ultimate differentiator.

In the end, when you start living the four terms of the leadership contract, you will redefine how you lead. You will be the accountable leader your organization truly needs you to be. The future of leadership is you!

I wish you success in your leadership journey.

ACKNOWLEDGMENTS

The first edition of *The Leadership Contract* was released in July of 2013. At that time, I would not have predicted that the ideas of the book would be so meaningful to so many leaders and companies around the world. I'm humbled by the response, especially now that the third edition of the book has also been released. Accomplishments like this are rarely done single-handedly.

I have so many people to thank for their contributions over the years, whether it was in shaping the ideas of the book, supporting the production of learning materials, certifying global facilitators, or bringing our leadership accountability solutions to our clients worldwide.

I want to express my personal gratitude to my many clients around the world. Without your commitment to my work, none of what has been accomplished would have happened. I have been blessed with many deep and longstanding relationships over my career. I'm also grateful and indebted to those of you who brought the ideas of *The Leadership Contract* into your organizations.

I want to also thank the many readers of my books and blogs. I deeply appreciate your support. I also especially valued when you have reached out to me to share how my ideas have helped you become a more accountable leader. It is personally gratifying to receive this feedback. I'm always thrilled to hear from a leader who has applied the ideas and made them better.

There are also several colleagues from Lee Hecht Harrison who I would like to acknowledge:

- Peter Alcide, president and COO and the rest of the executive team for enabling me to share my ideas with the world.

- To Claudio Garcia, EVP Corporate Strategy and Development, for his ongoing support of my work.
- Thanks also to my peers on the corporate team: Greg Simpson, Jim Concelman, Jeanne Schad, Beth Rizzotti, and the rest of the team members. Your contributions have been many and deeply appreciated.
- A big thank you to my many global colleagues and peers. There are simply too many names to mention, but know that your collective efforts have helped us spread the ideas of this book. You each made an invaluable contribution whether it was in organizing customer events in your cities, designing and translating learning materials, certifying trainers, and sharing our thought leadership via social media. I'm personally grateful for your commitment and great work.

I want to also recognize several of my colleagues from The Adecco Group:

- Thank you to Alain Dehaze, CEO, for your support and for writing the Foreword to this book.
- To Stephan Howeg, chief marketing and communications officer, thank you to your team for being a constant cheerleader and supporter of my work. Thank you also for recognizing *The Leadership Contract* with the first ever Adecco Thought Leadership Award. That was a special moment for me and my team.
- To Shanthi Flynn, chief human resources officer, for your vision and passion.

To my own team in the leadership transformation practice: Tammy Heermann, Alex Vincent, Tess Reimann, and Joey Edwards. Your commitment and passion are constant motivators for me. I'm lucky to work with each of you every single day. An extra special thank you to Razia Garda for your tireless efforts to keep me organized and productive—you are my secret weapon!

Thank you also to Dr. Nick Morgan, Nikki Smith-Morgan, Sarah Morgan, and Emma Wyatt of Public Words. Your full commitment to me and my ideas are deeply valued.

A big thank you goes to the team at John Wiley & Sons, who contributed greatly to this project. A special thank you Shannon Vargo, my editor for the past five years. Thanks also to Elizabeth Gildea, Chris Webb, Peter Knox, Dawn Kilgore, and Kelly Martin.

Writing a book while managing the demands of an executive role, consulting on global client projects, conducting speaking engagements, and leading a busy home life could only be accomplished with the support of my family.

Thank you to my parents, Camillo and Maria; my mother-in-law, Carmela; my brother, Robert; my sisters-in-law, Mary and Rosanna; and my brother-in-law, John; and nephews Owen and Nicholas.

To my children, Mateo, Tomas, and Alessia. You are the constant inspiration in my life. I am proud of the young leaders you are. Once again, an extra thank you to my daughter Alessia and your inspiration for the original design of the book cover.

Finally and most importantly, to my wife, Elizabeth. Once again you amaze me with your support and encouragement. Nothing I do is possible without you. Thank you!

NOTES

Introduction

1. J. Hemerling, D. Dosik, and Rizvi Shaheer, A Leader's Guide to "Always-On" Transformation, The Boston Consulting Group, 2015.

2. Studies consistently show that the vast majority of us routinely click Agree or Accept buttons without reading the terms and conditions of online contracts: Rebecca Smithers, "Terms and Conditions: Not Reading the Small Print Can Mean Big Problems," *Guardian*, May 11, www.guardian.co.uk/money/2011/may/11/terms-conditions-small-print-big-problems.

Chapter 2: What's Wrong with Leadership Today?

1. Maeghan Ouimet, "The Real Productivity-Killer: Jerks," *Inc.*, November 15, 2012, www.inc.com/maeghan-ouimet/real-cost-bad-bosses.html.

2. Shelley DuBois, "Why CEO Loneliness Is Bad for Business," *Fortune*, June 29, 2012, http://management.fortune.cnn.com/2012/06/29/ceos-loneliness-isolation.

3. Maritz Research, "Maritz Poll: Managing in an Era of Mistrust: Maritz Poll Reveals Employees Lack Trust in Their Workplace," April 14, 2010, www.maritz.com/Maritz-Poll/2010/Martiz-Poll-Reveals-Employees-Lack-Trust-in-their-Workplace.aspx.

4. Geoffrey Nunberg, *Ascent of the A-Word* (New York: Public Affairs, 2012).

5. Barbara Kelleman, *The End of Leadership* (New York: HarperCollins, 2012).

6. Jeffrey Pfeffer, *Leadership BS: Fixing Workplaces and Careers One Truth at a Time* (New York: HarperCollins, 2015).

7. Seth Godin, *Tribes: We Need You to Lead Us* (New York: The Penguin Group, 2008).

Chapter 3: The Leadership Accountability Gap

1. Vince Molinaro, *Building Leadership Accountability: A Critical Business Issue for HR Leaders* (Lee Hecht Harrison in partnership with HRPS, 2015).

2. The study deployed a threefold data collection strategy that included an online survey, a series of international customer events, and interviews with select customers to validate the emerging findings. As a company, we are a global partner to 70 percent of Fortune 50 organizations and to 60 percent of Fortune 500 organizations. This allowed for an accurate cross-section of 2,084 participants in senior HR and business executive roles. The online survey had 1,116 respondents. It explored leadership accountability in a broad way by exploring three dimensions of leadership accountability: the behaviors typically demonstrated by accountable leaders; the organization's practices, which help build strong accountability among leaders; and, finally, the key attributes of leadership culture that are important to sustaining leadership accountability. The online survey distribution by role was as follows: 29 percent C-suite executives (CEO, COO, EVP), 27 percent senior HR executives (CHRO, EVP, VP), 27 percent HR professionals at the vice president and director levels, 8 percent HR consultants, and 9 percent in the Other category. A strong cross-section of more than twenty industries was represented, suggesting the findings of this study apply to a broad range of companies in several sectors. A series of events was held in thirty-three cities with a total of 968 customers in attendance. Each respondent completed a short-form survey. In addition, the events were leveraged to cultivate insight on the emerging findings of the survey data. A series of one-on-one interviews with a select number of customers was employed to validate and further explore the themes emerging from the surveys and customer events. A consistent interview guide was used during the interviews, across all industries and segments.

3. Vince Molinaro, *The Leadership Accountability Gap* (Lee Hecht Harrison, 2017).

4. In the book, *Leadership Solutions* (San Francisco: Jossey-Bass, 2007), my co-authors, Dr. David Weiss and Dr. Liane Davey, provided a holistic framework to help organizations understand and improve their leaders by looking at three key dimensions: the behaviors of leaders, the organization practices put in place to build strong leadership, and the leadership culture attributes needed to sustain strong leadership in an organization.

Chapter 4: Why We Need a Leadership Contract

1. Fox News, "7,500 Online Shoppers Unknowingly Sold Their Soul," April 15, 2010, www.foxnews.com/tech/2010/04/15/online-shoppers-unknowingly-sold-souls.

Chapter 5: Leadership Is a Decision—Make It

1. Paul Ziobro, "Target CEO Memo: Less Committee, More Leadership," *Wall Street Journal*, June 9, 2014.

Chapter 6: Leadership Is an Obligation—Step Up

1. Kip A. Wedel, *The Obligation: A History of the Order of the Engineer* (Bloomington, IN: AuthorHouse, 2012).

2. Oliver J. Sheldon and Ayelet Fishbach, "Anticipating and Resisting the Temptation to Behave Unethically," *Personality and Social Psychology Bulletin* (published electronically May 22, 2015). doi:10.1177/0146167215586196.

3. Geoff Colvin, "Sam Palmisano's Legacy of Leadership at IBM," *Fortune*, November 18, 2011, http://management.fortune.cnn.com/2011/11/18/sam-palmisano-ibm/.

4. Bill George, "How IBM's Sam Palmisano Redefined the Global Corporation," *Harvard Business Review* (blog), January 18, 2012, https://hbr.org/2012/01/how-ibms-sam-palmisano-redefin.

5. Rosabeth Moss Kanter, "Five Self-Defeating Behaviors That Ruin Companies and Careers," *Harvard Business Review* (blog), November 20, 2012, https://hbr.org/2012/11/five-self-defeating-behaviors.html.

Chapter 8: Leadership Is a Community—Connect

1. Naomi Eisenberger and George Kohlrieser, "Lead with Your Heart, Not Just Your Head," *Harvard Business Review* (blog), November 16, 2012, http://blogs.hbr.org/cs/2012/11/are_you_getting_personal_as_a.html.

2. The research demonstrates that those of us with high-quality or a large quantity of social networks have a decreased risk of mortality compared with those who have low-quality or a low quantity of social relationships. Social isolation is often identified as a major risk factor for mortality. Maija Reblin and Bert N. Uchino, "Social and Emotional Support and It's Implication for Health," *Current Opinion in Psychiatry* 21, no. 2 (2008): 201–205, www.ncbi.nlm.nih.gov/pmc/articles/PMC2729718.

INDEX

reflections on the future of leadership
and, 207–208; signing the, 53,
142–149; understanding the personal
and moral nature of a, 61–62. *See also*
Leadership contract terms; Turning
points of leadership
"The Leadership Contract" (Conference
Board speech), 129
The Leadership Contract Field Guide, 198
The Leadership Contract for Teams
solution, 198
Leadership contract foundational
practices: 1: understand and share your
personal leadership story, 168–171; 2:
define your value and desired impact
as a leader, 171–172; 3: have the tough
conversations, 172–175; 4: be a
community builder, 175–178;
illustrated diagram of, 167*fig*
The Leadership Contract (Molinaro), 76,
140, 191
Leadership contract regular practices:
create your own personal leadership
contract, 182–183; daily actions,
178–179; quarterly and annual actions,
179–181; sign leadership contract at
each turning point, 182; solicit
feedback from others, 181
Leadership contract signing: a copy of
what you'll be signing, 146; at every
turning point, 182; everything changes
after the, 145; experiencing hesitation
over, 143–144; final thoughts on,
148–149; Gut Checks on, 53, 149;
remember that it is an agreement with
yourself, 144; you cannot stay in your
leader role without the, 145
Leadership contract signing scenarios: you
have confirmed a decision you already
made, 148; you realize that you don't
want to lead, 147; you want to sign,
but you don't feel ready, 148
Leadership contract terms: introduction
to the four, 59*fig*–61; leadership is a

community—connect, 59*fig,* 60–61,
124–141, 143, 208; leadership is a
decision—make it, 59*fig*–60, 63–81,
142–143, 208; leadership is an
obligation—step up, 59*fig,* 60,
82–101, 143, 165–167, 208;
leadership is hard work—get tough,
59*fig,* 60, 104*fig*–123, 143, 208; Mary
Barra's story on living the, 165–167,
168–169, 175. *See also* Leadership
contract
Leadership culture: assess your current,
203; attributes of accountable, 49–52;
author's personal journey in
understanding, 2–19; changing it from
a zombie to an accountable, 184–187;
facilitating relationship-building
among leaders, 48*fig,* 49; importance
of values in a strong, 12–13; leader
role in creating a vibrant, 13–15; as
leadership accountability dimension,
43*fig*–44; league of heroes rooted in a
charismatic personality, 129–130;
share employee engagement data to
drive stronger, 49; stable of
thoroughbreds, 130–132; stories
serving as examples of toxic, 8–11;
strategies driving strong accountable,
187*fig*–206; Zinta's story on leader
role in changing, 3–7, 13, 18–19, 23,
69, 128; zombies working in a weak,
128–129, 184–187. *See also* Culture
change; Organizational culture
Leadership culture attributes: celebrating
success in achieving key milestones,
50*fig,* 51; clarity about leadership
expectations, 50*fig,* 51; commitment
to "one company" idea, 50*fig,* 52;
common leadership experience across
organization, 50*fig,* 51–52; culture
with minimum of internal politics,
50*fig,* 51; leader modeling of
organization values, 50*fig,* 51; leaders
encouraged to give constructive

ABOUT THE AUTHOR

Vince Molinaro, PhD, travels the world helping organizations success-fully transform themselves by building strong leadership cultures with highly engaged and truly accountable leaders.

A *New York Times* bestselling author, speaker, and leadership adviser, Vince is the Global Managing Director of the Lee Hecht Harrison Leadership Transformation Practice.

As a senior executive himself, Vince doesn't just preach leadership accountability—he lives it every day. His passion for strong leadership extends to his writing and global research. He is a go-to source for media, and his writing has been featured regularly in some of the world's leading business publications, including *The Harvard Business Review, Forbes, Inc.* magazine, and *The World Economic Forum.*

Vince's bestselling book *The Leadership Contract* (Wiley, 2018), now in its third edition and available in several languages, is a must-read for all leaders. It currently serves as the foundation for culture change and leadership development at companies around the world. He is also the author of The Leadership Contract Field Guide (Wiley, 2018). In addition, Vince has also co-authored two other books: *Leadership Solutions* (Jossey-Bass, 2007) and *The Leadership Gap* (John Wiley & Sons, 2005).

He believes that a company's ultimate differentiator comes from building a strong community of leaders and so he shares his weekly insights and best practices on leadership through his *Gut Check for Leaders* blog (www.theleadershipcontract.com). He can also be followed on Twitter @VinceMolinaro and Facebook.

Vince and his family live near Toronto, Canada.

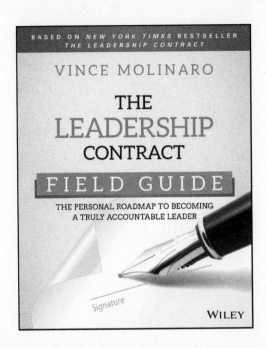

Commit to Great Leadership and Implement it Today

The Leadership Contract Field Guide provides a practical blueprint for implementing the Leadership Contract. Reading is one thing, but new ideas cannot be useful until they are put into practice—so now it is time to commit. Review the major tenets of great leadership, internalize them, and look around at your organization; what does your organization currently need the most? Where is the clear deficit? What do your people most need *right now* to work to their full potential? That's where you start. Decisions? Make them. Obligations? Fulfill them. Hard work? Toughen up. Leadership is a privilege and a responsibility, and this book shows you how to move from *conceptualizing* "great leadership" into *practicing* great leadership—starting today.

This guide summarizes what you learned in *The Leadership Contract*, and integrates that knowledge into real-world actions that make you more effective, while new discussion on accountability draws from research and case studies from major organizations to give you fresh perspective and valuable insight. The result is a clear roadmap to high performance, and you're standing on the starting line—are you ready to go?

• Review the key points of what it means to lead
• Focus on accountability and fulfilling obligations
• Identify and accommodate organizational needs
• Implement the Contract to become a more effective leader

Your employees are your biggest, most valuable asset, and you should be theirs. You need to equip them to succeed, motivate them to achieve, and inspire them to new heights with each and every interaction. In word and in deed, you must walk the walk every single day. This is what great leadership looks like, and it is already inside of you. *The Leadership Contract Field Guide* gives you a systematic blueprint for unleashing your very best and achieving so much more.

Bring *The Leadership Contract* into Your Organization to Build Strong Leadership Accountability

We offer a number of solutions based on the powerful ideas in the best-selling book *The Leadership Contract: The Fine Print to Becoming an Accountable Leader (Third Edition).*

Keynote Presentations

Many companies have taken advantage of our thought-provoking and practical presentations to share the ideas in *The Leadership Contract* with their leaders as part of management retreats, leader forums, development programs, or kicking off large transformation initiatives.

Learning Programs

We offer a series of learning programs to help leaders step up and become truly accountable in their roles:

The Leadership Contract™ Seminars and Workshops. Our hands-on Leadership Contract seminars and workshops (instructor-led, virtual instructor-led, blended) transform how leaders think about their roles and shift their mindset of what it means to be a truly accountable leader.

The Accountable Manager™ – A Front-Line Management Fundamentals Program. The Accountable Manager is a blended learning program for new or experienced front-line managers. This modular program (instructor-led, virtual instructor-led, blended) develops the core skills that front-line managers need to be successful and helps them step up to their leadership accountabilities.

Leadership Development for Mid-Level Leaders. This modular program (instructor-led, virtual instructor-led, blended) targets the specific capabilities that mid-level managers need to excel in their roles and helps them step up to drive real organizational impact.

Advancing the Development of Women in Leadership Roles. This program helps organizations address their diversity and inclusion priorities by specifically helping women accelerate their personal growth and development in their leadership roles.

The Leadership Contract for Teams. A powerful one-day classroom experience that translates the ideas from *The Leadership Contract* to build truly accountable teams.

The Leadership Contract for Human Resources Leaders. This program helps HR leaders and teams truly step up to help their organizations drive leadership transformation and build stronger accountability at all levels.

Consulting

We offer a series of services to help organizations build strong leadership accountability.

Leadership Accountability Audit. This solution is ideal for organizations that need greater insight into the state of leadership accountability at all levels. The insights from our audit become an important foundation to implement targeted solutions.

Leader Forum Design & Facilitation. We work with leading organizations to build strong leadership cultures among senior leaders by designing and facilitating dynamic meetings and off-sites.

ABOUT THE ADECCO GROUP

The Adecco Group is the world's leading provider of workforce solutions, transforming the world of work through talent and technology. Each year, The Adecco Group provides more than one million people around the world with career opportunities, guidance, and insights. Through its global brands Adecco, Modis, Badenoch & Clark, Spring Professional, Lee Hecht Harrison, and Pontoon, The Adecco Group offers total workforce solutions, including temporary staffing, permanent placement, career transition, talent development, and outsourcing. The Adecco Group partners with employers, candidates, colleagues, and governments, sharing its labor market expertise and insights to empower people, fuel economies, and enrich societies.

The Adecco Group is a Fortune Global 500 company, based in Zurich, Switzerland, with more than 33,000 FTE employees in 60 countries and territories around the world. Adecco Group AG is registered in Switzerland (ISIN: CH0012138605) and listed on the SIX Swiss Exchange (ADEN).

THE ADECCO GROUP

ABOUT LEE HECHT HARRISON

Lee Hecht Harrison helps companies transform their leaders and workforce so they can accelerate performance. In an era of continuous change, successfully transforming your workforce depends on how well companies and their people embrace, navigate, and lead change.

We bring our expertise in talent development and transition to deliver tailored solutions that help our clients ensure they have the people and culture they need to evolve and grow. We are passionate about making a difference in people's careers and building better leaders so our clients can build a strong employer brand.

A division of The Adecco Group—the world's leading provider of workforce solutions—Lee Hecht Harrison's 4,000 colleagues work with more than 7,000 clients in more than 60 countries around the world. We have the local expertise, global infrastructure, and industry-leading technology and analytics required to manage the complexity associated with executing critical talent and workforce initiatives, as well as reducing brand and operational risk. It's why 60 percent of Fortune 500 companies choose to work with us.

LEE HECHT
HARRISON